Heroic Women

Mary Cresp rsj

Heroic Women

The Sisters of Perpetual Adoration 1874–2014

Mary Cresp rsj

ATF PRESS
Adelaide
2024

ISBN
978-1-923206-82-3 Soft cover
978-1-923206-83-0 Hard cover
978-1-923206-84-7 Epub
978-1-923206-85-4 PDF

SCAN ME

Published by:

Making a lasting impact
An imprint of the ATF Press Publishing Group
owned by ATF (Australia) Ltd.
PO Box 234
Brompton, SA 5007
Australia
ABN 90 116 359 963
www.atfpress.com

This book is dedicated to
the Sisters of Perpetual Adoration
whom I have known and loved.
They have always been heroic women.

Table of Contents

Chapter Four

Chapter Five

Chapter Six

Chapter Seven

Chapter Eight

Chapter Nine

Chapter Ten

Prologue

Before telling the story of the Sisters of Perpetual Adoration we should take into account the religious environment from which they emerged. What would prompt a small group of women in 1870s Australia to dedicate their lives to praying night and day in adoration before the Blessed Sacrament? Why would they trust a young, charismatic priest to make this possible? What beliefs led them to persevere in this quest, despite formidable odds? To answer these questions, we must situate ourselves into the background that ploughed the soil and planted the seed that produced the eventual founding and growth of the Sisters of Perpetual Adoration.

At the heart of Christianity is the remembrance of the risen Christ present in his body, the church. We enter into this remembrance each time we celebrate Eucharist. 'Re-membering' goes beyond recall. We are re-membered into the body of Christ. As the body of Christ we gather, we receive the word and we enter into and become one with the action of Christ, life given once for all for the life of the world. Within the implications of Eucharist lie all we want to say about discipleship of Jesus Christ.

From the beginnings of Christianity, the disciples of Jesus gathered to celebrate the Eucharist. From Justin Martyr who lived in the second century, only fifty years or so after St John's Gospel was written, we have this account:

> On Sunday we have a common assembly of all our members, whether they live in the city or the outlying districts. The recollections of the apostles or the writings of the prophets are read, as long as there is time. When the reader has finished, the president of the assembly speaks to us; he urges everyone to imitate the examples of virtue we have heard in the readings. Then we all stand up together and pray. On the conclusion of our prayer, bread and wine and water are brought forward. The president offers prayers and gives thanks to the best of his ability, and the people give assent by saying, 'Amen'. The Eucharist is distributed, everyone present communicates, and the deacons take it to those who are absent.[1]

The fact that the Eucharist was taken from the assembly to those who could not be present reveals a basic understanding of the ongoing presence of Christ in the consecrated species even after the conclusion of the liturgy:

> For we do not receive these things as common bread or common drink; but as Jesus Christ our Savior being incarnate by God's Word took flesh and blood for our salvation, so also we have been taught that the food consecrated by the word of prayer which comes from him, from which our flesh and blood are nourished by transformation, is the flesh and blood of that incarnate Jesus.[2]

Periods of persecution meant that distribution of the Eucharist to the sick and those in prison had to become more circumspect, and so between times it was in a box and hidden away, the precursor of the later tabernacle or aumbry set in a niche in the wall of the sanctuary. By the late third century which saw the rise of monasticism, the Eucharist was often reserved in the chapels of monks and nuns, likewise for distribution to the sick.

With the edict of the Emperor Constantine in the fourth century proclaiming toleration of all faiths and that of Theodosius making Christianity the state religion, many nominal 'conversions' took place for various social reasons, among them being promotion in government ranks. Bradshaw points out that since many of these 'nominal converts' lacked understanding of the Christian faith, they acted inappropriately during the liturgy:

> According to John Chrysostom, for example, they pushed and pulled one another in an unruly manner during the services; they gossiped with one another; young people engaged in various kinds of mischief; and pickpockets preyed upon the crowd.[3]

In their efforts to instil a sense of awe and solemnity around the liturgy, church leaders introduced various alterations to the way the Eucharist had been celebrated, including liturgical vestments and formalities such as processions and ceremonial actions. John Chrysostom was particularly insistent that purity of life should be observed by those approaching communion. As often happens, exhortations meant to challenge can have the opposite effect, and therefore many of the faithful stayed away from receiving communion because of 'unworthiness'. With the Eucharist now celebrated in basilicas holding large crowds, the 'central table' or altar was moved to the end opposite the western door of the building's entrance. However, since the celebrant still faced east, the direction of the rising sun recalling the Resurrection, he now had his back to the congregation. Eventually, we have the situation where the celebrant becomes the 'doer' of the Eucharist and the congregation is silent, unable to see what is happening except when the priest turns to them or lifts the consecrated bread and wine for them to adore. 'Thus', says Hardon, 'the principal focus of the Eucharist came to be seen as making the bread and wine into the "real presence" of Christ which took place at the moment the "words of consecration" were uttered.'[4]

From the tenth to the twelfth centuries, controversies about the 'real presence' caused serious unrest in the western church. In some cases, these philosophical arguments led to reactionary literalism featuring 'carnal' interpretations of the doctrine. It was a period when, for example, accounts of hosts dripping blood and suchlike took hold. To combat both extremes of denial and literalism, St Thomas Aquinas and other theologians (using the philosophical terminology of 'transubstantiation') clarified what belief in the 'real presence' meant—that the sacramental encounter is a real encounter with the risen Christ, not merely symbolic or allegoric. For the general populace, devotions emphasising the 'real presence' were introduced. The fact that these devotions called for the participation of the faithful increased their popularity. Exposition of the Blessed Sacrament, Benediction and visits to the Blessed Sacrament reserved in church tabernacles made it possible for ordinary people to play an active role in worship.[5] The Feast of Corpus Christi instituted by Pope Urban IV in 1264 was celebrated with joyful processions through towns and villages.[6] 'Acts of Spiritual Communion' became common, whereby those unable to communicate expressed the wish in their hearts of being united to Christ while the priest actually consumed the Host. These acts of worship stood in stark contrast to the passivity of the faithful during the Mass as it was then celebrated.

This was a time when the majority of lay men and women were illiterate. With Latin being the language of the liturgy and the educated elite, the general populace depended on the visual arts, symbols and ritual practices to convey meaning. As in all cultures, some practices were abused and doctrine distorted. For example, when the consecrated Host became an object separate from the context of the Eucharistic celebration, adoration of the Blessed Sacrament became a mere 'private' devotion. On the other hand, we read of people 'running from church to church just to see the Host'—as though the consecration of the Host at Mass was the work of a magician.[7]

Such abuses offered prime fodder for leaders of the Protestant Reformation in the sixteenth century. Among others, Calvin and his followers denied the 'real presence' as defined by Aquinas, maintaining that the presence of Christ in the Eucharist should be understood 'figuratively'. In response, the Council of Trent (1545–1563) reaffirmed the church's belief that, 'in the august sacrament of the holy Eucharist, after the consecration of the bread and wine, our Lord Jesus Christ, true God and man, is truly, really, and substantially contained under the species of those sensible things'.[8] Regarding the 'cult and veneration to be shown to this most holy Sacrament', the Council declared:

> The only-begotten Son of God is to be adored in the Holy Sacrament of the Eucharist with the worship of *latria* [that is, worship that is due to God alone], including external worship. The Sacrament, therefore, is to be honoured with extraordinary festive celebrations (and) solemnly carried from place to place in processions according to the praiseworthy universal rite and custom of the holy Church. The Sacrament is to be publicly exposed for the people's adoration.[9]

One of the early responses to this statement was the introduction of the Forty Hours Devotion to Rome by Pope Clement VIII in 1592. As its title suggests, the devotion consists of a period of forty hours during which worshippers pray continuously before the exposed Sacrament. The retrieval of such Eucharistic devotions during the sixteenth and seventeenth centuries featured in an era of intense spiritual renewal throughout Catholic Europe as an immediate reaction to Protestant denial.

However, with the heresy of Jansenism arising in the Belgium in 1640 and quickly spreading through the Low Countries, France and Italy, the renewal movement was influenced in a way that discouraged people's participation in the Eucharist.[10] The basic premise of Jansenism was the 'otherness' of God before whom one was to bow in submission and adoration:

> According to Jansen, people were naturally corrupt in the absence of God's grace which was only given to those who were pre-destined to heaven. Among the legacies of Jansenism was a misguided belief that Holy Communion was a reward for the virtuous and should not be received frequently or by those who were unworthy.[11]

These aspects of Jansenist thought became particularly popular in seminaries, due in large part to the influence of cardinal and statesman Pierre de Bérulle (1575–1629) who founded a society of priests, the Oratorians.[12] Oratorians worked especially to improve the theological education of priests throughout France. They set up seminaries and were largely responsible for the spiritual revival of French clergy during the seventeenth century. They placed strong emphasis on the priesthood being aligned to that of Jesus Christ and consequently on the awe that surrounds that role.

Bérulle's spirituality was one of complete surrender to God–self-emptying in order to be filled with Christ. It was embraced by people from all walks of life and resulted in a wholesome outreach of charity to those living in poverty and ignorance. Its underlying Jansenist stance, however, placed the human at a distance from God's majestic presence and gave undue honour to those whose lives were consecrated to God, such as priests and those in religious life.

Various efforts were made to counteract the impact of Jansenism. The Jesuits promoted the immanence of God particularly through devotion to the Sacred Heart of Jesus–which symbolised his passionate love for humanity. They urged people to receive Communion more frequently, especially through a devotion known as the 'Nine First Fridays'. This devotion involved people attending Mass and receiving Communion on the first Friday for nine consecutive months with the intention of offering reparation to God for the sins of the world.[13] Still, even in these efforts, the sense of the sinfulness of humanity and fear of God's judgement prevailed. Devotions such as the adoration of the reserved Blessed Sacrament could allow one to approach the Holy without risking the presumption that one was 'worthy' to receive Communion.

In the sixteenth and seventeenth century Age of Enlightenment, the dichotomy between the things that were 'of God' and those that supposedly were not, took on the shape of alienating 'worldly' science from religion. At the social level, the dichotomy favoured elitism. This was threatened as the push for a more equal classless society and the separation of church and state gained momentum. The French Revolution followed in 1789–1799, and thousands of priests and Catholic laity of high rank fled to England to escape persecution. So it was that when, from 1829, Catholicism was able to be practised openly in England once again, it was heavily influenced by the piety, traditions and practices brought to the country by Catholic refugees from France.

This was the England into which Julian Tenison Woods was born in 1832. Although he was baptised a Catholic it was not until he was fifteen years of age that he came under the influence of two priests who were to confirm his Catholic allegiance. The first was Father Frederick Oakeley. Before he became a Catholic, he had been deeply influenced by the Tractarian movement of the 1830s that sought to remind the Church of England of its Catholic inheritance and taught the central importance of the Eucharist. The second was Father Frederick Faber, also a convert from the Church of England, who in 1849 had founded a community of Oratorians in London. He had formed close friendships with priests of the Society of Mary (Marists) who ministered to the expatriate French Catholic community.[14] At different times Julian lived with both these men and received instruction from them. At the age of nineteen he had been professed as a Passionist, but when his health failed, he was advised to leave and test his vocation with an order whose rules were less demanding.

Through Father Faber's connections, Julian was then accepted into the Marist novitiate in Lyons in France in 1853. The next year saw him teaching in a Marist college at La Seyne-sur-Mer on the south coast of France. There he lived with Father Peter Julian Eymard as his spiritual director. Author John Hardon considers that the influence of Eymard extends into our day:

> Among the apostles of perpetual adoration for the laity, none has had a more lasting influence in the modern world than St Peter Julian Eymard. In 1856 he founded the Blessed Sacrament Fathers in Paris and two years later, with Marguerite Guillot, he established the Servants of the Blessed Sacrament, a cloistered contemplative congregation of women. Peter Eymard's published conferences on the Real Presence have inspired numerous lay associations.[15]

When Julian Woods lived with him, Eymard was still a member of the Marist Fathers. In his *Memoirs*, he later recalled that his spiritual director 'was shy and retiring with a deep hidden devotion, a spiritual life with the spirit of the Blessed Eucharist, for the honour and adoration of which he founded his order.' Julian was inspired by Eymard's spirituality. Years later, following his example, he would with Catherine Gaffney and her companions, found a religious congregation: the Sisters of Perpetual Adoration of the Blessed Sacrament.

The effects of Jansenism were still present in the spiritual revival of nineteenth century France, but those emphasising the immanence of God such as devotion to the Sacred Heart were much stronger. Eymard impressed on Julian that he should receive Communion frequently. Later, in Australia, Julian would write:

> Go often to Communion–never leave longer than a month between your Communions. Go every week and every Feastday if you can, and oftener if your director will allow you.[16]

Julian saw adoration as the primary response to Christ's presence in the Eucharist:

> If, like the shepherds at Bethlehem, we came to the stable and saw the poor little baby, we should kneel down and adore Him. Jesus tells us that He is God. And if we see the consecrated Host lifted up, we kneel down and adore it, because Jesus Christ says, 'This is my Body'.[17]

However, there is a certain literal physicality in Julian's explanation of 'real presence' that borders on former 'carnal' interpretations. Why was he drawn to these? Perhaps it was because he grew up in the era of Romanticism where people appreciated poetic imagery. An example of this literalist description is where Julian likens the presence of Christ in the consecrated Host to Jesus in earthly life:

> But in this He puts Himself very much in the power of His creatures. He came to be lifted up and carried about for the living and the dying—and alas! He came to be insulted and ill-used. But love for us makes Him consent to all that.[18]

While we have no personal records of the understanding of Eucharist and adoration that inspired the first Sisters of Perpetual Adoration, we know they came from a mainly Irish background.[19] The Irish church had been suppressed until Catholic Emancipation in 1829, and its few priests had received their training in France. A strong Catholic revival was instigated in Ireland in the 1850s by the Archbishop of Dublin, Cardinal Paul Cullen (1803–1878). He had been educated in Rome and, like most of Ireland's priests, had absorbed many of the Jansenist ideas that still prevailed in Europe. He also happened to be the uncle of Bishop James Quinn, the first Bishop of Brisbane, who gave his approval of Father Woods' rule for the Sisters of Perpetual Adoration.[20]

The soil which gave rise to Sisters of Perpetual Adoration in Brisbane in 1874, therefore contained seeds sown over hundreds of years of the history of the Catholic Church. Its first shoots sprouted at a time when, as David Walker points out, Australian Catholics shared a world view that 'was largely created and sustained by the basic vision of the French school [of spirituality]'. He adds further: 'The local church and also the universal church was able to sustain such a world view because by and large it was acceptable within the whole society within which the church existed.'[21]

Having described these circumstances in which the Sisters of Perpetual Adoration were born, we now follow that story through as they adjusted to changes in the worldview of the years of their birth. The fruits that they produced would nourish both church and society in Australia.

Chapter 1

For any organisation, its founding story is important. Foundation stories can shape the character of an organisation. They tell us about the beliefs and cultural aspirations of those who laid down those foundations. The founders' story has power. As it unfolds, its vision transforms into core principles and values that continue to resonate down the years. These are the principles and values we will see demonstrated in the history of a group of heroic women, the Sisters of Perpetual Adoration. We will be introduced first to a group of women who, like Abram of old, were called to step into the unknown to follow a dream: 'Go forth from your country, and from your relatives and from your father's house, to the land which I will show you.' (Gen 12:1).

Beginnings

It was Monday 15 June 1874, three days after the Feast of the Sacred Heart.[1] In Brisbane, three young women, Anne Lafferty (thirty-three years of age), Ellen Connolly (twenty-nine) and Catherine Gaffney (nineteen) took occupancy of a small rented cottage on the corner of Russel and Merivale Streets in the city's south. Newly-arrived from Sydney, they had made the three-day journey by ship at the instigation of Father Julian Tenison Woods who had assisted them in paying the fare and had made arrangements for them to be met at the Brisbane wharf by a Sister of St Joseph, Sister Clare Wright.[2] She had also been entrusted by Father Woods with finding accommodation for the three women, obtaining a sewing machine for them so that they could immediately begin to earn their keep with needlework, and helping them settle into the way of life he had outlined for them. For Anne, Ellen and Catherine considered themselves the first members of a new Religious community, the Sisters of Perpetual Adoration of the Blessed Sacrament.

Anne and Ellen were Irish-born and had lived in Sydney for some years before embarking on this new journey. Details of Anne's family are unknown. However, from what we can glean from his letters, it is obvious that Father Woods trusted her and that she was very responsible.[3] Ellen, who had emigrated to

Australia with her family, was the daughter of Bridget Costello and Thomas Connolly, farmer, and was born in Barnaderg, County Galway, on 22 May 1845. She and Anne had been introduced to Father Julian Woods in 1872 by their spiritual director, Father Angelo Ambrosoli. Father Ambrosoli was an Italian missionary who had arrived in Sydney in 1855. He and his confreres had been sent by the Pontifical Institute for Foreign Missions to help establish Catholicism on the islands of eastern Papua. However, the attempt failed. Sick and exhausted, Father Ambrosoli had been cared for by the Sisters of Charity at Potts Point, Sydney, before taking on the role of chaplain to the Benedictine Sisters at Subiaco.[4] It was there he met Anne, Ellen and another friend, Mary Libskin who had expressed their desire to enter a religious order dedicated to adoration of the Blessed Sacrament. Knowing his friend, Father Woods, hoped to found such an order, he had referred the women to his guidance.[5] Since then, while gaining a small income from needlework, they had visited various churches to pray and had received instruction from Father Woods about their future Religious Life.

Catherine Gaffney had been born on 13 November 1855, near Deloraine in Tasmania. Her father, Hugh Gaffney, was a migrant from Ireland. Her mother, Catherine Whelan, was born of Irish parents in Tasmania in about 1836. One of eleven children, six girls and five boys, Catherine was well educated both academically and in religious knowledge. Like the rest of the family, she would often walk the seven miles from her family's farm, 'Early Rise', to the Catholic church at Deloraine to attend Mass.[6] When Father Woods had come there in 1873 to give a mission, she had been inspired by his idea of forming a religious order of Sisters of Perpetual Adoration. A few months later, on 22 May, 1874, she left her home 'without even looking back' to join the three women in Sydney. She carried with her a letter of introduction written by Father Woods:

> The bearer, Kate Gaffney, is to join the Perpetual Adoration sisters. She is going to Brisbane to wait for you there. I want you to help her and encourage her all you can. I have given her £5 to help you in going to Brisbane. If you like to keep Kate with you for a few days you can do so.[7]

Since Anne, Ellen and Catherine had arrived in Brisbane by 15 June, they must have boarded the ship soon after Catherine reached Sydney. At journey's end, they stayed with the Sisters of St Joseph at Kangaroo Point, observing their way of life until they were ready to move into the premises obtained for them. Mary Libskin travelled separately and would not join them until some two years later.

Father Director, Julian Tenison Woods[8]

Father Julian Woods was already well-known in the Brisbane diocese for he had conducted missions and clergy retreats there at various times over the past two years. It was at one such retreat that he had heard of Bishop James Quinn's intention to bring a contemplative religious order to his young diocese.[9] In subsequent conversations he had told the bishop of his hopes to found an order devoted to adoration of the Blessed Sacrament and of the group of possible candidates that he was directing in Sydney. The result was that Bishop Quinn had offered to support the enterprise in his diocese. However, sensing the bishop's enthusiasm—he was 'full of plans'[10]—and fearing he would take them over, Julian asked the three women to proceed slowly, making sure that everything was in place before actually leaving Sydney for Brisbane.

Julian had every reason to be cautious. Past experience with bishops in Hobart, and Adelaide. had already caused him problems. He had come from England to Hobart in 1854 at the invitation of Bishop Robert Willson. It had been explained to the bishop that Julian had suffered a series of disappointments in his desire to be a priest. The suggestion that he could teach in Hobart and continue his studies with the view of being ordained there was seemingly an answer to prayer. However, when he arrived at his destination, Julian found that the conditions were not as described. Disillusioned, he set out to Adelaide to visit his brother James there. Hoping to earn his passage back home to England, he obtained employment as reporter and sub-editor at the *Adelaide Times.*

Catherine Gaffney

Julian Tenison Woods

Bishop James Quinn

First house, Russell Street 1874-1878

Second Chouse, corner of Russell & Manning Streets. (Shop front added in the early 1900s)

A chance discussion with Bishop Murphy of Adelaide, however, changed his plans. The bishop—in urgent need of priests for his diocese—arranged for Julian to complete his interrupted studies with the Austrian Jesuits at their college at Sevenhill in the Mid North of South Australia, and he was ordained on 4 January 1857 at the age of twenty-four. Julian was then appointed to a newly-formed mission of 22,000 square miles (57,000 square kilometres) covering the South East of South Australia, with its centre in Penola. For the next ten years he served his people with enthusiasm and zeal. He was popular with Catholic and Protestant alike, making significant contributions to the civic welfare of the community, particularly its Aboriginal inhabitants. To help raise much-needed funds he wrote books and articles about his geological and general scientific observations of the area.

A severe need in this thinly-populated area was the religious and secular education of children. Julian was thwarted in his attempts to get qualified teachers to stay in such an isolated district. It was only in the early 1860s, when Mary MacKillop responded to his idea of a establishing a group of Religious Sisters dedicated to teaching under these stringent conditions that he could find an answer to the problem.[11] On 19 March 1866 the dream became reality with the birth of the Sisters of St Joseph in a renovated stable in Penola. The third bishop of Adelaide, Laurence Sheil, subsequently gave his approval to the rule that Julian drew up for Mary and the many women who soon joined her, especially after schools were opened in Adelaide when Julian was appointed as Director of Catholic Education for the diocese.

It is obvious that Julian considered himself well-qualified to oversee the formation of candidates for Religious Life. He himself had entered the Passionist Congregation in London in 1850, but after two years, having lived as a Novice and then as a professed Brother, his superiors advised him that his health could not sustain the life. Doctors recommended that he go to a warmer climate, so, still longing for the priesthood, he took the opportunity to enter the Marist Fathers in the south of France. It was there that he not only extended his personal experience of religious life, but he met people who would greatly influence him later in Australia. In the Marist community, he lived with Father Peter Julian Eymard who would go on to found two religious congregations, the Blessed Sacrament Fathers for men and the Servants of the Blessed Sacrament for women.[12] While travelling in the Auvergne region, Julian had met a congregation of religious women who greatly inspired him. They were the Sisters of St Joseph founded at Le Puy in 1650 and now serving in small villages around France. As the priest in charge of the South East Mission, he realised that these Sisters' way of life offered a model suitable for conditions in Australia. Years later when he dictated his *Memoirs*, Julian recalled his personal hesitations before the Penola venture:

> I was continually thinking of such a foundation, yet it seemed so wild a scheme and so utterly impracticable that I scarcely dared to hope for it, and certainly never spoke of it to anyone. Yet the idea haunted me in the strangest way and I felt that I were resisting an inspiration when I turned aside from it. I could not help remarking likewise that I felt extraordinary pleasure in reading the lives of all those who had been founders of religious orders.[13]

By 1874, the Sisters of St Joseph were firmly established, but not without the founders having been deeply wounded. Three years before, Julian had suffered a major burn-out and had lost the confidence of Bishop Sheil. Hostile clerics had convinced the bishop that Julian's management of finances and his direction of the Sisters warranted a complete overhaul. His defence fell on deaf ears. As a consequence, Julian was exiled to the eastern colonies, the Rule of Life that Julian had written for the Sisters was to be drastically changed, and Mary MacKillop was excommunicated, the victim of calumny. After the bishop's death and Mary's reinstatement, an official enquiry into the whole affair was conducted by two bishops. As a result, Julian was no longer to be the Sisters' director; instead, the Jesuits took over his role. Further, his original rule was changed by church authorities when Mary travelled to Rome in 1872 to get pontifical approval. Julian had lost all control over the situation.

In his dealings with the proposed Sisters of Perpetual Adoration, it is as though Julian was saying, 'I'll never let that happen again!' Certainly, he needed a bishop's approval for his dream of the Sisters of Perpetual Adoration to become reality, so he was grateful that Bishop Quinn would welcome them to Brisbane. But he did not want the bishop to take over. Therefore, in a letter written in January 1873, he made it clear to the group in Sydney: 'All I ask of you is that you will follow my directions exactly.'[14] He was aware that the bishop considered the primary need in the diocese to be teaching, so he warned them: 'Wherever you go it must be to commence the Perpetual Adoration and nothing else.' Again, he asserted his role: 'In future I shall sign myself F. D., which means Father Director.'[15] When the bishop was travelling to Sydney and asked that the women visit him there, Julian gave them the exact wording they were to use—they were to explain that they propose only 'Perpetual Adoration and to work for the Church', and that, whatever plans are made, they 'will do what Father Woods tells (them)'.[16] Rather than be in a 'hurry' to begin, they were to wait until everything was in place, 'as the work must be slow to be sure'.[17]

Early Days

Now settled in the five-roomed house at Highgate Hill, South Brisbane, Anne, Ellen and Catherine set about living their life as Sisters of Perpetual Adoration.[18] Father Woods had already written a rule of life for them and had sent it to them while they were still in Sydney.[19] In fact it was very like the rule he had drawn up for the Sisters of St Joseph, except for the substitution of the words 'adoration of the Blessed Sacrament' for descriptions of apostolic works. They followed this rule now as best they could. St Mary's Church was nearby on the corner of Merivale and Peel Streets, South Brisbane, so they visited there for a time each day keeping watch before the Blessed Sacrament and attending Mass whenever it was available. According to instructions from Father Woods, they set aside one of the rooms in the house as an oratory. There they met for common prayer and meditation three times a day, framing a schedule of prayer, work and recreation. There were particular prayers they said at different times of the day. For example, upon rising they were to pray while dressing:

> Clothe me, my Lord, with the robe of innocence, and adorn my heart with all the virtues that are pleasing to thee, especially with humility, obedience, purity and an exact fidelity to my holy rule and vows.[20]

Father Woods had also told them not to wear a habit as yet and not to announce themselves to the bishop as having arrived to start the congregation. Being in Tasmania, he wanted them to wait until he could get to Brisbane. As rent for the house was 15 shillings per week, it was imperative that the women quickly obtain orders for needlework. This involved crossing the Brisbane River at least three times a week to take samples of their work to local shops and leading businesses in the main part of the city. A permanent order from the Finney Emporium for items of apparel boosted both their finances and morale.

In a letter sent on 23 June, Father Woods indicated that he had just learnt that they had left Sydney for Brisbane. The surprising request in this letter was that Anne should immediately come to Hobart where there was a rich woman 'who takes an extraordinary interest in the establishment of the Perpetual Adoration, and will do anything to forward or help it.' He sent a Post Office Order for £10 via Sister Clare for the passage, and explained that, 'now that you have seen Brisbane and know what you require', it would be best to speak to the benefactor personally. He instructed the group, 'Don't speak of the lady's name, especially as she is very well known and wants to keep quiet in this matter'.[21] There is no record of what the precise outcome of this visit was, and we can only presume that Anne did indeed make the trip.

A postscript to this letter included another surprise. From now on, he directed, they were to be addressed by their religious names. So by August there were six 'Sisters' crowded into the little cottage—Sister Teresa (Anne Lafferty), Sister Gertrude (Ellen Connolly), Sister Stanislaus (Catherine Gaffney) and three more who had come from Tasmania, Sister Mary Joseph (Sarah Breen), Sister Francis (Alice Downs) and Sister Aloysius (first name Frances, but surname unknown).

New Premises

It soon became obvious that the Sisters would have to find a larger house. Five rooms, one of them being an oratory, another a kitchen and the third a workroom, were not sufficient. By September 1875 there was seven women in the group, Bridget Lillis, now Sister Mary John, having joined them.[22] Soon after her arrival, the Sisters heard of a larger house on the corner of Russell and Manning Streets in South Brisbane which held possibilities. 'Park Cottage', set in attractive grounds opposite Musgrave Park, belonged to an elderly couple, John and Deborah Beach.[23] By now the Sisters were becoming well-known in the area, and when the old man became ill, he sent for them to make a bargain. He told them he would give them the house and property when he died, on condition they would then provide a room for his wife and take care of her. They willingly consented to this proposal.

For the next two years, they continued to put up with the restrictions of the rented cottage. It would not be surprising if by now they were feeling discouraged about the establishment of the Sisterhood. Father Woods was occupied with his missions in Tasmania and seemed unable to find the freedom to attend to the group other than by letter. When they learned that he would be in Sydney in December 1877, Sister Teresa and a companion went there to see him, but it is unknown what they discussed.[24] During that time, two women—one of whom was Mary Libskin who had been in the original group in Sydney—did became part of the community but stayed only a few weeks. The numbers therefore remained static.

After the death of John Beach in January 1877, the Sisters prepared to move up the two blocks along Russell Street to their new home. Building alterations had to be attended to first. Another large room had to be added to the house for Mrs Beach to live in, and various modifications for an oratory and community-living made. The estimated cost was £200. The amount, otherwise prohibitive, was able to be paid because of money brought by Bridget Lillis. On his arrival from Ireland in the 1850s, Thomas Lillis, the father of Sister Mary John (Bridget Lillis) had 'struck it rich' on the goldfields of Ballarat, Victoria. Then, when gold was found at Gympie, Queensland, in 1867, he had moved his family there. Somehow, young Bridget, only sixteen years of age, had heard of the proposed Sisters of Perpetual Adoration in Brisbane and asked her parents' permission to join them. When she left home, her father had given her £200 to take with her.

By 28 January 1878 all was ready, and the seven Sisters and three postulants who had recently joined them took up residence in their new home. Mrs Beach moved to the newly-built room and the Sisters saw to her wants, taking her meals to her on a tray. As one of the Sisters described her, '[Mrs Beach] posed as the most gentle lady in the land.'[25] For the time being, all went well.

Visit of Father Woods

It was not until November of that year that Father Woods could visit the Sisters in Brisbane. He did not come as a stranger. Even those who had never met him would write to him frequently and he wrote personal letters in reply. We might say he directed by correspondence. His letters were full of endearing terms and, for those not reading with Victorian-era eyes, quite flowery. Even in physical absence, Father Woods was a powerful presence in the community. Nevertheless, the few visits he did make to Brisbane were remembered as having laid the foundations on which their Congregation was built.

During this first visit, Father Woods celebrated Mass for the first time in the Sisters' new oratory on 19 November, 1878. Now he could introduce the community to Bishop Quinn who had approved their rule and promised continued interest in their welfare. As yet they did not have the numbers required for perpetual adoration. But, the bishop pledged, if during the next seven years enough candidates joined the group, he would give his approval and recognise the Sisters of Perpetual Adoration as a Diocesan Congregation.

Another significant happening for the Sisters during this visit was Father Woods' blessing of the simple, black dress and veil that they wore. This was not an attire then recognisable as a 'religious habit', but one that would nevertheless earn them the title by which they became affectionately known for at least the next forty years, 'the Black Sisters'. Their house, too, was blessed and re-named as 'Villa Maria'—a name Father Woods asked that the Sisters always give their homes from now on.[26]

Grote Street Adelaide, 1886, showing the Bishop's House and St Patrick's Church in which Julian Woods was ordained on 4 January 1857. Photo: State Library of South Australia: B1938.

St Joseph's Church, Penola, built by Julian Woods in 1861.

Sisters Agnes and Irene Kelvin in the dress of the 'Black Sisters'. With them is their mother.

Victoria Bridge looking from North Quay to South Brisbane, about 1875, John Oxley Library, State Library of Queensland, Negative number: 18790. The Sisters crossed this bridge when taking their sewing to sell in the city.

During the time he was in Brisbane, Father Woods gave spiritual instructions to the Sisters whenever he could. However, he was concerned about their day-to-day interactions and whether they really understood the spirit of the rule. For over a year he had spoken about getting 'Sister Ignatius' to live with them and teach them the ways of Religious Life.[27] This was Mary Jane O'Brien who had left the Sisters of St Joseph after Father Woods was dismissed as their Director. He had suggested to her and other former members that they should form yet another group of Religious Sisters, the 'Sisters of the Compassionate Heart of Mary', so they gathered in Sydney awaiting the time when this could be formalised.[28] It never was, but they remained together, living as a group of pious women. In August 1879 Father Woods chose 'Sister Margaret Mary' (Mary Anne Fox) from their number to go to Brisbane to instruct the emerging Sisters of Perpetual Adoration. He was anxious that they should not be influenced by Sisters who had not been taught by him: 'As for you going to a community of Nuns to be taught work—that is, the Sisters of Mercy—that would never do, and would only result in complete failure and surely much painful misunderstanding.'[29]

Sister Margaret Mary was to stay with the group as temporary Superior for the next two years. From Port Douglas, Father Woods had written: 'I have given directions to Sister Margaret Mary to make certain changes, which I am sure you will help her to carry out.'[30] We don't know what those changes were, but the lives of the Sisters were certainly different from the time of her arrival. There was obvious friction for which evidence suggests Sister Margaret Mary could well have been the cause. Community problems had already followed her from Bundaberg in Queensland to Adelaide in South Australia while she was a Sister of St Joseph. Mary MacKillop, in a confidential letter to the then Provincial of the Queensland Sisters of St Joseph had written: 'Sister M. (Margaret) Mary is a great trial to us all—you know what a temper she has—it seems to get worse instead of better.'[31] The minutes of a Council Meeting held at Kensington on 2 April 1879 record: 'Sister Margaret Mary's wish to abandon religion also discussed and it was unanimously decided that in consequence of bad health and being incapable for community duties she should be allowed to seek a dispensation.'[32]

Evidently, Sister Margaret Mary's temper came with her to the Sisters of Perpetual Adoration. From November 1879 through to August 1880 the letters of Father Woods to the Sisters constantly focus on the need for charity: 'All I ask for you is perfect charity to one another'; 'Let me beg of you all to try and let charity reign amongst you'; 'When anything goes wrong, take your complaints to St Joseph'; and most pointedly. 'Supposing your Spouse makes one of His spouses seem to show temper, but in what she means well—. . . Is it evil? We, and those who love her, will say No.' No doubt, Sisters' letters of complaint had been following Father Woods on his travels. A solution, he suggests over and again, is for them to keep strict silence as stipulated in their Rule:

> Silence shall be kept in every room except during recreation in the community room. If necessity obliges, the Sisters may speak in other places, but in a whisper and as briefly as possible.[33]

Optimistically, Father Woods thought that not talking might calm the situation.

However, it was not to be. The spirit of unrest seeped beyond the house to the room in which Mrs Beach resided. She began to interfere in the Sisters' lives and circulated stories about them in the neighbourhood. Externally, the Sisters tried to act as if everything was normal. Bishop Quinn took an interest in them and visited them regularly. Even though their house now accommodated them better, they still had poor furnishings. To save a Sister from getting a box to sit on when he visited, he would often sit on the corner of the table, speaking in a friendly and informal manner.

Internally, the Sisters struggled. Matters came to a head when Sister Gertrude wrote to Father Woods, asking him to re-install Sister Teresa as superior of the community. This did not happen. In June 1880, Sister Teresa (Anne Lafferty) left the Congregation and returned to Sydney where her former Director, Father Ambrosoli, was now chaplain to the Sisters of Charity at Potts Point. In August, Sister Gertrude (Ellen Connolly) did the same. Later, by February 1882, both women had entered the Sisters of Charity.[34]

The departure of these two Sisters rocked the small community. Oral history records this watershed moment when the remaining six gathered to consider their future:

> They fasted and prayed God to direct them to do his holy will. At this time there were some doubts among them as to which of two courses they should follow. They gathered together to discuss their future and problems. Would they return to their homes and relatives who wanted them to abandon the idea of a new religious order, or would they carry on? One of the group a very young woman at the time, Sister Mary John Lillis, solved their problems and doubts by saying, 'We can't go away and leave Him alone', pointing to the oratory. Their decision was made; they would stay and pray; If it was God's will, the work would prosper. 'So they struggled happily on', one of the group could tell us later.[35]

In an attempt to console them, Father Woods wrote to the group at the end of August:

> Now, my dear children, I hope your faith and confidence in God will enable you to see His hand in all that has happened. Unless the changes which have been made had taken place, the Order would remain languishing for many years. Now, however, you will see that all will soon be flourishing . . . I say to you all without any hesitation that you must not regret what has happened, but to see how good Our Lord has been, what warnings He gave and how patient He was before He struck the blow.[36]

He must then have realised how distant these words would sound, for two days later he followed up with another letter, only two sentences long but more empathetic and signed affectionately, 'Ever your own Father':

> I am sending you a big blessing, and can do no more but beg you to have courage and now try to keep the Rule with all your hearts, for God will help His work on rapidly. I am full of hope and confidence and courage, and send you my heart with this.[37]

The first sign of 'flourishing' was the entrance in October of a postulant, Bridget Hayes, who took the name 'Sister Clare'. In the same month, Father Woods returned to Brisbane to give missions and retreats. On at least six days in November and December he devoted himself to giving instruction to the Sisters. The notes they took of these talks were meticulously written out to be passed on to future generations. To their great joy, this precious time with Father Woods culminated on 28 December with Bishop Quinn giving his approval for the Blessed Sacrament to be reserved in the oratory. The hours of adoration were restricted to between 6 am and 9 pm, since the community would have to be much larger if there were to be 'perpetual adoration'. But this event had enormous significance for the group. They had reached a milestone that marked and gave expression to their purpose.

Meanwhile, the difficulties with Mrs Beach were taking a nasty turn. The Sisters' lives, now adhering to the strict interpretation of the rule that Sister Margaret Mary insisted upon, were constantly disrupted by interference from the old lady. Moreover, her gossiping among neighbours was putting them in a very difficult position. Finally, they sought the bishop's advice and he recommended that they look for another house where they would have the privacy they needed.

A property in Leichhardt Street on the north side of Brisbane offered opportunities that were very favourable. It was a large house with an attic, close to the city centre, and where St Patrick's Church in Fortitude Valley and St Stephen's Cathedral were within walking distance. But no sooner had they made definite plans to move there than they received another blow. It was found the Russell Street house on which they had spent all their means was mortgaged and so the money they had contributed could never be redeemed. They had lost everything.

During January 1881 two more postulants joined them.[38] So, now eleven in number (Sister Margaret Mary being with them still), they packed up whatever they had and arranged for its transport. On the last Thursday of the month, they set out for their new abode, Kenyon House in Spring Hill.

Chapter 2

Once more the little group known as the 'Black Sisters' were venturing into a new land. They had made friends in South Brisbane. Here in Spring Hill they were strangers once more. There was little time, however, to adjust to their new surroundings. They now had security in housing, but they needed more than that. To face difficulties ahead, they would need to feel secure in their chosen way of life. Strong spiritual foundations would now be more important than ever.

Leichhardt Street

One of the articles of furnishing that the Sisters made sure came with them to the house on Leichhardt Street was a *prie-dieu* on which they knelt during their allocated time of adoration. Many years later, during their centenary year of 1974, Sisters would treasure this legacy:

> Today, . . . the Sisters kneel on the same prie-dieu of cedar wood and beautifully carved. On the arm rest are two grooves in the wood worn over the years from constant use. This is a very precious link with our foundation Sisters.[1]

With the privilege of having the Blessed Sacrament reserved in the oratory in this new house, their second 'Villa Maria', the little group entered whole-heartedly into living the rule, uninterrupted by the previous troubles of Russell Street. When possible they attended Mass daily, either at the Cathedral or at St Patrick's:

> They organised to go in twos at different times to either place so they could keep the perpetual adoration going without interruption. This must have required great effort and sacrifice on their part, remembering we fasted from midnight for Mass and Holy Communion those days.[2]

The Sisters still had to earn their living, so filling the sewing orders was a necessary concern, often working until midnight on a rush order. Rent for the house, which was owned by Arthur Kenyon, was high. To guard against the financial pressures they had experienced in South Brisbane, they made a number of resolutions. First, they would put by the amount needed for rent before buying anything else—'they would rather starve than have the Lord evicted'. This meant that 'many a night their tea consisted of bread and dripping'. Second, they would never allow themselves to run into debt. Third, they would never complain to anyone else about difficulties they were experiencing.[3]

The Sisters' hard work and discipline did not go unnoticed among their new neighbours. Because they could not afford to have the material they needed for sewing delivered, two Sisters would be regularly seen rolling the large bales home from the suppliers. Shop owners noticed the poor fare the Sisters were buying. In later years, these early Sisters would tell stories of this time when it became obvious that they lacked food, and 'a certain good woman of the laity would organise a supply which would be delivered in a push-cart by one of her sons'.[4] Soon, children would drop by on their way to school with a batch of scones, damper, vegetables or fruit sent by their mothers for the 'Black Sisters'. The local baker often gave them his left-over bread. On St Joseph's Day (19 March), Father Woods would write, 'Be content with everything you get, for there is great peace in making the best of everything.'[5]

Light and Darkness

In June 1881, Father Woods returned to Brisbane and was able to give more talks to the Sisters, ending with what they called 'The Great Retreat' at the end of the month. Since the beginning of the year Bishop Quinn had suffered severe ill-health. When his condition worsened in July, he sent a message to the Sisters asking them to pray for him and expressed his wish that they should have 24-hour adoration as soon as it could be arranged. This began on the Feast of the Assumption, 15 August. The Sisters felt they had at last their primary goal had been achieved. On the same day, another postulant Bridget McGrath (Sister Raphael) joined the group.[6]

Their joy was impinged by sadness three days later when news came that Bishop Quinn had died. They grieved his passing; for he had proved himself a true friend. Despite his reputation of being authoritarian, especially in his dealings with women Religious, he had been kindness itself to the Sisters of Perpetual Adoration, at ease and relaxed during his many visits to their home.[7]

A strong theme in Father Woods' letters during the months after Bishop Quinn's death was the familial connection with the Sisters and their heavenly patrons. On the feast of St Michael, for example, he encouraged the Sisters to be brave, since the archangel was their 'defender and guardian'.[8] They were to align themselves with the sufferings of the Holy Family and of Saints through the ages whenever they experienced difficulties: 'Disappointments you are sure to have, but remember that Jesus and Mary had no comfort of any kind on earth'.[9] The mindset of being 'family'—be it spiritual and temporal—was one that would have influenced the Sisters' relationships with those around them. By now, the Sisters were a familiar sight in the district, visiting the sick and tending the needy. Parents would send their children to the Sisters for catechism lessons in preparation for First Communion and Confession at St Stephen's Cathedral. Soon, a group of friends formed around the Sisters to unobtrusively attend to their welfare. They were 'family'.

Bishop Quinn's successor was Robert Dunne who was consecrated as second Bishop of Brisbane on 18 June 1882.[10] By that time further changes had taken place at Villa Maria. Early in February, Father Woods had recalled Sister Margaret Mary to Sydney. At Easter time, a letter described her new role: from now on she was to be 'like a visiting provincial' to guide and give advice as necessary to Sister Stanislaus, now appointed as the superior.[11] Had Father Woods recognised during his stay in Brisbane that Sister Margaret Mary was, indeed, a problem in community? While no explanation was given, we might surmise, first, that Father Woods thought that the Sisters were now strong enough to live the rule on their own, and second, that by appointing her 'Provincial', he could 'save face' for Sister Margaret Mary by giving her a role that held prestige. However, there is no record that Sister Margaret Mary did continue to visit the community, although it is known that she did keep in contact with Sister Mary John (Bridget Lillis) for many years.[12]

The little community had been devastated when Sister Francis (Alice Downs) died on 26 February of that year. Father Woods' letter to them a week later had typically reminded them of her fundamental connection with them still:

> The first bitter sting of our grief is over, and we think less of the parting with one so dear, and more of the glory of having one foundation stone placed in Heaven, and one advocate to please our cause and watch over our interests. Is it not a great thing to think that one of our members has joined the Perpetual Adoration in Heaven?[13]

However, her 'heavenly' adoration did not fill a time-slot in the Sisters' schedule of ensuring someone was praying before the Blessed Sacrament twenty-four hours a day. It meant more sacrifice on the part of the ten who remained. The coming of a new postulant, Mary Leavy, on 6 May provided comfort and practical help. Mary took the religious name of Sister Josephine.[14] But hardly had the Sisters adjusted when, again, they mourned the death of another loved member, Sister Clare (Bridget Hayes), who died on 20 May. A few days later, Frances Oliver joined the group and assumed the religious name Sister Clare.[15]

A further blow had arrived on the Sisters' doorstep when Finney's Emporium, who 'took our whole output and paid us well', suddenly and regretfully cancelled their contract. Relatives had arrived from Scotland, and 'blood being thicker than water, they were given the work which had hitherto kept the wolf from the door.'[16]

The only solution was for the Sisters to take on private orders. Sister Aloysius, accompanied by the young Sister Josephine, now 'sallied forth in search of custom'. Sister Josephine told stories of going from door to door, showing samples of their work:

> They visited private homes and Sister said many a door was banged in their faces, other times they were greeted with abusive language. Sometimes Sister Josephine said she felt she couldn't take any more of it and would say to Sister Aloysius, 'Let's go home'. Nothing doing. Sister Aloysius would say, 'No Sister, we will keep trying, we must get some orders to take back to Mother Stanislaus'.[17]

The 'Black Sisters' were already well-known as expert needlewomen, and it was not long before they were busier than ever. They expanded their skills into making trousseaus for brides and other luxury items. Another anecdote fills out the challenge of those days:

> Lady Lilley, wife of Judge Lilley, headed the honour roll of private customers, the victims their two sons, for whom the Sisters made suits. . . . A number of little boys, here and there around Brisbane, climbed from childhood to boyhood in convent-made suits. It is with regret we have no record that some of these manly little fellows hardly appreciated the greatness thus thrust upon them, but their mothers did, God bless them.[18]

As November 1882 approached, the Sisters hoped that, since the seven-year probation set by Bishop Quinn was now completed, Bishop Robert Dunne would give his approval to the Sisters of Perpetual Adoration as a diocesan congregation.[19] Father Woods had written to them in April advising them 'to have some kind of cap' designed as part of the habit they planned to show the bishop when he visited them. When and where the Sisters did eventually meet the bishop we do not know.[20] We are simply told that he 'gave the Community his blessing and desired them to continue the work of Perpetual Adoration'.[21] At the end of November Father Woods again wrote to the Sisters, commenting:

> This month has been a month of suffering to you all. But that should encourage you because it shows that Our dear Lord is not forgetting you.[22]

He saw disappointment at not receiving the approbation they hoped for, not as an obstacle, but as a guarantee of success, since the cross leads to victory.

Father Woods' Travels

At the end of the year, Father Woods was invited by his friend, Sir Frederick Weld, to explore for mineral resources in South East Asia.[23] The expedition was to leave Brisbane on 14 August 1883, so the Sisters were thrilled when Father Woods arranged to spend some weeks with them on his way to Singapore. He arrived in Brisbane on 21 June and was able to give them seventeen talks, faithfully recorded and later bound with others that he had given into a notebook, 'Instructions to the Sisters of Perpetual Adoration.'

The next time the Sisters saw Father Woods was in 1886. During the time he was away he had sent many letters and parcels of souvenirs to them, so in one way they had travelled with him throughout Indonesia,

Malaya, French Indo-China, Hong Kong, Japan and the Philippines. He had instructed them to 'consult your geography and your maps' in order to follow where he was writing from.[24] His letters were a thread that kept them tied to him. As they had gathered to hear his talks to them before he left, they now gathered to hear his letters and to rejoice: 'When my letters come you may have recreation for a quarter of an hour after they are read.'[25]

Their prayer for him was, of course, constant. In requesting their prayers, he had often introduced them to new friends who were now part of his life—as in October 1884: 'I want you also to remember especially in your prayers the following persons who have been very kind to me Captain Bickford, Major Coffey, Mr & Mrs Creegh, the French Missionary Fathers and their missions.'[26] It was as though the Sisters were his primary family, and to them belonged the privilege of sharing the details of his daily situation.

When he wrote of illnesses, they had worried for him. Of most concern was Father Woods' frequent reference to failing eyesight: 'I am sorry to say that my eyes are very weak, and I am not able to write very much'[27]; 'I am not in the humour for writing, my own darling children, for my eyes are sore and I am not very well.'[28]

They had rejoiced with him when he shared his delight, an example being when, from Manila he had written:

> Yesterday was the feast of St Joseph. I saw the day kept up as I have never seen it in any country. The churches were crowded and there were signs of rejoicing everywhere. All day long bands were playing and at night the city illuminated. Indeed I feel so happy to think that my darling Saint was (celebrated) so much, however though, I can't be quite happy anywhere when I am so far away from all those that I love.[29]

In turn, the Sisters wrote to him, keeping him informed about their daily lives. On occasion, this meant that they might be reprimanded: 'Don't talk quite so loud at recreation—what you say can be heard across the road.'[30] And Leichhardt Street, now St Paul's Terrace, was not narrow!

Father Woods Returns

It was not until half-way through 1886 that a telegram came from Father Woods saying he was at last back in Australia. He had travelled on the HMS *Flying Fish*, arriving in Port Darwin on 23 June. However, it would be four months before he could leave there, since passenger ships from the Northern Territory to other Australian ports were few and far between. In the meantime, he accepted an assignment from the South Australian government to do geological surveys in the Northern Territory.[31] This took him to the area along the Victoria River and across Arnhem Land. Having submitted his report to the authorities, he then gave a public lecture in Darwin about his Asian trip to raise money for the Catholic Mission.[32] At last, at the end of October, he was able to secure passage to Brisbane on the ship *Menmuir*, and the Sisters joyfully obtained accommodation for him in another house owned by Mr Kenyon next door to their own. In fact, Mr Kenyon did not charge Father Woods for rent and made sure the room was always available so that priest could come and go as he pleased.[33]

Despite ongoing ill-health and severe problems with his eyes, Father Woods committed himself from 20 October to 1 March to give instructions to the Sisters on their spiritual and community life. Again, notes of these conferences were copied to be handed on to future generations of Sisters. Topics ranged from those dealing with fundamental religious matters such as personal relationship with God, the ministry and passion of Jesus, issues of conscience, and the Religious Vows, to those more trivial, such as 'Story of an irritable monk' and 'Religious decorum'. The Sisters remembered that he did not face them when he gave these talks. 'He sat and faced the tabernacle, . . . and spoke often in the third person, as if our Lord was speaking to them through him.'[34]

While Father Woods was overseas, the community had increased in number. Sister Maria Joseph (Sarah Meagher) had joined them on 19 March in 1885.[35] Now, during Father Woods' stay with them, Annie Shannahan entered on 9 November and took the religious name, Sister Mary Baptist.[36] However, even with two extra members to help, the community was struggling financially, as Father Woods himself was. He had taken on the extra assignments in the Northern Territory primarily to earn more funds to send to his brother Terry who was ill in Sydney. But he also was ill—his hands and legs were constantly swollen, he suffered from bouts of fever, and he often had to sit for much of the day in the dark, with wet bandages over his badly inflamed eyes. He was conscious, then, that his need for nursing was proving to be another burden on the Sisters. On the last day of February, he explained his situation to them:

> I'm going to say a few words to you about the month of St. Joseph [March], and how to spend it to please him. Before doing so I want to speak to you about a matter that I have mentioned to you before. I would not speak of it again were it not to spare you further pain. You must not be disappointed if I do not see you all every day, it seems hard to say but each day I feel less able to talk to you. I am so taken up with my own pains and little sufferings that I cannot talk to persons who come to speak to me, and when you come I scarcely hear half what you are saying, but you must not be disappointed or think you are forgotten or passed over. . . . One thing, whether I see you or not I make some little offering to our Lord for each of you every day.[37]

On 15 March, he wrote to his sister-in-law Sarah (Terry's wife): '[The doctors] all advise me to get out of Queensland and so I will as soon as I am able to travel which I am not at present.'[38] While the Sisters would have been aware that it was necessary for him to leave Brisbane, they relished his presence with the, since it was his vision that had first drawn them into Religious Life. Still unsure of themselves, they were dependent on his approval. Therefore, they grieved when at last he was able to make definite plans to return to Sydney. There he would live with the group of former Sisters of St Joseph led by 'Gertrude Abbot' (Mary

Jane O'Brien—'Sister Ignatius').[39] He would leave on 18 May, just a week after the diocese of Brisbane had been created an Archdiocese.[40] His parting gift to the Sisters was a statue of St Joseph. Years later, the Sisters found a note folded up in the hollow of the statue. It read as follows:

> St Joseph's Day 1887.
> I consecrate this community to our glorious father St Joseph for the Honour of the Sacred Heart of Jesus in the Adorable Sacrament of the Altar; the Immaculate heart of our sweet Mother and the glorious and faithful heart of St Joseph. I appoint St Joseph father and keeper, guardian, guide and protector of the community, to keep it from danger, to fill the members with graces, to be the support of the house and guard the door, to give the community the grace of confidence in St Joseph, their souls the grace of a happy death and the glories of heaven at the feet of Mary and Joseph.[41]

Father Woods in Sydney

From the time he left Brisbane until October of that year, Father Woods wrote to the community every week. He was still with them in spirit: 'My heart burns with longing love to Villa Maria'[42]; 'I love to place myself by your sides when you are at Adoration' [43]; 'My own loving and faithful children, my heart turns towards you.'[44]

From then on, due to the swelling in his hands, he found it more difficult to write and letters to the community as a whole became less frequent. Evidently, he still answered the letters of individuals, but even these had to be gradually curtailed. On 15 August 1887 he wrote to the young Sisters apologising: 'The truth is I cannot write to all . . . it is only fair therefore that the youngest and latest should be the first to go without letters since someone must.' Soon, he had to resort to writing with a pencil, 'so much easier' for his swollen hands,[45] and eventually, from 5 February 1889, the letters were dictated.

The prie-dieu brought from South Brisbane.
Photo permission:
Archdiocese of Brisbane Archives

Kenyon House, Leichhardt Street
The Sisters moved here in January 1881.

Bishop Robert Dunn

Sir Frederick Weld

Father Woods in Perak, 1884.

533 Elizabeth Street Sydney (Photo 1968 before demolishment).

Terry Woods

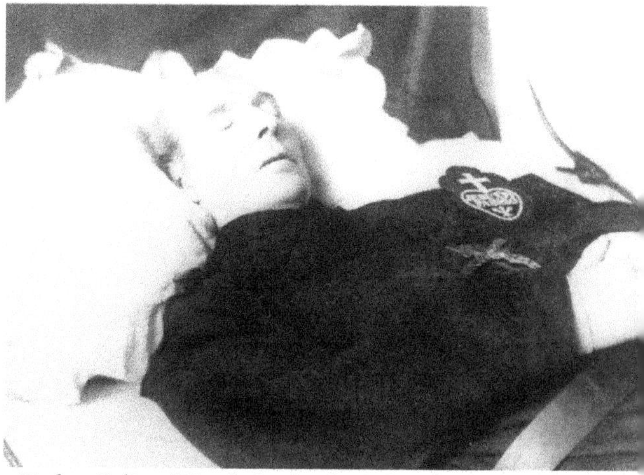

Father Julian Woods in death, 7 October 1889.

Father Joseph Canali

St Stephen's Cathedral, 1922
Photo permission: Archdiocese of Brisbane Archives

At the urging of the women caring for him, he also dictated his Memoirs to one of the Sydney community, Anne Bulger, who wrote in the Introduction:

> In December 1887 Father consented to give a few particulars for me to take down writing. At this time he was more or less a complete invalid and the little exertion of dressing in the morning fatigued him so much that he was obliged to rest for some little time, lying down. It was at this time that I got from him the notes in the following pages, and they have been transcribed in the very words in which they were given.[46]

Later, the Sydney community would entrust this precious Memoir to the Sisters of Perpetual Adoration. Every memory and report of what Father Woods was doing during these years of infirmity was stored up as part of his legacy to them. They knew that shortly after arriving in Sydney he had visited his dying brother Terry, but his own illness prevented him from attending Terry's funeral.[47] A number of priests, friends and fellow scientists visited him often at the Elizabeth Street house, and considerable time was taken up with his dictating reports and articles on scientific matters for publication. But gradually he was confined to his rooms. To his friend, William Archer, he had written in 1888:

> I have not walked 50 yards for some months and even the trifling shaking of a drive in Sydney is more than I can bear. It seems to me that my active work is done and perhaps it may not be our Lord's will to let me labour again as of old.[48]

The Sisters also knew that Father Woods did not fear death. When Sister Gabriel (Emily Francis) died in Brisbane on 9 June that year, he grieved with the community on reading 'the account of darling little Gabriel's happy death', but assured them that 'when you are called home that will indeed be a happy time.'[49] As it became obvious that Father Woods' own death was near, Mother Stanislaus and Sister Maria Joseph hurried to Sydney to see him. However, they were too late: 'he was unconscious and never knew the effort they made to visit him.'[50]

The travellers knew, however, that Father Woods was at peace. His friend, Father Ambrosoli, was his confessor and weekly visitor. It was he who had told Father Woods that the doctor predicted his life was entering its final stages. His reply was simple: 'I am in God's hands, He may do what He pleases with me.'[51] He had received the consolation of Viaticum, and over the days that followed, people whom he had known through the years came to thank and comfort him. The visits of other religious priests, including friends from the Marist Fathers and especially the Passionist Fathers, at the time giving a mission in a nearby parish, provided a connection with events in his earlier life. One of the missioners, Father Marcellus, arranged for him to be dressed in the Passionist habit—not as a sign of being received back into the Order, but according to a devotional practice whereby the faithful could be buried in the habit of a Religious.

Father Woods died on the Feast of Our Lady of the Rosary, 7 October 1889. Two days later his requiem Mass was celebrated at St Mary's Cathedral by Cardinal Moran. He was buried at the Waverley Cemetery, overlooking the Pacific Ocean. His tombstone today is mounted by two tributes, one erected by a group of scientists 'Commemorating the Scientific Work of Rev J. E. Tenison Woods FGS, FLS, FRGS' and the other honouring him as founder by the 'Sisters of St Joseph of the Sacred Heart in 1866 at Penola, S. Australia' and the 'Sisters of Perpetual Adoration of the Sacred Heart in 1874 in Brisbane'.

Life without Father Woods

When they returned home to Brisbane, Mother Stanislaus and Sister Maria Joseph visited Archbishop Dunne who asked them why they had travelled without asking his permission. Sister Dympna, writing in 1974, related the story as it was told to her:

> Mother said, 'Because I was afraid you would not let us go.' His Grace answered, 'I would never have stopped you from going down to your Father.'[52]

Up to now, the Sisters had depended on the advice of their founder mainly through correspondence, since there had been very few times when he was physically present with them. While they had preserved his written words, his death threw them back on their own resources more than ever before. Father Woods himself was conscious that there would be many details that would remain unresolved after he died. In his letter earlier that year on 26 April 1889 he had remarked that Sisters had raised matters which he did not then have the strength to attend to: 'There were some questions to answer, but you know what my answer would be without my writing, and, if not, I'm sure your little Mother can tell you.'[53] Mother Stanislaus knew enough of his heart that he considered she could interpret what was needed from now on.

When Father Woods died, the community consisted of eleven Sisters. In 1888 Mary Dinan had entered and had taken the religious name Sister Clare.[54] While numbers had remained almost static since August 1881, the Sisters had faithfully adhered to the 24-hour adoration that Bishop Quinn had entrusted to them. However, Archbishop Dunne had left them to their own devices since then. As biographer Neil Byrne explains, Bishop Dunne's focus was primarily on the pastoral care of families and on building up Catholic education in the early days of his bishopric. Besides that, he had a certain wariness about religious life for women owing to the negative experience of his own sister in Ireland.[55] Towards the end of his life, however, this changed with his friendship with the Sisters of Mercy at All Hallows. These factors, plus very bad health, would probably have contributed to his seeming distance with regard to the Sisters of Perpetual Adoration.

Providentially, soon after Father Woods's death, another priest, Father Joseph Canali, became a frequent visitor and confident.[56] The Sisters understood that the Archbishop had appointed him as their chaplain-director. It was more than likely, however, that aware of the death of Father Woods, he had taken on the role himself. This would have been true to his reputation for 'filling in' whenever there was a gap. He lived with other priests at the presbytery of St Patrick's Church in Fortitude Valley, so the Sisters were certainly within the boundaries of the parish. So, too, was the then Brisbane General Hospital (now the Royal Brisbane and Women's Hospital) where he was its much loved, self-appointed chaplain.

As a layman, an engineer-architect, Joseph Canali had been invited by Bishop Quinn to oversee the completion of St Stephen's Cathedral.[57] From his native Italy he had travelled with Bishop Quinn to Australia at the conclusion of the First Vatican Council. A number of the buildings he erected for Brisbane's Catholic institutions, including a classroom at St James Christian Brothers' School at Spring Hill, still stand today.[58] Despite his broken English which, it seems, never improved, he had been tutored in theology and was ordained by Bishop Quinn on 5 January 1879. Having taken the 'Black Sisters' to his heart, Father Canali became a source of practical help to them. Sister Stanislaus in particular came to depend on him for his wise counsel.

Before a group could be recognised as an established Religious Congregation, their bishop was required not only to give his own approbation but also to get the approval of the Congregation for the Propagation of the Faith in Rome which was responsible for Religious Life in Australia, since Australia was classified as a 'mission country' at the time. In 1890–1891, Archbishop Dunne made his *ad limina* visit to Rome[59] and took with him the Constitutions of the Sisters of Perpetual Adoration. There he was informed that the text of Father Woods needed modification.[60]

On his return, the Archbishop sought the advice of a Redemptorist priest, Father Edmund Vaughan who was then living at Singleton, New South Wales.[61] However, he was recalled to England in 1894 and it was a visiting Jesuit, Father George Buckeridge, who offered the Archbishop a workable solution.[62] Father Buckeridge had recently come to Australia from Ireland where he had known of a small religious community called the Sisters of Perpetual Adoration in Wexford. While he was in Brisbane giving retreats to priests and to the Sisters of Mercy, Archbishop Dunne asked him 'to give a retreat also to the group of pious women at "Villa Maria" on the Hill.'[63] Reporting that these were 'good, pious, sincere and virtuous women', he advised that they should be given 'the opportunity to prove themselves'.[64] His suggestion was that four of the Sisters should spend up to two years as Novices with the Wexford community, to receive training in Religious Life. The Wexford Constitutions could then be adapted to conditions in Australia.

Being Irish, the Archbishop was reassured, and soon wrote to the Wexford Sisters to make arrangements. But the 'Black Sisters' were faced with two huge concerns. The first was the number of Sisters needed to maintain the schedule of adoration which was their primary purpose. Two recent arrivals helped alleviate with that worry. In 1893, Mary McNulty (Sister Juliana) and Catherine Breen (Sister Michael, blood-sister of Sister Joseph) had entered and were now Novices.[65] The second concern was finance. There was no way they could afford to send four Sisters overseas. Nevertheless, they scrimped and scraped over the next two years, sometimes sewing up to 1.30 in the morning to fill extra orders. Eventually they earned enough money to send two of their number, Mother Stanislaus and Sister Maria Joseph. In December 1895 these two Sisters set sail for Ireland.

Chapter 3

Once again, the Sisters of Perpetual Adoration were loosed from their moorings. Mother Stanislaus and Sister Maria Joseph were on the high seas as they made their way to another country. In the 'new land' they believed God was showing them, they would have to be ready to explore a new way of being Eucharistic adorers. Meanwhile, the Sisters back home in Brisbane were venturing into what was a 'new land' for them. With Mother Stanislaus' absent, what little security they had felt was gone. Financially they lived with uncertainty and want. This part of the journey would be, for the Sisters of Perpetual Adoration, a time when, like all pilgrims, they would have to strip away anything that might have tempted them to pause and settle.

Wexford

No record survives to describe the journey of around three months that Mother Stanislaus and Sister Maria Joseph made when they left Brisbane for Ireland in December 1895. Nor do we know details of their arrival at Wexford and their reception into the convent community. On their way around the southern coast of Australia to the Indian Ocean, they are known to have stayed briefly with the Dominican Sisters in North Adelaide, South Australia. This Order, like theirs, was devoted to perpetual adoration of the Blessed Sacrament while also engaging in apostolic activity.[1]

It is probable that the travellers sailed first to England where in London it is likely they were guests of the Poor Servants of the Mother of God.[2] When they arrived in Dublin, they would have proceeded southeast to Wexford at the mouth of the River Slaney. They would have been impressed by the town's medieval appearance with its old town walls, narrow lanes and the ruins of a twelfth century abbey. At the marketplace they would have noticed a statue marking the rebellion against British rule a hundred years before.

The Catholic Church in Wexford was within the diocese of Ferns, this being a large town north of Wexford. In 1896 it was led by Bishop James Browne, second successor to Bishop Thomas Furlong who had founded the Sisters of Perpetual Adoration in Wexford. They were an enclosed Order whose purpose was to engage in continuous adoration of the Blessed Sacrament and to pray for the people of the diocese. Unlike the Brisbane Sisters, their members were divided into two: Choir Sisters who concentrated on adoration and recitation of the Divine Office, and Lay Sisters who saw to the domestic needs of the community. They had been established on 1 January 1875; so in that respect, at least, the Wexford and Brisbane groups were of similar age. When Mother Stanislaus and Sister Maria Joseph arrived at the convent, then located on Bride Street, Wexford, they were warmly greeted by the superior, Mother Mary Rose.[3]

The only surviving letter from Mother Stanislaus in Wexford was written on 28 August 1896. By that time the travellers were well ensconced into the life of a novice. Mother Stanislaus writes briefly, telling the Sisters that her Adoration times are 3 pm and 4 am, and that she continually keeps them in her prayer. She adds a note of pathos:

> I got a letter the other day from my poor Mother: when she heard we were passing though Melbourne she rushed over [from Tasmania] to meet me and was there three days after we left, poor thing. I was sorry, as it was a rough journey for her.[4]

During their time in the Wexford community, both Sisters took notes, commenting about differences between the Wexford rule and that of Father Woods. On their arrival, Mother Rose had given them a copy of the Wexford Rule that she had written by hand. Compared with the rule that Father Woods had written, it was more detailed, containing legislation for a host of community roles—not only for the 'Mother Superior', 'Bursar' and 'Mistress of Novices' as in Father Woods' rule, but also for the 'Mistress of Health', the 'Infirmarian', the 'Cook', the 'Refectorian', the 'Commissionaire' (the Sister who attended to maintenance), the 'Portress' and the 'Librarian'. Father Woods' 1873 Rule, on the other hand, simply named roles without minute instructions:

> The Sisters shall perform all the offices of their household for themselves. To one shall be allotted the preparation of the food, to another the refectory and so on. The Sisters in turn shall wash the dishes. The offices shall be changed every month, and where the work is heavy, they shall be ready to help each other in all charity, as in the Holy Family.[5]

Another difference between the two rules was the context in which they were written. In Father Woods' rule, legislation was not in a separate section but had to be derived from his description of daily living and its spirit. For example, there is no explanation of the vow of chastity in his rule. Instead, there are constant reminders that the Sisters 'must never forget that they come to give themselves completely to God and to belong wholly to Him';[6] '. . . the hearts of the Sisters should be fixed upon God and every occasion removed which would keep them attracted to external things';[7] '. . . the true Religious has no thought, no wish, and no desire except to love, to serve and to know God'.[8] On the other hand, the Rule Book for the Wexford Sisters is precise and clear: 'The Sisters in making their profession bind themselves by the vow of chastity to observe celibacy and moreover pledge themselves in virtue of the vow itself to abstain from any act opposed to the 6th and 9th commandments.'[9]

While much in the Wexford rule did not apply to them as non-enclosed Religious, Mother Stanislaus and Sister Maria Joseph did benefit from what they learnt of the requirements of Roman authorities for Constitutions to be accepted, and also from the friendships that were formed during that time. Because many of the Sisters back in Brisbane had originally come from Ireland, it seems likely the two visitors would have been in touch with Sisters' relatives while they were there. Certainly they visited Sister Maria Joseph's cousins—one of them, Bridget Meagher, decided to travel back with them to join the Congregation. Her brother, a prosperous Dublin publican, paid the fares for the three of them to make the return journey. This enabled them to spend around a fortnight in Rome where they stayed with a community of English Sisters, the Poor Servants of the Mother of God whose main work of charity was the care of older women.[10] Their foundress, Mother Magdalen (Frances Margaret Taylor) and Mother Stanislaus became very good friends. While in Rome they were able to visit churches, shrines and other places of interest. Years later, novices would press Sister Maria Joseph to tell them about this visit:

> What really amused her was having to ride about the streets of Rome in rickshaws. She said she was always afraid of falling, as they went so fast.[11]

Stories about these two weeks in Rome continued to be told during recreation for years to come, with special reference to the highlight of the whole trip—attending Mass celebrated by Pope Leo XIII and being given a personal audience with him.

In Brisbane

While they were in Ireland, Sister Mary Joseph had been left in charge of the Brisbane community. One of the earliest members of the community, Sister Mary Joseph (Sarah Breen) had fond memories of Father Woods who had fostered her vocation to the Sisters when he was giving a mission in Tasmania in 1874. By him she had been well-versed in openness to the Will of God, shown in an attitude of obedience to her superiors.

Sisters remembered Sister Mary Joseph as being 'very kind, but always firm'. She spoke well, and one of the Sisters' 'most vivid recollections' of her was her fluent pronunciation of Latin:

> For many years Sister Mary Joseph read the third lesson of the third nocturn of the Office of the Blessed Sacrament. We loved to hear her read this lesson—every word perfectly pronounced. It was really an inspiration to hear her. Her whole heart and soul were in her prayers.[12]

Despite her excellent pronunciation, she had her own way of emphasising the importance of obedience. When Margaret Daly (Sister Margaret Mary) joined the community in August 1896,[13] no doubt Sister Mary Joseph greeted the new postulant with what she said to all newcomers with her distinctive pronunciation:

> No use you coming here unless you will be obejent, You must be obejent, do you hear?[14]

Being only eleven in number, the community had struggled to maintain the 24-hour adoration while at the same time meeting deadlines for sewing orders and attending to daily tasks. For the two years that Mother Stanislaus and Sister Maria Joseph were away, the night adoration had been divided into four shifts—8 to 11 pm; 11 pm to 1 am; 1 to 3 am; 3 to 5 am. However, while they were able to manage this arrangement, the income from their needlework was small, and sometimes the food cupboards had been 'as bare as Mother Hubbard's'.[15]

Consequently, when the travellers arrived back in Brisbane in January 1898, they found that the health of some of the Sisters had begun to fail. The reception of Bridget Meagher as a postulant took place on 13 January and she took the Religious name of Sister Berchmans.[16] After that, Mother Stanislaus organised for the Sisters to go on their first holiday. She rented a house in Sandgate, and the Sisters went there in twos or threes until all had spent some time away. She even encouraged them to go for a swim. While there, Sister Aloysius, 'a very gifted and talented woman', took the opportunity to train some of the Sisters in painting and design. As a result, the community was able to embark on a new venture, the sewing and adornment of church vestments and banners.[17]

Since the return of Mother Stanislaus and Sister Maria Joseph to Brisbane, the Sisters had excitedly looked forward to the day when Archbishop Dunne would give his promised approval to them as a Congregation. He had already urged them to design a habit to be worn as a recognised Diocesan Congregation. But when he was presented with a model of what the Sisters wore in the Wexford community—a white habit with a red scapular and red shoes—he had remarked dryly: 'Won't ye look pretty getting round Brisbane like that!'[18] So the Sisters had designed a more acceptable model, and when at last the date was fixed, they placed their new habits in the oratory where the blessing would occur and awaited the Archbishop's arrival:

> The hour came and went, but Archbishop Dunne did not. They sent to the Archbishop's residence to enquire discreetly if His Grace was coming. They were told that His Grace was administering Confirmation in Cunnamulla.[19]

As the new century approached, the Archbishop made no further mention of approbation. It was thought advisable to adopt the rule followed by the Wexford Sisters with some alterations in terminology for example the term 'Sister Guardian' instead of 'Superior', as the Archbishop was not in favour of Father Woods's rule.[20] Whatever personal disappointment the Sisters suffered from the Archbishop's actions is not recorded. In her diary, Mother Stanislaus noted only matters of business:

1899 Jan. 23 Father Lee's vestment £2.15. Paid £1.
Mrs Willie owes £3.
Mrs Evelyn Lily pinafores making 3/- each.
Mrs Mooney dress, 6/6.
Making flannel shirt 1/9. With collar 2/-.
Dressing gown 17/6.[21]

Indeed, money matters were always pressing. A crisis occurred when several of the Sisters came down with influenza and sewing had to be put aside. For the first time they found they did not have the amount they needed to pay the rent. Then, the night before the rent was due, a knock came at the door. A gentleman whom they had never met greeted them and said he wanted to make a donation in thanksgiving for God's blessing. It was the exact amount needed for the rent. The Sisters were convinced that it was St Joseph who had visited them, proof of his protection under which Father Woods had placed them.[22]

Arthur Kenyon, owner of the house they rented, died in November 1896. From Ireland, Mother Stanislaus had asked Archbishop Dunne to inquire whether Mr Kenyon's son would sell to them. This was not agreed to. Since then, the Sisters began thinking about looking for a property that they might call their own. It was Archbishop Dunne who had suggested this first of all, since he did not deem it suitable that the Blessed Sacrament should be reserved in a place from which the Sisters could be ousted at a moment's notice. Besides that, he considered the state of Kenyon's house to be unsafe, and he feared for the Sisters' health.

Precarious as the Sisters' lives might be, in the neighbourhood, their presence had become even more valued. In adulthood, Mrs Nancy Tiernan remembered that 'the "Black Sisters", in their black dress and bonnet, and the hats and veils they wore when they left the convent', were poor but always happy—'people loved them'.[23] Father Frank Masterson who grew up in Spring Hill recalled his family's gratitude to the Sisters when they visited. It was Mother Stanislaus who had taught him to be an altar-boy which, he later realised, had sown the seed for his call to the priesthood.[24]

During 1898 a property came up for sale at the corner of Warren and Leichardt Streets, close to where the Sisters lived. William Maher, the baker who frequently sent left-over bread to the Sisters, urged them to buy it.[25] Again, lack of finance was the obstacle. So the neighbourhood stepped in. A committee was organised by the Gallagher and Casey families to raise funds and take subscriptions, William Maher's contribution of £200 heading the list.[26] Brisbane's Catholic newspaper, the *Age*, reports on 1 July 1899:

> For the past two months. a large and energetic committee have been working very hard to make the social held on Friday night in the Centennial Hall in aid of the Sisters of Perpetual Adoration a pronounced success, and judging by the magnificent result achieved, nothing had been left undone. The hall was beautifully decorated with pot plants, flags, and evergreens, placed in every conceivable manner to obtain the best and most graceful effect possible, whilst the supper room which was curtained off from the dancing portion of the building, was draped with flags and adorned with foliage, and the table which

The only photo that the Sisters of Perpetual had of Mother Stanislaus was that taken before she came to Brisbane. In the 1940s a photographer used that photo to place an impression of the head-dress worn by the 'Black Sisters' around it.

The habit of the Sisters of Perpetual Adoration, Wexford, Ireland.

The Wexford Convent

Mother Stanislaus' Grave
Nudgee Cemetery

The only photo of Mother Maria Joseph in the archives of the Sisters of Perpetual Adoration is an out-of-focus snapshot taken in her senior years.

> literally groaned under the weight of delicacies, showed at once the amount of labour bestowed on them by those to whom this portion of the evening's enjoyment was entrusted, and heartily do we congratulate them on their effort which would have been very difficult to surpass.[27]

A series of fetes, balls and other fund-raising events followed. A solicitor (and bachelor) who lived in Thornton Street, Mr Corbett, offered his services to the 'Black Sisters' to enable them to make the down-payment on the property.[28] The idea was put forward that the dilapidated house in the corner block could be demolished and replaced by a chapel, and that a second cottage also for sale next to it, be bought for the Sisters. Because the Sisters now numbered twelve and would be expected to increase, they needed more space than what they had become used to. Mr Corbett suggested that he himself would pay what was lacking for the second deposit. This the Sisters could not accept, and it was only when he changed his offer to a loan to be repaid when they could afford it that they agreed.[29]

The next few months passed in a flurry of activity. The house on the corner was demolished free of charge, by a neighbour who was a carpenter. He carefully saved any timber or roofing that was re-usable. Soon, with the help of anyone who could hold a hammer, the first Chapel of Perpetual Adoration in the southern hemisphere was erected. Perched on the ridge of Leichhardt Street, it looked down on the city, its bell 'ringing gently across the valley' as it called the Sisters to prayer.[30] Lady Lilley donated some rich materials from which the Sisters sewed the tabernacle veil and other furnishings[31] and William Maher, the baker, donated a 'handsome marble altar' for the sanctuary.[32]

The century turns

By early January 1900, renovations to the second house had been completed and the twelve Sisters were able to move in. They had their own convent at last. There was not enough money to have their few belongings and furniture delivered to their new home so the people of Spring Hill helped carry them down, using wheelbarrows and carts and whatever came to hand. The remark of one Sister was recorded: 'Thank God it is down and not up we are going!'[33]

Soon the Sisters had resumed their timetable of adoration, prayer, visiting the sick and the poor, and attending to the various activities of life in community. One difference was that the chapel was now separate from their convent, so they had to take care, especially at night, as they crossed the yard in all types of weather to take their turn for adoration. Donations continued to trickle in to help the Sisters in their efforts to pay off the debt.

In 1902 a chance decision marked the beginning of what would be a turning point for the Sisters:

> One morning a lady came to the convent and asked Mother Stanislaus if she would visit her mother during the day as she was very ill. The daughter had to go to work. Mother told her not to worry; she would take care of her. This was when Mother realised there was a great need for a place for the elderly

> to be taken care of and nursed. Mother Stanislaus gathered the Sisters around her and told them she felt the time had come when they should devote their lives to caring for people. She mentioned the sick lady she had visited and who had been taken to the General Hospital. When she was ready to come home the Sisters found room on a verandah for her for the time being.[34]

Perhaps Mother Stanislaus felt the Sisters had learnt from their experience in South Brisbane and could do better this time. Perhaps her friendship with Mother Magdalen in Rome gave her assurance. But it was not long before the Sisters took on another risk 'by mortgaging their home to purchase an adjoining cottage for the work'. For the Sisters of Perpetual Adoration, the ministry of caring for 'aged and infirm ladies' had officially begun.[35]

The new cottage was called 'Loretto', and soon all the rooms were occupied.[36] In an effort to maintain the women's dignity, the Sisters insisted that they be called 'boarders' instead of 'patients' or 'inmates'. Some did indeed pay what they could for their upkeep. Mother Stanislaus' diary notes: 'Mrs Atkins came to board, giving us £200 for her support.' However, those who could afford nothing were never turned away.

Within months another cottage, 'St Joseph's', was added. Then, over the years, the Sisters gradually bought more adjoining cottages. While 'the convent' housed an increasing number of Sisters, more accommodation was needed for women coming to them for help. Mr Corbett took care of their financial affairs, so the Sisters felt they could proceed with confidence. Another benefit was the fact that opposite the chapel was a private hospital, the Lady Lamington. The matron befriended the Sisters and instructed them in the care of aged persons. She and the doctors would visit the sick when called upon. When Sister Michael (Catherine Breen) died at the hospital in 1907, the bond between the two establishments grew even stronger with the Sisters pledging never to forget their indebtedness to the Lady Lamington.

There was a stream flowing through the property, created by water seeping through the rock-formation of the hill. A group of men who did odd jobs for the Sisters on weekends suggested the slopes of the stream could be utilised to supply fresh vegetables for the ladies and flowers for the altar. It was decided also to build a fowl house, and when various neighbours contributed a hen or two, fresh eggs and sometimes chicken broth were on the menu. To keep the grass down in Victoria Park, the Brisbane Council had given permission to the people around Spring Hill to pasture cows.[37] So when the Masterson family presented the Sisters with two cows, they accepted them with gratitude.[38] Each morning and evening two Sisters would go to the park to bring the cows home for milking and then take them back, although many a young boy would be sent by his mother to carry out the chore when the rains came. A separator was procured, which meant that not only milk but also cream and butter were produced. It was all hard work, but savings were made and debts were paid.

The Sisters continued their needlework for which they were renowned. When a young tailoress, Ann Kelvin (Sister Irene) entered in 1905, the Sisters' 'Tailoring Department' received a boost.[39] Some Sisters still taught catechism lessons, and each year the little chapel would be filled as families celebrated their children's First Communion. But gradually, care of the aged came to occupy first place in the Sisters' ministry.

During these years, the leadership of Mother Stanislaus heartened the Sisters and, indeed, the neighbourhood. During the illness and then death of Mrs Bridget Maher, wife of William, their benefactor, Mother Stanislaus and other Sisters of Perpetual Adoration were 'in constant attendance'.[40] In 1909 the Catholic newspaper the *Age* reported:

> Many Brisbane residents are cognisant of the good work achieved in an unobtrusive way by the nuns of the Perpetual Adoration Order, more generally spoken of as the 'Black Sisters' (in view of the habit worn by them), whose convent is situated in Leichhardt Street, at the top of Warren Street. Theirs is truly a life of devotion and self-sacrifice, and there are many poor families in our city and its suburbs who could gratefully testify to the benefits, material as well as spiritual, conferred upon them through the benign ministrations of the Black Sisterhood.[41]

The Sisters' title for Mother Stanislaus was 'Little Mother'—a term of affection, but also reminiscent of Father Woods' wish that the superior of their communities should not be 'Mother Superior' as in many other religious congregations, but rather 'Little Sister'. He had also impressed on the Sisters that the atmosphere in the convents should reflect the life of Jesus, Mary and Joseph, the Holy Family. It is this spirit of family that came to mark the relationship between the Sisters and 'boarders'. To foster this spirit among the Sisters, Mother Stanislaus would write a personal letter of appreciation to each on the feastday of the Saint after whom she was named. The Sisters took a sisterly interest in the welfare of priests, remembering Father Woods' comment about how some 'poor priests' are 'never loved or compassionated as they should be'.[42] As Father Woods had done in letters and, on occasion, in person, Mother Stanislaus gave regular spiritual talks to the Sisters. The text of only one of these talks survives—one given in 1891—where she reminds the Sisters that God has given them the privilege of Religious Life, but that this does not mean that they are thereby saints: 'We see how imperfect our lives are'. She points out that holiness is not found only in Religious Life: there are 'pure souls in the midst of the world'.[43] It is obvious that common sense informed the piety of this loved woman.

Death of Mother Stanislaus

The first indications that Mother Stanislaus was suffering from kidney disease is recorded in her diary of 1911:

> 16 August: Went into the Mater Hospital for some weeks.
> 4 September: Came home from the Mater Hospital.

However, when she arrived home, it was business as usual. On the very day she left hospital, her diary notes: 'Mrs Navy came to board at Antonia.'[44] Then on 20 September: 'Mrs Johnston came to board at Antonia. Paid 10 shillings in advance.' Functions continued to be organised by the Sisters' friends, as more cottages were purchased. An article in *The Age* in 1913 describes one such fund-raiser:

> A most enjoyable trip to the bay was indulged in by over twelve hundred excursionists last Tuesday evening. The occasion was the annual excursion in aid of the Sisters of Perpetual Adoration. The commodious steamer *Koopa* had all her available deck and cabin apace occupied to the fullest capacity commensurate with the comfort and enjoyment of the excursionists. The run down the river, with a beautiful cool breeze coming up from the bay, was a distinctly enjoyable experience after the. sweltering heat endured in the city during the day.[45]

In early 1914 Mother Stanislaus again spent time at the Mater Hospital, and there learnt that her condition was terminal. She wanted to die 'with her own dear Sisters around her', so she returned to the convent where the doctors and nurses of the Lady Lamington Hospital attended to her. The Sisters had put her bed in the parlour as she could not walk to the dormitory upstairs. However, because the Sisters provided breakfast in the parlour for the priest who offered Mass in the chapel each week, she stayed there only a few days and then determinedly dressed and returned to St John's dormitory where Father Canali gave her Communion. The Archbishop visited her and suggested that she put her wishes in writing which Father Canali would convey to him. This she did, Father Canali writing as she dictated to him:

> 9th June, 1914.
> If God in His mercy calls me out of this world into His glory through the merits of Our Lord Jesus Christ, I appoint Sister Maria Joseph, called in the world 'Sarah Meagher', born in Templemore, Ireland, as head of the Sisters of Adoration, in the Diocese of Queensland, City of Brisbane, residing at Villa Maria, corner of Leichhardt and Warren Streets. I also wish that if opportunity or necessity requires it, Sister Margaret Mary, called in the world, 'Mary Daly', should be appointed Mistress of Novices. I recommend to all my dearest Sisters of Adoration to be holy, charitable, kind; and ask them for the sake of God and Jesus Christ, to make light to their superior the heavy burden of her office.
> Signed this day, the 9th of June, 1914.
> Sister Mary Stanislaus, called in the world 'Catherine Gaffney'.
> Witness: GA Canali.[46]

When the Sisters of Mercy visited her, she was able to receive them and conversed with them. After a few days, however, it became obvious that death was near. The Sisters' reminiscences of her death are best told in their own words:

> When the end was drawing near the Sisters noticed Mother's breathing becoming weaker. . . . They could see she would not last long. All the Sisters knelt around her bed (except for the Sisters at adoration). Rosary after rosary was recited. Litanies and aspirations were repeated, the Sisters answering amid tears and sobs. . . . Mother died on the 20th June, Trinity Sunday, 1914, after a long painful illness. She was nearly 60 years of age.[47]

Mother Stanislaus never saw the episcopal approbation of the Sisters of Perpetual Adoration. However, she left a group of Sisters who now numbered thirteen, witnessing to the compassionate love of God in simple, down-to-earth lives, beloved of the Church community and, on its behalf, gathering in adoration around the eucharistic presence of Jesus. She had led the Sisters through years of struggle and disappointment, showing outstanding courage, wisdom and deep love. As Father Tom Boland said, the little group of Sisters had persevered in spite of enormous setbacks because 'they did not know when they were beaten'.[48] No one would contest that it was through the practical, steady hand of Mother Stanislaus, co-founder of the Sisters of Perpetual Adoration, that they did so.

Chapter 4

Even the best of succession plans cannot avoid the trauma of a leader's death. A period of turmoil and readjustment will inevitably follow the loss of one who was loved and revered as was Mother Stanislaus was. However, while they would face continued uncertainty, the Sisters of Perpetual Adoration did not lose their sense of direction. Perhaps it was because their true, unseen leader was present with them always in the sacrament of the Eucharist. Whatever the cause, the Sisters now faced a new phase of their journey with characteristic doggedness and hope for the future.

Mother Maria Joseph

The choice of Sister Maria Joseph by Mother Stanislaus as her successor was a wise one, since Archbishop Dunne would have no objection to her, seeing she had shared with her the training from the Wexford Sisters that he had required. Still, this assurance did not change the fact that the Archbishop seemed to have forgotten that the Sisters had been awaiting his approbation of them as a diocesan sisterhood for as long as he had been Archbishop. Mother Stanislaus had died with that wish unfulfilled. Now, having assumed the title, 'Mother' Maria Joseph inherited also the frustration of uncertainty about their status as a religious congregation.

The Sisters' recollections of Mother Maria Joseph described her as 'a bright, happy cheerful person, always smiling'; 'Mother had an Irish accent not too broad; she was softly spoken and all prayers were said from her heart'; 'When Mother Maria Joseph would go to the *prie-dieu* for adoration, she would look up at Our Lord in the Blessed Sacrament and smile.' Novices had especially fond memories:

> She was a loveable person and even when she would reprimand us, before night there was some small way she would make known to us that all was forgiven. For instance, she would say, 'Sister, if you go around to my room there is an apple there for you.'

During her assigned hour of night adoration, 10 to 11 pm, Mother Maria Joseph would always have a Novice with her. That did not mean they would then go to bed:

> You would never know . . . what job Mother had in store. Most nights it would be a tour of the invalid ladies to see if they were alright. Other times it was to lift all her pot-plants out so they could get the rain. It didn't matter about the Novice getting her share of the rain too! The night might be as black as ink, thunder and lightning everywhere—the Novice might be frightened, but nothing daunted Little Mother.[1]

When Mother Maria Joseph took office on 5 July 1914, the world was on the edge of a cataclysm. On 4 August 1914, Britain and Germany went to war, and the Australian government pledged to send troops to support Britain. Locally, Archbishop Dunne was failing in health, and in 1912 a coadjutor, Bishop James Duhig had been appointed to assist him.[2] For the time being, neither the archbishop's health nor the World War had direct impact on the daily lives of the Sisters of Perpetual Adoration, although the span of their prayers would have encompassed both.

What did have a profound effect on the Sisters was the death of Father Canali a year later, on 15 August 1915. For the past twenty-six years he had been their chaplain and friend, a link with their founders and one upon whom Mother Stanislaus had relied. Throughout Brisbane he was known as a second *Curé d'Ars*, renowned for his holiness and pastoral care of the disadvantaged, the sick and the dying, especially at the Brisbane General Hospital.[3] His habit had been to read the Office while he was travelling by tram from one place of ministry to the next. On this occasion, absorbed in his prayer and sitting by the open doorway, he had been thrown out when the tram lurched around a corner. He seemed to recover, but after a few days he had been taken to hospital and died of his injuries.

The whole city mourned the loss of this good man. On the day after his death, his body lay in state in St Stephen's Cathedral and thousands of people filed past to pay their respects and to pray. Civic leaders, members of parliament and four Anglican clergymen, his friends, were among those who attended his funeral. Bishop Duhig was away at the time and Archbishop Dunne was too ill to attend, so his Requiem Mass was celebrated by Father O'Flynn from the Fortitude Valley parish where Father Canali had lived for so long. His panegyric was preached by the Cathedral Administrator, Father James Byrne,[4] who declared:

> His history is best told in the wards of the General Hospital and in the countless chambers where he brought the last consolations of religion to the sick and the dying. As long as Brisbane is Brisbane, his name will stand, and when its ecclesiastical history comes to be written, no name will go down to posterity with more euloquiums (sic) of respect and sincere veneration than that of Father Canali.[5]

Another loved friend, Mrs Catherine Bragg, died suddenly on 29 October 1916. When her husband, Joseph, had died in 1883, she had taken over the family bakery he had established in Ann Street, Fortitude Valley, and had generously supplied the Sisters with pastries, especially when they began caring for aged women. When the Sisters heard she had collapsed they visited and were with her 'in her last moments'.[6]

However, the supporters of the Sisters continued to increase. Their committee organised various fund-raising events every few weeks as cottages were bought or adapted for the aged. Each year, for example, a Moonlight Trip was advertised as being 'under the auspices of the Sisters of Perpetual Adoration'; the *Koop* would 'leave Kennedy Wharf at 7.45, music and refreshment on board'.[7] As a young boy, Father Frank Masterson remembered: 'Sometimes after school and at weekends I would help clean the yard and often helped on stalls at fetes and house functions (games of Euchre and so on) in order to raise funds for them.'[8] The Sisters were a focus of community, giving and receiving life and care. Obituaries published in Brisbane's Catholic newspaper, the *Age*, frequently noted that the Sisters of Perpetual Adoration had been with the dying person, one such example being Mrs Rhea Hughes, niece of Sister Margaret Mary (Daly).[9]

After the death of Father Canali, Father William McGoldrick was appointed chaplain to the Sisters of Perpetual Adoration as part of his ministry in the Cathedral parish. In later years he remarked that the appointment involved little more than bringing Holy Communion on occasion to the sick or to Sisters unable to be at early parish Mass, and to 'giving Benediction on Sundays and the First Friday'. For Benediction there was a 'choir master'—Sister Aloysius—whose singing voice would run 'like a saw through you when she raised it'. Another memory that stayed with him was the 'dreadful heat' in the chapel in summer months when the candles would bend over 'double'.[10]

In 1916 the Jesuits made a foundation at Toowong in Brisbane, and Bishop Duhig asked them to give 'spiritual care' to the 'Black Sisters'. For three years Father Richard Murphy SJ endeared himself to the Sisters, acting as confessor and giving them regular spiritual talks.[11] When he left at the end of 1918, Father John Roney SJ did likewise.[12] Father Robert Little SJ gave the first of what would be many retreats to the Sisters in July 1916.[13] It would seem that if the Sisters were to survive, they would need to be well-known not just in the neighbourhood but among the clergy in general, since in a hierarchical Church they had influence. Certainly, the Jesuits were to play a prominent role in the Sisters' lives from now on.

Local Approbation

With the aging Archbishop Dunne becoming more and more frail, Bishop Duhig had taken on greater responsibilities for the Archdiocese. However, while he had been aware of the Sisters of Perpetual Adoration, he did not have the authority to make good the lack of diocesan approbation for which they longed. The death of Archbishop Dunne on Saturday, 13 January 1917, meant that Bishop Duhig automatically succeeded him as Archbishop. Immediately the Sisters noticed the change. When he learnt of their longing to have Exposition of the Blessed Sacrament during adoration, he made arrangements that this could be done for the time being on First Fridays and on other occasions depending on Father McGoldrick's availability.[14] This was the first sign the Sisters had that one day they would achieve their ultimate goal—to have Exposition on a permanent basis.

The Archbishop's interest in them was welcome. There were now eighteen Sisters, and he was concerned by the conditions in which they lived. Their convent was in a poor state of repair, they had to walk or run from cottage to cottage to attend to the ladies, and, no matter what the weather, they had to make their way across the yard to the chapel with a hurricane lamp at night for rostered adoration. Soon, he raised the possibility of them replacing the wooden chapel for a more secure brick one. Further, he suggested, they might build better accommodation for themselves.[15]

However, a more important event for the Sisters occurred when the Archbishop made a move in December 1920 that filled them with joy. He wrote to Mother Maria Joseph: 'Acting on authority granted by the Sacred Congregation of Religious in Rome to my predecessor, the Most Rev. Dr Dunne, . . . I hereby approve of your Congregation known as the 'Sisters of Perpetual Adoration' as a Diocesan Institute, subject to the Ordinary of the Diocese.'[16] The moment the Sisters had been waiting for since 1881 had arrived. However, the Archbishop explained, this approval would have to be ratified by the Holy See, and therefore the Sisters' Constitutions would have to be prepared for presentation to Roman authorities. That meant producing a clean copy of the rule by which they had been living and having it translated into Latin.

Here, the assistance of Father Little SJ proved invaluable. On her return from Ireland in 1898, Mother Maria Joseph had adapted the Wexford rule which was composed for enclosed nuns, to one that suited them, the non-enclosed Sisters of Perpetual Adoration. Now she and Father Little re-wrote this rule according to the requirements of the Sacred Congregation of Religious. By the time Archbishop Duhig announced he would pay his *ad limina* visit to Rome in April 1922, the documents were ready.

'Real Nuns'

For the Sisters, diocesan approbation gave them legal security regarding their place in the Church as Religious. However, externally, no one knew this. There was a Catholic saying that 'the habit does not make the monk'. But, the Sisters felt, it would not be until they could wear what was then a recognisably religious habit that they would be regarded as 'real nuns'. Further, they were uncertain as to whether Roman ratification was necessary before they could do so. In 1915 Mother Maria Joseph had written to Australia's first Apostolic Delegate, Archbishop Cerretti, seeking clarification about the status of the Sisters of Perpetual Adoration, but she had received only a polite note in reply, ignoring her question and simply sending his best wishes to the Sisters.[17] In 1920 she had written to the next Delegate, Archbishop Cattaneo, repeating the request.[18] It seems Father Roney SJ also wrote, as it was to him, not to Mother Maria Joseph, that Archbishop Cattaneo sent a letter of reply on 13 January 1921 regarding the 'Black Sisters':

> Quite recently I had a conversation with the Archbishop of Brisbane on this subject, and he told me that some time ago he gave episcopal approbation to the Sisters of Perpetual Adoration. The time is not yet ripe—as far as I know—to take steps for the formal approval as an Institute *Juris Pontificii* (Roman Approbation).[19]

In July of that year, another Jesuit, Father William Lockington from Sydney gave a retreat to the Sisters.[20] Whether or not he then spoke to the Archbishop on their behalf we do not know, but at the end of March in 1922, a few weeks before he was due to set sail for Rome, the Archbishop wrote to Mother Maria Joseph to say that Father Lockington was soon returning to Brisbane for a visit and that he might well be present at their 'Clothing Ceremony' to be held on 5 April. This was the first indication to the Sisters that their approbation would now be known by the general public. The date the Archbishop named for the ceremony was a Wednesday, so only the Sisters and 'boarders' could be present. But quietly, the sign of recognition for which the Sisters longed had arrived. In Church politics, men could achieve what a woman's efforts could not.

Archbishop James Duhig

The foundation stone of the chapel and convent, 1925.

The new convent and accommodation (left), the new chapel (back right), the original timber chapel (front right)

Villa Maria Chapel, opened in 1927.

In writing her reminiscences years later, Mother Philomena Callaghan recorded the 'Clothing Ceremony' quite simply:[21] 'On 5 April 1922, assisted by Father W. Lockington SJ, His Grace blessed the Sisters' monastic habits which proved we were recognised as a religious community.'[22] In the community, however, the Sisters could hardly contain their excitement. Brother Anthony Keenan CFC was teaching at St James' College at the time and was a regular visitor to the convent. He tells what happened when he was introduced to the habit:

> Usually the door was answered by a cheerful Sister of medium build, wearing not the customary style of a nun's habit, but a black dress with white collar and cap with a short veil resembling the dress worn by postulants of other orders. . . . One day the front door was opened to me by a joyful Sister, radiant and almost unrecognisable in a new habit complete with veil, guimpe and cincture . . . A large metal cross was shown to me and its symbolism explained. [She was then joined by] several other Sisters anxious to show off the new habit and there followed great chatter, the Sisters folding their hands in their ample sleeves in orthodox nun fashion.[23]

The explanation of this habit by one of the Sisters was recorded by Father Joseph Gates SJ:[24]

> The habit is black and has a scapular back and front. It has long sleeves and a cincture of leather and a silver cross, Celtic in design. We have a white coif and guimpe of dimity and a veil. Such things have significance. The habit means regeneration, the cincture is in honour of the penance of Saint John the Baptist, the coif is the helmet of salvation, the guimpe resembles purity of soul, the cross and beads remind us that we belong to Jesus crucified, and the scapular reminds of God's free grace with which we clothe ourselves. When we go to Chapel we wear a long white muslin veil. And when we go out we wear a black mantle just a little shorter than our habit.[25]

Even if official ratification of Archbishop Duhig's approbation was yet to come from Rome, externally, at least, the twenty-two Sisters of Perpetual Adoration were now 'real nuns'.

Altar Breads

For the Sisters, the wearing of the habit was the highlight of 1922. Yet, another happening in that year would have repercussions for them that would prove to be highly significant. When Mother Maria Joseph was at Wexford, she had, as part of her duties in the Novitiate, been taught how to bake and cut altar breads for use during Mass. On their return trip to Australia, she and Mother Stanislaus had purchased a small baking and cutting machine, and since then the Sisters had produced the breads they needed for their own use.

One day in 1922, a priest (un-named) whom the Sisters had known when they lived in South Brisbane, came to them in distress.[26] He had found he was short of altar breads, and with the weekend approaching, he could not obtain any and did not know what to do. The Sisters were able to help, and word soon got around that the breads made by the 'Black Sisters' were superior to any obtained from interstate suppliers.[27] More orders came in. It was not long before two Sisters were assigned to the baking and distribution of altar breads full-time, as it was recognised that this was a most appropriate ministry for a Congregation devoted to Eucharistic worship. Eventually, electric machinery replaced the hand-cutters, with the Sisters supplying thousands of altar breads each week for the whole of Queensland and beyond.

A New Chapel

On the Archbishop's return to Brisbane from Rome later that year, no further mention was made of the Roman authorities ratifying the Sisters of Perpetual Adoration as a Diocesan Congregation. Once again, Mother Maria Joseph had to accept that personal intervention was impossible and that she must await the outcome of a bureaucracy in which she had no power. By now there were thirty-six women under the Sisters' care. The community had grown to twenty-three, so the Sisters' own accommodation was being stretched to the limit. So, at the Archbishop's urging, the focus was put on a building program to build a new chapel and a hostel to house the 'boarders' and Sisters.

It was not for nothing that Archbishop Duhig became known as 'James the Builder'. Duhig's biographer, Father Thomas Boland points out that 'in his lifetime he was responsible for some hundreds of church buildings, large and small'; many of them were on hilltops and other prominent sites.[28] The Chapel of the Sisters of Perpetual Adoration was not the least among these. While the Archbishop left it to the Sisters and their supporters to pay for the construction, it was he who arranged for architects and consultants to advise the Sisters and to oversee the building process. The committee that had raised funds for the Sisters for so long was revamped to become the 'Building Committee'. The Archbishop's architect JF Hennessy was engaged.[29] The contract price was cited at £46,000, an enormous sum for those days and a long way out of the reach of the Sisters' savings. It was only with difficulty that a loan was raised, as the banks refused to advance the money given the small amount the Sisters could offer as security. It was the intervention of an unnamed businessman 'who was on the Board of Directors of an insurance company' that a loan of £25,000 was obtained. Archbishop Duhig laid the foundation stone for the chapel and hostel on 6 December 1925.[30]

The Sisters and their supporters then became caught up in a relentless effort to raise the necessary funds. At one stage it looked as though all building operations would have to cease because money had dried up. The Sisters could draw only on what the boarders offered and what they earnt by their own hands in the production of vestments, banners, articles of clothing and, lately, altar breads. When a Father Ryan died and left £100 to the Sisters of Perpetual Adoration, the suggestion was made by the *Age* that his 'recognition of the silent charitable work performed by these Sisters might well be imitated by others when leaving money for charitable and other purposes'.[31] The Building Committee held a host of functions—garden parties, jazz and euchre parties, concerts, Florin Evenings, Art Shows, grand fetes, dances and balls, raffles, river trips—all advertised in the Catholic publications and listing there the prize-winners and those who made donations.

Looking back, the Sisters later reflected that these activities, including the naming of contributors, 'fostered friendships' and helped build up an even stronger sense of community around 'Villa Maria'.[32]At the same time Archbishop Duhig was making his own appeals for funds to complete St Stephen's Cathedral, so the demands being made on ordinary Catholics must have been enormous.

Somehow, money crises were overcome—the Sisters attributed that to 'divine Providence'—and the building continued.[33] We might also attribute it to the fact that Brisbane Catholics 'owned' the Sisters: as the *Age* pointed out, 'Brisbane has the honour of being "the foundation centre of a religious order of Nuns of Perpetual Adoration."'[34] Perhaps, too, given the influence of priests over parishioners at the time, the Sisters' efforts to cultivate friendships with clergy bore fruit. The Sisters of Perpetual Adoration were by this time well-known and well-regarded, at least in the Catholic world. In almost every edition of the Catholic newspaper, they are mentioned. When Father McGoldrick joined the Irish Mission to China in 1923, the Sisters' presentation to him of a 'travelling altar' was praised in the *Age* as being a most 'valuable gift'.[35] Brisbane Catholics welcomed the newly-ordained Father Brian Bolton back from Rome in September 1924. He celebrated his First Mass 'in the beautiful little Chapel attached to the Convent of the Sisters of Perpetual Adoration where his aunt, Sister Sebastian, is one of the community'.[36] While today we might consider social-media opportunities to have been limited in the 1920s, word got around that the Sisters needed financial help and people responded.

By April 1927 the Convent and Hostel were nearing completion. On 14 April, Brisbane was celebrating the visit of the Duke and Duchess of York. Crowds and processions filled the streets. Coincidentally, the funeral of a Sister of Perpetual Adoration was also held on that day. Sister Mary Teresa had joined the Sisters in 1920 at the age of 31 years and made her temporary profession in 1923. Soon afterwards she succumbed to a serious illness. On 9 April 1927 Mother Maria Joseph had received her Final Vows and the next day Sister Teresa had died.[37] Father Archibald Mills contrasted the two events of 14 April—the one with cavalcades, cheering and excitement, the other in silence and sombre respect—as he wrote for the *Age*:

> There were two processions that day and two kingdoms. She had chosen the one that fadeth not away, and so passed Sister Mary Teresa of the Sisters of Perpetual Adoration to her eternal reward.[38]

There was plenty of cheering at Villa Maria on 14 August that year when Archbishop Duhig blessed and opened the first stage of the building project, the new chapel and convent at the corner of Leichhardt and Warren Streets, Fortitude Valley. In his address given for the occasion he congratulated 'the Sisters of Perpetual Adoration and their large circle of friends' for what they had achieved against the odds:

> The new Chapel is a delightful piece of architecture and will be a permanent adornment to the fine site on which it stands. The Convent and Hostel are in keeping with the Chapel and when the whole block is completed there will not be many buildings of its kind in the Commonwealth to surpass it.[39]

Pontifical High Mass was celebrated in the Romanesque-styled chapel and the marble altar was consecrated. There could not have been a greater contrast between the new chapel and the tiny wooden building that had served the Sisters and people for twenty-seven years. This lofty chapel, able to hold 350 worshippers, had tall, arched windows and a large, semi-circular apse beneath a towering dome. When the celebrations were over, the Sisters placed the humble *prie-dieu* they had brought from South Brisbane at the foot of the grand Sanctuary and began their adoration of the Blessed Sacrament in its magnificent new setting.

Accommodation completed

The Convent opened by the Archbishop comprised three storeys, the top floor being reserved as the Sisters' residence, the first for some of the boarders and the ground floor for dining and the various works conducted by the Sisters. There were now twenty-six Sisters, only six of whom had lived at South Brisbane and Kenyon House. For the first time they had adequate space and shelter from the elements.

Hardly had they settled into these new quarters, however, than they had once again to attend to fund-raising for the completion of the Hostel (which involved the demolition of the old chapel) and the payment of outstanding debts. As early as the next month, Archbishop Duhig was scheduled to 'open a fete in the Convent grounds of the Sisters of Perpetual Adoration' on 10 September.[40] Again, the Building Committee drew up a calendar of events that extended well into 1928, with dignitaries attending whenever possible. So it was that the Governor (Sir John Goodwin) and Lady Goodwin were present at the Annual Fundraising Ball held in the South Brisbane City Hall on 13 June 1928.[41] Colonel NAH Campbell, ADC and Mrs Campbell accompanied the Vice-regal company. The strategy of inviting prominent people to such functions not only drew the crowds but also introduced the presence of the Sisters to the wider community,

On 3 June 1928 the Hostel for Aged Women was blessed and opened, again by Archbishop Duhig. While both *The Age* and *The Catholic Advocate* gave full coverage of the event, the latter newspaper considered the comments by various speakers 'on the worth and qualities of the Sisters' to be 'eulogistic'. Today we squirm upon reading the Archbishop's praise of the Sisters, informed as it was by 1920s attitudes to women:

> Although the building has cost £30,000 and is not yet complete and the Sisters have spent only £19,000 out of £25,000 borrowed from a friendly source, this shows men how economical a woman can be. Usually they are thought to be spendthrifts, but if you have a good woman at the head of your affairs, your household will be run economically. All the [ventures] of the Sisters are financially sound, and they have already paid on this building £45,000. This is an asset to the Church and above all to the Sisters themselves and the city of Brisbane.[42]

The Archbishop saw the new buildings as featuring in what he envisioned for the whole of this area overlooking the city, with Leichhardt Street a tree-lined boulevard where stately mansions and tall government building might rise. In his vote of thanks, the Minister for Works, Michael Kirwan, said that he 'endorsed the remarks made by His Grace regarding Spring Hill', and agreed that the new buildings contributed much to Brisbane: 'The brick work is as good as you would see in any part of the world.' He extended the thanks of the Sisters to the workmen and all who were involved in the construction of the building, paying particular tribute to the memory of Father Canali and 'also the late Mr Wm. Maher and the late Mr John Casey, who had taken such a keen practical interest in the Sisters and their work.'[43]

The Sisters had fulfilled the hopes of the Archbishop so far, but there would still be years of fundraising events to organise and friendships to cultivate in order to pay off the outstanding debts. Meanwhile, their work of providing accommodation to elderly women continued to expand. No sooner was the new Hostel blessed and opened than more applications came in:

> In a short time every available room was occupied by ladies who wished to find a home away from home; and whose house or condition would warrant not their maintaining their own homes. They told their friends they had found peace and happiness, free from cares and worries to spend their remaining years under the roof with the Blessed Sacrament.[44]

The influx of numbers requesting haven at Villa Maria meant that on the section of land facing Gotha Street, the cottages bought over the years continued to house 'boarders'. There were still difficulties, despite the improved conditions. But the atmosphere of peace referred to was striking. Father Joseph Gates SJ commented:

> The almost magic influence which these Sisters possess of spreading contentment among the boarders is a puzzle to me. One of those 'boarders', a bedridden patient, yet perfectly bright and happy, once confided that the source of her joy was the fact that the Sisters loved her.[45]

'The Sisters loved her.' A commendation indeed!

Chapter 5

The 1920s had been good to the Sisters of Perpetual Adoration, even though they were now left with an enormous financial debt. They now had the official approbation of the Archbishop and were recognised as a genuine religious congregation. They had secure housing. However, as the next two decades approached, the Sisters, with the rest of society, would find themselves vulnerable to forces outside their control. Vulnerability can be met with two opposite reactions—either withdrawal and anxiety or compassion and outreach. How the Sisters of Perpetual Adoration navigated their way through these years takes us into another phase of their story.

The Depression

In October 1929 the Great Depression, sparked off by the Wall Street stock market crash in the United States of America, hit Australia. Although Queensland was somewhat shielded from its immediate effects in that the state was more dependent on farming and primary products than on manufacturing, unemployment grew from 11.6% in 1930 to more than 30% the next year.[1] Nevertheless, the Building Committee (now calling itself the 'Appeal Committee') continued to do whatever they could to raise funds on order to pay the debt of the new buildings that comprised Villa Maria. Letters were sent to prospective benefactors, acknowledging the effects of the Depression which meant that 'many who were desirous of helping were unable to do so', but appealing to the generosity of the recipient:

> We are sure you will not be wanting in admiration of the courage and grand spirit of the Sisters who have once more thrown their all into the work of God. The prayers of the good Sisters will be poured out for you perpetually. Besides you will have the gratitude of Him whose ear is ever open to the petitions of the kindly hearted people who give in His name.[2]

As with convents and presbyteries everywhere, the Sisters of Perpetual Adoration were called upon to provide food for unemployed men and swaggies especially during the Depression. The effect was often personal. For example, when the brother of Sister Mary Paul (Mary Baggot) lost his job, he 'used to come to the convent for food', and 'Sister felt this very much'.[3]

In these years of anxiety and hardship, a depiction of peace and contentment would have been alluring. By now, Villa Maria was housing around eighty women. In his booklet *An Australian Mustard Seed*, Father Thomas Dunphy invites the reader to 'visit' Villa Maria, where these women 'find shelter and friendship for their declining years'. The visitor proceeds first from the 'threshold' to the 'great chapel':

> Within the sanctuary there kneels the silent figure of one of the Sisters, her black habit hidden under a snowy mantle which the nuns wear when at their supreme duty of adoration . . . Let's go upstairs. Here we find the star boarders of the whole establishment. They are numerous groups of elderly ladies who have placed themselves under the care of the Sisters . . . Along the shaded verandahs are little groups of these elderly women reading, chatting, knitting, finding a home from home among the nuns . . . In the courtyard that opens off the inner verandah there is erected a stage for plays and concert parties . . . If they wish it, these ladies can enjoy the privilege of morning Mass and frequent Communion; they are free to visit the Chapel whenever they wish; they are close to the city whence may repair to do a little shopping or window gazing, and within the walls of the convent . . . the grey years of old age are brightened by spiritual and material kindliness.[4]

When the Sister began caring for the aged in 1902 there were no old age pensions. The situation of the aged, unless they were supported by their families, was dire, and the Sisters' ministry filled an obvious need. The Federal Government did introduce these pensions in 1908, but, of course, they could not provide antidotes to the prevailing problems of ageing, such as the lack of nursing care and the tendency to omit meals and retire into isolation. During the Depression, social problems were exacerbated. It is no wonder, then, that the people of Brisbane approved of what the Sisters were doing for the elderly. The building program would not have met with disapproval, since the development of infrastructure, such as the construction of the Storey Bridge across the Brisbane River, was a commonly-used ploy by governments to boost employment. In these circumstances, the Sisters of Perpetual Adoration became more popular than ever.

Mother Philomena Callaghan

In 1917 the canons of the Catholic Church had been codified. Religious Congregations were required to re-write their constitutions to accord with the Code, and in 1921 the Wexford Sisters of Perpetual Adoration had done this. A copy of these constitutions had been sent to the Brisbane Sisters, as it was this rule that they lived by, with necessary adaptations made to suit them as a non-enclosed Congregation. One of the stipulations of the revised rule was the holding of a General Chapter every six years and time-limits on the length of time served by the major superior. The maximum time was two terms of six years. After a break, there was the possibility of re-election for a further two terms.

By 1932 Mother Maria Joseph had held the position of major superior for eighteen years—twelve years since their approbation as a Diocesan Congregation. It was therefore necessary to hold a General Chapter (or meeting of Sisters elected by their peers) to review their way of life and to elect another superior in place of Mother Maria Joseph. Sister Philomena Callaghan was chosen.

Ellen Callaghan had joined the Sisters in 1906 at the age of twenty-six years. Her family lived at Mount Walker, a farming district south-west of Brisbane. A story that has been handed down to the Sisters points out that she came from 'a well-known racing family'. She was a good cook, and even when she held the position of 'Little Mother', was known to have rolled up her sleeves when needed and cook the meal for the large number of 'boarders' at Villa Maria. On one particular occasion she was doing this. The stove ran on fuel, so the flames were confined to the top. Six novices stood at the ready with plates to be filled and served to the women. Suddenly, a rat appeared at the back of the stove. The eyes of Mother Philomena and the rat met:

> Mother, quick as a shot, grabbed the nearest weapon, a large wooden spoon, and whack!'. The rat dodged. Mother continued the serving. A minute afterwards Mr Rat appeared again. Another whack from Mother. Every time Mr Rat showed its head, Mother was alert and 'at the ready'. We stood around in a trance. As the ladies were waiting to be served there was no time to lose, but Mother was anxious to finish the fight. Now it was on. Mr Rat played hide and seek, pursued by Mother. Whack! Whack! Whack! At last, perhaps thinking of the serving, Mother gave a mighty one and we knew that at last she had won, leaving the broken spoon on the stove. . . . [After the meal was completed], a large-sized hole behind the wood heap became the burial place of the largest rat you ever saw from the quarry at Spring Hill.[5]

As the story illustrates, determination was one of the qualities Mother Philomena brought to the role of Superior. Like Mother Stanislaus and Mother Maria Joseph, she persisted in spite of the odds. She had heard of the founding days of the Congregation only from other Sisters. She had not known Father Woods, and had spent only a few years with Mother Stanislaus, the last three of which were when the foundress was ill. Yet when Ellen Callaghan entered, Sister Mary Joseph was heard to say, 'That girl will do great things for the Congregation.'[6]

To the depression years, Mother Philomena brought a common-sense attitude born of both her country background and her experience as a Sister of Perpetual Adoration. Mother Stanislaus had trained her and had given her responsibility during the short time she knew her.[7] Although there is no record of which Sisters formed the council that, according to the 1921 Wexford Constitutions, was to assist the major superior in governance, it is possible that Sister Philomena was a member of that council. In 1928, before she had been elected, she had written to a Mr Blake, thanking him for his help given at a St Patrick's Day luncheon.[8] As she wrote this on behalf of the Sisters in her own name rather than that of Mother Maria Joseph, we can conclude that she had assumed the authority of a leadership role.

Despite the hardships of the depression, the Building Committee continued during the 1930s to organise 'various functions to help pay the interest' even though 'funds were hard to get'.[9] Annual events, such as the 'brilliant' ball held on 25 July 1932 which 'Their Excellencies the Governor and Lady Wilson and Miss Marjorie Wilson attended', continued to be popular.[10] For the Sisters during these years the emphasis would have been on obtaining enough food and other supplies for the large number of women now under their care. Like society in general, they learned to 'make do' and to economise. For example, Sister Mary Raphael McGrath who had known and loved Father Woods, was 'a great gardener' who 'always had a garden full of vegetables' and fruits including grapevines.[11] One factor that caused some sadness to the Sisters, however, was their inability to visit people in the neighbourhood as much as they used to, since all their time was now spent in attending to the needs of their 'boarders'.[12]

In 1936, Mother Philomena was able to fulfill the sixty-year-old hope of the Sisters of Perpetual Adoration; to have permanent exposition of the Blessed Sacrament in their chapel. Since 1881 they had carried out adoration night and day and had had exposition on occasion since Archbishop Duhig had granted the permission in 1917. However, the request for 24-hour exposition had been consistently refused. Now Mother Philomena took up the cause again. When Father Samuel Hunter, a young curate newly arrived from Ireland, was appointed as their chaplain, Mother Philomena asked if he would ask the Archbishop to allow them to have exposition permanently.[13] Innocent of past experience, Father Hunter brought the matter up with Archbishop Duhig over breakfast next morning. In turn, the Archbishop pointed out that it would not be possible to do since a priest needed to be on hand to open and close the tabernacle as required and to place the Host in the Monstrance. Father Hunter later explained to the Sisters:

> I was able to explain to His Grace the case of the Poor Clare Nuns in my native parish in Belfast who had perpetual adoration with no priest in residence but an especially constructed altar for the purpose. He requested me to do a plan of the altar in Belfast which fortunately I knew well. When I brought this plan to him, he was very interested and said, 'Father, in the name of God, go on with it.'[14]

Immediately, the Sisters made the alterations that involved erecting a double tabernacle with a top level that was able to be locked and unlocked, opened and closed without the need to touch the Monstrance inside. A Sister could do this; no priest would be needed. To their delight, after so many years of waiting, the Sisters celebrated on 27 June 1936 when Archbishop Duhig exposed the Blessed Sacrament for perpetual adoration. It was the Feast of the Sacred Heart.

Equal determination was needed when Mother Philomena persisted in seeking the final approbation of Roman authorities for the Sisters of Perpetual Adoration as a Diocesan Congregation. Father Joseph Gates SJ was serving in Brisbane at the time, and so he was able to help Mother Philomena compose the letters to the Apostolic Delegate, Archbishop Giovanni Panico, and to provide once again the necessary documentation.[15] However, with the next General Chapter due in 1938, the Sisters' attention was deflected to its preparation. There is no evidence that the Apostolic Delegate replied to Mother Philomena's enquiry.

Re-election of Mother Maria Joseph

Mother Maria Joseph was now seventy-seven years old. There may have been some questions asked when the 1938 General Chapter re-elected her to lead the Congregation once again. Was this a simple, well-grounded challenge to ageist attitudes? Or was it a result of a growing culture among the Sisters that loyalty confined leadership roles to a 'chosen few' already singled out by former superiors? On the other hand, the uncertainties exacerbated by the Depression years may have led the Sisters to prefer the security and stability that they believed only Mother Maria Joseph could bring to the community.

There were, however, factors that would have been obvious to the Sisters. While Mother Maria Joseph was beloved by the Sisters for her kindness and gentle manner, she was admired also for her obvious ability to deal with business matters. Phase One of the building campaign had been successfully completed under her leadership in 1928. Now ten years later it was time to begin Phase Two. Who better than Mother Maria Joseph to deal with the complexities of a building program that she understood so well?

Mother Philomena

Villa Maria facing St Pauls Terrace, seen from the quarry.

Towards the end of 1938, Brisbane architects Cullen & Egan were engaged to plan and supervise the project. Both Desmond Egan and Francis Cullen were former pupils and draftsmen of Hennessy, Hennessy & Co, the firm that had been responsible for the first section of the building. Moreover, Francis Cullen was the nephew of Archbishop Duhig. Personal connections were important. Without doubt, Mother Maria Joseph had shrewd advisors who knew their way around the political world of the time.

Sisters of Perpetual Adoration were highly involved in the Corpus Christi Processions, held annually in the Cathedral parish.

Fr Samuel Hunter

By 11 August 1940, Archbishop Duhig was again at Villa Maria to bless and open the second stage of the building program. The architects had successfully incorporated the original external form and design laid down by Hennessy for the convent wing facing St Paul's Terrace, adding internal facilities for altar-bread making, sewing and laundry.[16] A lift tower was built at the junction of the first and second stages of the building. Until then, the Sisters had reserved for their use the top floor of the Hostel. Now they had a convent the Sisters could call their own.

The address given by Archbishop Duhig on this occasion must have sounded like music to the Sisters' ears. He began by praising the life and work of Father Julian Woods who had, for many years, given missions 'throughout the vast diocese of Brisbane' and had introduced the founding Sisters of Perpetual Adoration to the Catholic community. He went on to give a brief but appreciative history of the Congregation, emphasising the 'high esteem' the clergy had for the Sisters, and maintaining that 'he did not know of any other community that had got into the hearts of the people like the Sisters of Perpetual Adoration'.[17]

Hostel for Business Women

With Australia's involvement in the World War II having been announced by Prime Minister Menzies in September 1939 and conscription to the Citizen Military Forces two months later, many roles in business and other civic occupations that had previously excluded women became open to them. Additional government departments and agencies needing clerical workers were opened in the cities as a result of the war. This resulted in an influx of women into Brisbane. Archbishop Duhig grew concerned for 'Catholic girls from the country, who are in employment in Brisbane and are seeking a good Catholic home'.[18] Therefore he asked Mother Maria Joseph if the Sisters would provide accommodation for such young women.

The decision to do so was not made easily. Sisters worried about the effects of mixing the old with the young and the possible conflicts that might ensue. Having specialised in care of the elderly for so long, they felt themselves inadequate in understanding the needs of young people. They were not parents, yet they would be required to take on a parent's responsibilities. They would have to provide conditions that would fulfill parents' expectations that, with the Sisters, their daughters would receive the support and guidance that would shield them from moral and physical harm. At a personal level, it meant also that the Sisters would lose their own recently-won privacy, having to give over the basement of their convent for dormitories. In addition, the aging cottages now vacated by the elderly in the Hostel would have to be renovated for more lodging.

Despite the problems, the Sisters went ahead and, 'according to all reports, the girls found in the accommodation at St Pauls Terrace a religious atmosphere and generous freedom that was truly the mark of the Catholic home'.[19] On the other hand, the Sisters experienced physical strain due to the extra work involved. It was impossible to hire domestic help, since, as the war progressed, the government conscripted single women between the ages of twenty and thirty as auxiliaries to the armed forces. The requirement to blacken all windows presented a huge undertaking, especially in the chapel where the arched windows extended as high as two storeys. As the numbers of boarders and Sisters increased, space became scarcer, and with that, the stresses inevitably created by over-crowding. However, over the next four years, tensions were usually resolved and the family atmosphere which had always characterised Villa Maria was able to be sustained. If today we acknowledge the outstanding response made by women during World War II, the Sisters of Perpetual Adoration should be recognised for their own remarkable contribution to the war effort in establishing the Hostel for Business Women in Brisbane.

War Years

It is amazing that during the years of the war, the Building Committee continued its fundraising unabated, organising two or three events every month. The presence of the Sisters of Perpetual Adoration was thus constantly brought to the attention of the people of Brisbane. In death notices they were frequently mentioned as having visited the dying person or the family of the bereaved. Often, too, as in the case of Mrs Marion Moore, the person who had died was a resident of the Villa Maria Hostel and her funeral Mass had taken place in the chapel there. There is a certain pathos in the closing sentence of her death notice: 'She is survived by her son, daughter-in-law and grandson, the latter serving with the RAAF abroad.'[20]

Another event, stereotypical but sad, also focussed attention on the Sisters of Perpetual Adoration during this time. A four-month-old baby was abandoned on the porch of the Villa Maria convent during the night of 18 January 1944. Police managed to trace the mother. Then 'it was learned that she was on her way to visit a desperately ill parent, and that baby Paul's father was an Allied Service man, killed in New Guinea six months ago'.[21]

In 1942 the Sisters mourned the loss of Sister John Lillis who died on 30 May. One of the founding Sisters, she had lived in all six 'Villa Maria' houses—South Brisbane's Russell/Merivale and Manning Streets in South Brisbane, Kenyon House, the first convent, the top floor of the Hostel and finally the new convent opened in 1940. For some years she had been very frail, able to walk only a few steps and needing constant care. Now, having moved to the new quarters, she discovered that the convent floor she lived on was on the same level as the gallery of the chapel, with no stairs to be negotiated. She begged the doctor to let her go to the gallery so that from there she could look down at the monstrance enthroned on the altar. Permission was granted, provided two strong Sisters accompanied her:

> It was a great event. Several of us gathered to witness the occasion. After a lot of struggling and juggling the Sisters arrived at the gallery. It would have been a couple of years since Sister John walked so far. Sister gripped the edge of the gallery, looked down at the altar and cried out, 'Jesus, Jesus, you are here!' The Sisters were terrified she would go head over heels over the gallery wall.[22]

Corner of St Pauls Terrace and Gotha Street showing unfinished section of St Stanislaus Wing, the rear of the Chapel and one of the Gotha Street cottages

The oldest cottage along Gotha Street. Accommodation for the Business Women was provided on the first floor of St Stanislaus Wing and the cottages.

Sr Michael Brosnan

Sr Cordelia Constable

Sisters with residents: Srs Mary Paul Tyler, Philomena McAuliffe, Angela Turvey

After that she was allowed by the infirmarian to go to the gallery again only on condition that she promised to sit on a chair while she made her visit.

During the six years of the war, eleven women joined the Congregation, one of whom was 'Miss Gabriel Ansaldo of Red Hill' who, the *Catholic Leader* reported, was farewelled in 1943 by her parish 'at several functions and received some beautiful and useful gifts from her many friends'.[23] When she entered, Gabriel took the Religious name of 'Sister Rosarii'. She was destined to play an important role in the history of the Congregation.

In 1943, Archbishop Duhig, to whom the Sisters were ultimately responsible, made his official visitation of the community. Evidently he found problems. One of them must have involved the Mistress of Novices. In a letter of 15 June letter to Mother Maria Joseph, he said he had been in touch with the Apostolic Delegate, and that 'it has been deemed advisable to relieve the present Mistress of Novices of her office, principally on account of the state of her health.'[24] The Mistress of Novices was not named. Mother Stanislaus had expressed the wish that after her death Sister Margaret Mary (Daly) should be assigned this role. Did she still hold this office in 1943? There are no records to consult on this question. But it could well be the case, given that Mother Maria Joseph had also served in leadership since 1914. Sister Margaret Mary, revered and well-loved, would have been eighty-five years old in 1943. Externally, the Sisters of Perpetual Adoration had taken huge steps that involved risk, courage and daring. It could be judged, however, that internal structures were more conservative, favouring conformity rather than divergence or innovation.

Re-election of Mother Philomena

These internal structures required the next General Chapter of the Sisters to be held in 1944. Mother Philomena was re-elected as Superior. The Sisters apparently appreciated what she had already demonstrated—that preserving the 'traditions and practices that had been handed down from the past' was an important part of her leadership role.[25]

However, with the end of World War II in August–September 1945, Mother Philomena was faced with a new world which would again challenge the past. It would have been unusual if life for the Sisters could go on as before. The continuation of the Hostel for Business Women provided one of those challenges. The first was overcrowding, with the continued expansion of opportunities for women's employment:

> They came from every part of the state, often unannounced and apparently buoyed up with a youthful, cheerful optimism that presumed, 'Of course the Nuns will find a corner for me.'[26]

For some time the Sisters struggled. Some were finding that with regard to the young women, life was changing too quickly. These were not 'school-girls' and neither were they as 'pliable' as the boarders during the war years seemed to have been:

> The Superiors did not want to be too strict but had to safeguard them just the same. Experience taught them that rules and regulations had to be changed when necessary for the good of the girls. They may have at times vehemently opposed these, but the Superiors were able to make the girls realise they were acting for their own good.[27]

Stories abound as to how these young women were able to get around these rules—windows surreptitiously left open beyond curfew and so on—but more frequent are the comments that strong friendships were formed between the Sisters and the women, who came to regard Villa Maria as their second home.[28]

During the war, the Sisters had supplied altar breads to most chaplains of the armed forces from Australia and the United States of America fighting in the northern campaigns. At the completion of the war, they found that, instead of orders growing less, they actually increased. By 1947 they were dispatching 6,000 large hosts and around 70,000 small hosts each week to all parts of Australia, New Zealand and the Pacific Islands.[29] The number of Sisters dedicated to this work had grown to four, and for them this was a full-time ministry.

By this time, the number of older people living in the Hostel had increased to more than two hundred. The logistics of supply were enormous. Among that number of women were many who were infirm and needed consistent nursing. There were a few Sisters who were qualified nurses, but most were not. The requirements of safety in these circumstances demanded an exact observance of procedure, and the Sisters, well-known for their 'obejence' (a term popularised by Sister Mary Joseph in the early days of the Congregation), continued to give care of the highest quality, despite the odds.

Home for Crippled Children

During the 1930s and 40s, a series of epidemics of poliomyelitis had occurred in Australia, resulting in thousands of children being infected and many paralysed.[30] In 1946, a group of Catholic professionals and businessmen known as the 'Xavier Society' purchased a former convalescent home for returned soldiers at Coorparoo, a suburb south-east of the city, with the intention of establishing it as a home for children with polio. They renovated the house, providing suitable accommodation and facilities for staff and the treatment of ten children, including an area in which, it was hoped, Religious Sisters might reside and take charge of the project.

On 19 June 1947, it was announced in Brisbane's Catholic newspaper, the *Catholic Leader,* that the Archbishop had invited the 'progressive Religious Order' of the Sisters of Perpetual Adoration to undertake this work.[31] What conversations had taken place beforehand between the Archbishop and the Sisters is unknown. However, two weeks later, Mother Philomena wrote to the Archbishop (at the time in the United States), saying that while she was willing that the Sisters should 'undertake the work at the desire of Your Grace, and should do all in our power to give satisfaction', she was not satisfied with the terms being offered by the Xavier Society. While she did not name which aspects of the agreement were not acceptable, she was sure 'they would not meet with your approval'. She enclosed a copy of the document for the Archbishop's perusal, having informed the Xavier Society that she wished to let matters stand for the time being.[32]

The prospect of taking on this new ministry had its attractions. Mother Philomena was particularly drawn towards the Sisters making a foundation outside central Brisbane, since the original rule written by Father Woods had presumed the Congregation would spread to other places in order to spread devotion to the Blessed Sacrament. Some of the younger Sisters were excited by the possibilities for wider horizons in ministry. However, there were many points of concern, mainly about the nature of the work itself. Justice to incapacitated and crippled children would require full-time attention on the part of the Sisters. Given that their primary focus was adoration of the Blessed Sacrament, they could not see how these two aims could be compatible. It was feared, too, that the long-term effects of deflection from their principal aim could give rise to a spirit entirely at odds with the Sisters' true purpose. Besides, clauses in the Xavier Society agreement restricted the Sisters' ability for decision-making—they would not be in control of the institution. One of the proposals stated: 'The control and management of the Home and all matters relating thereto, subject to His Grace the Archbishop, shall be vested in the [Xavier] Committee'.[33]

Despite reservations, the Sisters acceded to the Archbishop's wishes for the rest of the year by preparing for the new ministry. Three Sisters travelled to the Montrose Home for Crippled Children at Corinda or to the Mater Children's Hospital in the city each day for refresher courses in techniques of caring for children with disabilities. Sister Michael, a fully-qualified nurse, was chosen as the Matron for the new venture. Other Sisters took on the task of purchasing the necessary furnishings and linen required for such an undertaking. It was anticipated that by the time of the Archbishop's return to Australia in December 1947, legal agreements would have been decided upon, definite dates set and final plans made to begin the work at some time in the following year.

Papal Approbation at last

Of deepest concern for Mother Philomena was the lack of Papal approbation of the Sisters of Perpetual Adoration as a Diocesan Congregation. She had tried once, in 1937, to draw attention to this, but the Archbishop did nothing. One of the first things she did on her re-election as superior, therefore, was to take up this matter again. On 1 August 1945, she gathered up the required documentation and repeated her request for approbation to the Apostolic Delegate, Archbishop Panico. However, in his reply he pointed out that he would need Archbishop Duhig's letter of recommendation before this could be done. Things were going around in circles.

It took the personal visit of Archbishop Panico to Brisbane in July 1946 to break the impasse, the letter being given into his hands. He now forwarded this and other documentation to the Roman authorities. This led to another delay. In September, Archbishop Panico explained that the adapted Wexford Constitutions by which the Sisters had lived needed major revision and that a Roman canonist had been engaged to do this.[34] On 14 January 1947 he wrote again with a set of questions from the canonist. Mother Philomena found that the canonist had presumed that since they were not an enclosed order, they were free to take up any ministries whether or not they interfered with their availability for eucharistic adoration. Her insistence that the re-written Constitutions should reflect that their primary purpose was Adoration of the Blessed Sacrament and that other ministries were simply complementary, resulted in even more to-ing and fro-ing. As in the early days of the Sisters' history, church authorities found it difficult to understand Father Woods' vision in this regard.

At last, after months of negotiation, the Congregation for the Propagation of the Faith wrote to Archbishop Duhig on 4 July 1947 saying that all was in accord, and that he should give the Sisters his official approbation.[35] By the time that letter arrived in Australia the Archbishop was overseas. It was not until November that Mother Philomena received a letter from the Apostolic Delegate, telling her that Archbishop Duhig's approbation was now officially approved. He sent a copy of the new Constitutions and instructed her to have them translated into English 'by a competent priest'.[36]

On his return to Australia in mid-December, Archbishop Duhig notified Mother Philomena that he had received the communication. To all intents and purposes, Mother Philomena had achieved her aim. The Sisters would remember 4 July 1947 as being the date when they received papal approval. However, it was not until the following year that this was publicly announced. It was then that the Archbishop asked the Sisters to ensure people referred to them as 'Sisters of Perpetual Adoration' rather than the 'Black Sisters':

> On 17 January 1948, on the occasion of the final profession of three Sisters, Sister M Immaculata, Sister M Gerard and Sister M Michael, His Grace announced to the community the great news of final approval in Rome. That was a great day of rejoicing indeed. After many long years the order had fully blossomed.[37]

This latest episode in the saga of receiving final approbation had taken three years. In those three years Mother Philomena had led the Sisters through the uncertainties of post-war life to a place where they were ready to try new things but where Church strictures still kept them dependent upon clerical approval and control.

Chapter 6

The Sisters of Perpetual Adoration were now strong enough in numbers and attitude to consider expansion. Previous uncertainty about their ecclesial status had given way to a confidence in themselves as an authentic congregation commissioned by the church to carry out their work of Adoration of the Blessed Sacrament and its extension into the apostolate of caring for those in need. However, the Archbishop's wish that they take over the care of crippled children was causing anxiety to Mother Philomena and many of the Sisters. Would this assignment be a step too far? The resolution of this question would determine the paths taken by the Sisters in the following two decades.

Home for Crippled Children

Preparations for the furnishing and staffing of the Xavier Home for Crippled Children at Cavendish Road, Coorparoo, occupied the Sisters for the whole of 1948 and far into 1949. While Mother Philomena had had issue with some aspects of the agreement drawn up by the Xavier Society, it could be assumed that these matters were resolved, as there is no mention of them in subsequent communication.

On Sunday 15 May 1949 Archbishop Duhig blessed and opened the Xavier Home. Prior to the ceremony he had celebrated Mass in the chapel and had welcomed the Sisters to their new residence.[1] The event was attended by the Premier of Queensland, Edward (Ned) Hanlon, and other state and local dignitaries.[2] In the third annual report of the Xavier Society given in October, president TJ Pender recalled that the opening of the Home had 'provided an opportunity for the Mother Superior [Mother Philomena] and Sisters to meet the large number of our honorary medical consultants, vice-presidents and members of the council present.' During the year, the Apostolic Delegate, Archbishop Paul Marella, had visited the Home and had given his blessing to what was promising to be a 'most admiral enterprise'.[3]

However, all was not as it seemed. At the end of August, Sister Michael, who had been appointed as Matron of the Home, fell ill and spent the next two months in the Mater Hospital. The other Sisters who were to make up the community, Sisters Augustine, Cordelia and Matthew, continued their tasks, presuming that all was going ahead.[4]

> Everything was set for the departure of the four Sisters to take up the challenge. We had even given the Sisters a farewell concert and they were to depart in a few days.[5]

That all changed when the doctors attending to Sister Michael informed Mother Philomena that she was not well enough to assume leadership of the work. This setback compelled the Sisters to reconsider their involvement. Mother Philomena had already been concerned about what authority the Sisters had according to clauses of the agreement. She also knew of the unrest among her Sisters on the matter. Despite feeling obliged to accede to the Archbishop's wish that they undertake this new ministry, she once again asked for a deferral of final arrangements.

On 15 November 1949, the President of the Xavier Society reported to the meeting of the Executive that he and two other members, on receiving this information, had met with Mother Philomena and that, given the circumstances, she had stated 'they would be happy to be released from the arrangement whereby the Sisters of Perpetual Adoration would be in charge of the Xavier Home.' She informed the delegation 'that she would see the Archbishop regarding this matter.' The three men, too, had met with Archbishop Duhig who was 'disappointed', but advised them that 'he would try and make other arrangements'.[6] Publicly he made a wry announcement: 'Divine Providence has intervened, and the Sisters of Perpetual Adoration will not be taking on the running of the Home for Crippled Children at Coorparoo.'[7]

At Villa Maria, many Sisters were relieved that the project did not go ahead, even though it meant that the three years of hard work were apparently wasted. They had worried that the new ministry and the practice of Adoration of the Blessed Sacrament were incompatible. At the same time, Mother Philomena's attempts to have the Congregation spread its wings were thwarted. It would have taken courage and humility for her to acknowledge their inability to live up to the agreement made with the Xavier Society, especially as it had involved a lot of publicity. The Sisters of Perpetual Adoration had received accolades from church and society for undertaking this work.

Meanwhile, the Xavier Society began the search for another Religious Congregation to take over the project, and in 1951, the Franciscan Missionaries of Mary did so.[8] Sometime later they visited the Sisters at Villa Maria and thanked them for all they had done: 'One Sister remarked on the well-stacked linen presses, clothes marked and washed ready for use.' In turn, the Sisters of Perpetual Adoration considered that the Franciscan Missionaries of Mary brought a professionalism to their work that made the Home 'a successful place of care and training, combining Christian love with medical and educational skills.'[9]

The Ipswich Foundation

It was not in Archbishop Duhig's nature to give up. So when, in early 1950, 'Beaumont', an old mansion in Ipswich came up for sale, he prevailed upon Mother Philomena to look at the property and investigate possibilities for a new foundation there.[10] What she found was a two-storey building in a bad state of repair on Limestone Street, a busy thoroughfare close to the town centre. The house had been built in 1863. For many years, 'Beaumont' had been the family home of Mr G H Wilson, a successful businessman of the area. Doctor John Flynn and his wife Jane then lived there with their family until the 1920s and had changed the name to 'Marie Mont'.[11] Since then it had become a boarding house and was finally altered to serve as a group of flats. In his book *Quiet Women*, T. P. Boland quotes the *Queensland Times* as saying that by 1950 the building 'had reached its lowest stage since its establishment'.[12]

Mother Philomena moved quickly. She agreed that the building could serve as a home for elderly women, a ministry with which the Sisters were familiar. There were numbers of older women in Ipswich whose husbands had not returned from the war and who were now in need of care, as well as those who found themselves homeless. Indeed, no sooner had word got around that the Sisters were considering care for the elderly in Ipswich than women were making reservations for future accommodation.

On the Feast of the Sacred Heart, 15 June 1950, three Sisters were sent to found the new community. In charge was Sister Augustine Dobie who had done so much to prepare the Xavier Home for its operation. Her companions were Sister Cordelia Constable (who had also been named as one of the Xavier community) and the young Sister Aloysius Wallis.[13] On their arrival in Ipswich they first of all made a courtesy call to the parish priest, Monsignor Baldwin, and then proceeded to the house.[14] A frightening scene confronted them—the front door was jammed with old mattresses and there was mess everywhere. Straight away they set about trying to get some order in the place, but when, in mid-afternoon, they decided to get themselves some refreshments, a hurried search of their luggage revealed they had forgotten to bring food or cutlery with them. The former caretaker of the building happened to call, and seeing their plight, presented them with two fresh patty cakes. They had no chairs as yet so, sitting on packing cases, they enjoyed their first cup of tea in their new home. It was the 76th anniversary of the day their founding Sisters had gone to the first Villa Maria in Russell Street, South Brisbane, and here they were in Ipswich, re-enacting the scene.

Later that evening, the curate of the parish, Father Basil Bergin, called to welcome them to Ipswich and saw the difficulties in which the Sisters found themselves.[15] He quickly organised for foodstuffs to be delivered and rang Mother Philomena to ask for the missing items to be sent on. The parcels did arrive a few days later, minus the forks.

Over the next months the Sisters swept and scrubbed and did their best to 'transform the old place into something liveable'.[16] They called in carpenters to attend to urgent repairs. The Sisters' first concern was to convert Doctor Flynn's former surgery into a small oratory. As they did not yet have a phone they were dependent on 'Providence' to obtain specific items unavailable in Ipswich. Father Bergin was their answer to prayer when he called in one morning to tell the Sisters he was going to Brisbane and would do any shopping they wanted. Armed with a list of articles required for the celebration of Mass in the oratory he set off, returning in heavy rain that night with the precious goods.

Like their first Sisters in Russell Street, these pioneers had to go to the parish church for Mass and to spend some time there in adoration. In the now furnished oratory they prayed the Divine Office and performed other spiritual exercises as was customary for their Congregation. However, their aim was to have Mass celebrated in the oratory and eventually to have the Blessed Sacrament reserved. Having been told by Monsignor Baldwin that they would need the Archbishop's permission for this, they made their way to the Ipswich Post office to put in a trunk-call to the Archbishop's house. The receptionist informed them that no one was at home. Disappointed, they returned to the oratory and there complained:

> They went straight to the Sacred Heart, had a good talk to him and told him they would not take NO for an answer, and he would have no peace from them, or the Sisters at Villa Maria Brisbane, until their prayers were answered. . . . On the next Sunday afternoon [2 July], Feast of the Visitation, 1950, whilst the Sisters were saying Vespers, a car drove up to the front door. In it, to their great surprise, were Bishop O'Donnell [and two priests].[17] . . . The co-adjutor said he was there to see their chapel and bless it. But when he saw they had no tabernacle, he told them until they had a stationary tabernacle, they could not have the Blessed Sacrament reserved, but could have Mass. . . . On 3 July the first Mass was said in the temporary oratory.[18]

Renovation work was still in progress when the first six 'boarders' took up residence. Two of the women had daughters living in Ipswich and had strong ties to the town. Around the same time, Father Bergin asked the Sisters if an English migrant family could stay in that section still standing as flats, since arrangements for their accommodation had fallen through. By now, too, the Sisters were building friendships with the people of Ipswich. Their primary aim of having adoration of the Blessed Sacrament permanently in their oratory was finding expression in what can be understood as their instinctive awareness of the connection between the presence of Christ in both sacrament and community.

Eventually, the Sisters were able to purchase a tabernacle, and on Sunday 12 November, Archbishop Duhig blessed it, instructing the Sisters to let Monsignor Baldwin know that this had been done. The next morning, Monsignor offered Mass in the oratory and reserved the Blessed Sacrament. It was 13 November, the anniversary of the death of their foundress. Immediately after Mass, the three Sisters recited the *Te Deum*: 'Mother Stanislaus was very close that day.'[19]

In only five months, the Sisters had made significant progress. Still, while the local people could share their happiness at what had been achieved, they did feel cut off from the Brisbane community. They were thrilled, therefore, when Mother Philomena arranged for two Sisters to join them for Christmas. They came 'laden with gifts of every description.'[20] Physical distance might be a challenge, but this first venture into establishing other houses of the Sisters of Perpetual Adoration brought home to the little group the reality of a spirit that unites, no matter what the separation.

General Chapter and aftermath

While the Ipswich foundation had pushed the Sisters into unchartered waters in 1950, so, too, did their six-yearly Chapter that was held in July that year. Because of the new foundation, this meeting had to take into account the life of the community beyond Brisbane. Therefore a 'General' Chapter was held. Likewise, there was need now for a 'General' Superior to provide leadership for both communities. Her responsibilities would be different from those of a local superior. Fortunately, the coadjutor bishop Patrick O'Donnell, appointed only the year before, was a canon-law expert, so he guided the Sister-representatives on the Chapter through the new procedures.

At the General Chapter, elections were held according to this new governance framework. Mother Philomena was chosen as the Congregation's first 'Mother General'. The title 'Mother' was also conferred on her elected Vicar, Mother Gabriel, and on the three Councillors, Mothers Augustine Dobie, Stanislaus Fitzpatrick and Kevin Lewis.[21] However, although this fact is noted in the Chapter report, it seems that in practice only the Mother General retained that title in common usage.

As with any change, it took time for the Sisters to adjust to the different structures. Letters written to the Archbishop in subsequent years indicate some unrest among a few Sisters about the lack of transparency about how the Congregation was being governed.[22] However, on the surface, life proceeded as usual. In Brisbane, the members of the Building Committee continued to hold functions to raise money for the hoped-for completion of Villa Maria on Warren Street and St Paul's Terrace. The Sisters contributed by hosting fetes, card nights and other events, and continued to care for increasing numbers of elderly boarders and working women. In Ipswich, too, a Building Committee was formed so that major renovations of the building there could begin.

On 9 January 1951 builders began the work of partial demolition, reconstruction, remodelling and refurbishment of the old Ipswich house. Shortly afterwards, Father Robert Flynn who had been brought up in this house, paid a visit.[23] He was 'overjoyed' to see that his father's surgery had been transformed into an oratory, and informed the Sisters that the family intended to present them with a revolving tabernacle that could be used when a much larger chapel was built.[24]

The weather was a major obstacle. It rained heavily during those months, so that the Sisters and occupants had to negotiate mud, planks of wood and open roofs as they hurried from one area to the other. It was planned that the section for elderly women would be completed first, so, with no permanent quarters of their own, the Sisters found themselves constantly moving from one bedroom to the next to allow the workmen to proceed with the renovations. Work holdups increased the sense of uncertainty and displacement:

> It has been raining for days and no sign of the men. Every week there is something; it is either the difficulty of transport, failure to get the materials, bad roads . . . our decision is bad organisation![25]

Monsignor Baldwin, who had been ill for some time, died on 28 June 1951. Father Bergin, who had been such a great friend to the Sisters had already been transferred to another parish earlier that year. The Sisters found it a moving moment when, at his instalment on the feast of Christ the King, Archbishop Duhig presented the church keys to the new parish priest, Monsignor Timothy Molony.[26] They felt that some order was coming back into their lives after such a tumultuous year.[27] Two weeks later they moved into their own convent, as yet unfinished but habitable. The frontage of the house had been renewed, and the name 'Villa Maria' mounted by a cross was proudly displayed.

Alterations within the building included enlarging the oratory to make it a chapel suitable for the anticipated numbers of Sisters and residents—around forty people. Already there was a community of adoration forming: the Sisters had invited the resident boarders and local friends to join them for the daily recitation of the Rosary, and soon they found that for most of the daylight hours there was someone praying before the Blessed Sacrament. Every few weeks Sisters from Brisbane would come to stay for a few days. When an Ipswich Sister would go to Brisbane to make her ten-day retreat, a Brisbane Sister would take her place. Gradually, with more interchange, feelings of isolation between the two communities were overcome: Brisbane 'owned' Ipswich and vice versa. In fact, Mother Philomena and Council were making plans for the Novitiate to be shifted to Ipswich in the near future. From their conversations with other groups of Religious and aware of problems of overcrowding in the Brisbane convent, they recognised that it was best for the novices to do their training away from the demands of the large Brisbane institution and to have the space provided by a country setting for self-reflection as they discerned their future.

By mid-June 1952 all was ready for the opening of Villa Maria, Ipswich. About sixty parishioners, urged by Monsignor Molony, had helped clean the renovated building and its surrounds. A neighbour 'brought in her polishing machine and did the whole convent—left it looking like glass'.[28] The tabernacle donated by the Flynn family was blessed and installed by the curate, Father Power.[29] In the chapel of Villa Maria Brisbane, the small marble altar that had been donated for the original wooden chapel on the corner of Leichhardt and Warren Streets had been replaced by a larger one, so the Ipswich chapel now boasted this beautiful legacy of former days, much more suited to its size.[30]

A large crowd of dignitaries and townspeople gathered for the blessing and opening by Archbishop Duhig of Villa Maria Ipswich on 29 June 1952.

> A guard of honour was formed for the Archbishop by members of the Ipswich branch of the Hibernian Society, and Air Cadets from the Christian Brothers' College. His Grace blessed the chapel and the whole of the house before performing the opening ceremony.[31]

In his speech he referred to the Sisters' history and their 'very humble beginnings', but now 'they had one of the finest hostels in Brisbane'. He noted that 'the Sisters had the goodwill of everyone in Ipswich'. The Mayor (JT Finimore) agreed with this, commending the Sisters 'for pioneering this long felt want in the city': 'We realise the work the Sisters are doing here and they are welcome amongst us.'[32]

The Flynn family was present at the ceremony, and shortly afterwards Mrs Jane Flynn joined the community of residents who now numbered twenty. Her son was able to celebrate Mass in the chapel where his father had once sought to heal physical ailments and which now gave spiritual healing and nourishment.

Villa Maria, Ipswich, 1952

Sr Augustine Dobie

Sr Kevin Lewis

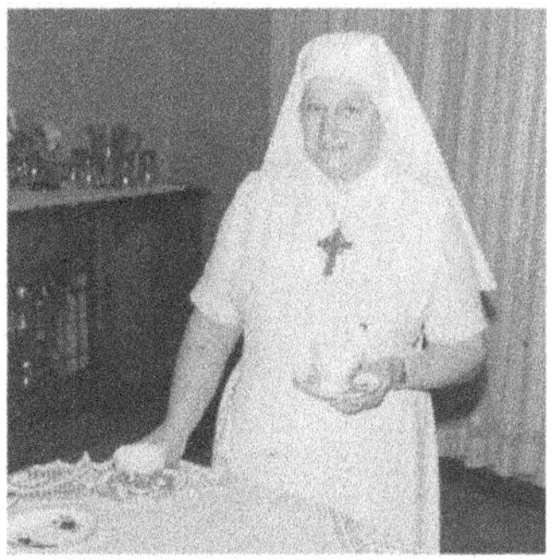

Sr Aloysius Wallis

The Novitiate, Ipswich, 1953

Sr Dympna McFadden with a group of residents at Villa Maria, Brisbane.

Beginnings and Endings

Only days after the Ipswich opening, it was reported to the Sisters that Mother Philomena had 'had an accident and was admitted to the Mater hospital in a critical condition'. 'Everyone is upset, and going about their duties in a dull, apathetic manner', wrote Sister Augustine.[33] Her recovery was slow, and at seventy-three years of age, she was no longer the determined 'ball of fire' she once was.

Later that year she submitted her first 'Quinquennial Report to the Holy See'—five years after the Final Approbation in 1947. The report followed a set format, seeking information on essential canonical matters, financial details and personnel statistics. There were at the time forty-eight Sisters who had made perpetual vows and two in temporary vows. Fourteen Sisters had died since the founding of the Congregation. Eight novices had been received over the past five years. It was hoped a Novitiate separate from the Mother House would be erected within a year. The report was co-signed by Mother Philomena and her Assistant, Sister Gabriel.[34]

The planned relocation of the Novitiate to Ipswich did go ahead at the end of 1953. It was the close of one era and the beginning of a new when the Novice Mistress, Sister Eucharia, a junior-professed Sister and two postulants left Villa Maria, Brisbane, on 27 November, and arrived in Ipswich to set up the new Novitiate.[35] However, with more postulants entering and more women coming to the hostel, space became a problem again. In December 1954 a nearby wooden house was advertised for sale. This was purchased, and 'at a cost of £8000, was moved in two sections to the Villa Maria grounds and renovated to accommodate the Novices'.[36]

During the week of Easter 1953 the Sisters at Ipswich had an unexpected visit from Pattie Menzies, the wife of Prime Minister Robert Menzies. In her diary, Sister Augustine noted:

> Mrs Menzies is a charming, wholesome, homely little lady. The boarders were delighted with her visit. She had a word with each person, inspected each room and expressed her pleasure and astonishment at finding Villa Maria so beautifully furnished and declared our work was not publicised enough.[37]

The Sisters regarded the 'work' of caring for the aged at Villa Maria Ipswich and Brisbane as a privilege. Right from the beginning of the ministry in 1902, 'boarders' and visitors commented on the family atmosphere, the peace and contentment they felt at Villa Maria. However, providing such care required hard, physical work. The first impulse of the Sisters of Perpetual Adoration was to do this work themselves rather than employing other staff to assist them. This was primarily for financial reasons, but it also had the effect of creating a bond between the women and the Sisters. The Sisters were the servants, but also the friends of their 'guests'.

The inevitable deaths of these 'friends' came at a cost. Sister Augustine's diary records the Sisters' reactions. When the first boarder died, they were shocked: 'We will miss her so much'. Another woman died unexpectedly:

> She had been to Brisbane for a few days, returned by the evening train, arriving in Ipswich 5.55 pm. Was anointed and dead at 6.10 pm. Appeared to be in splendid health.

The woman who had been the first boarder at Ipswich died shortly afterwards:

> Mrs James walked out on to the verandah and said she was dying. She was, too. The Sisters took her back to her room; we sent for the priest and doctor. She answered all the prayers and held the blessed candle herself. She died in her chair quite calm and resigned.[38]

On 14 August 1954 Archbishop Duhig, assisted by Monsignor Molony, blessed and opened the Novitiate of Our Lady of the Blessed Sacrament. Twenty-eight years before, on the same date, the Archbishop had been assisted by the then Father Molony when he had blessed and opened the chapel at Villa Maria Brisbane in 1927.

On 25 October Mrs Flynn died. Two days afterwards her son, Father John Flynn, celebrated an early Mass in the Villa Maria chapel. Then as many Sisters and staff as could be spared proceeded to the parish church, St Mary's, for her Requiem Mass and funeral.[39] Another era had passed.

The pattern of 'beginnings and endings' continued during 1955. At Ipswich there were the first ceremonies of Profession and the reception of Novices. Parishioners joined the many families and friends for the celebrations. On 23 March Sr Josephine Leavey died in Brisbane. She had entered the Congregation in 1882 and had great love for Father Woods. In old age she was blind, but with a mind 'clear as a bell' would happily relate stories of the early days to the younger Sisters. She maintained that 'Mother Mary [MacKillop] would never be canonised at the expense of Father Woods', and asserted, 'His name will be shouted from the housetops.'[40]

The death of Mother Maria Joseph on 1 July 1955 shocked everyone. The Ipswich Sisters were called to Brisbane when it became obvious she was seriously ill, and she died a few days later. Her joy had been to see Mother Stanislaus' hopes for the Congregation accomplished—the approbation of the Congregation and its 'new foundations' beyond Brisbane as the first Rule had envisaged.[41] The Sisters appreciated her direct links with their origins, but above all they remembered her kindness, especially to the younger Sisters and their times with her at the Cleveland holiday house:

> Mother took three postulants away with her to Cleveland for holidays which were from Sunday to Sunday twice a year. We would walk up and down the veranda and say the rosary and Mother's trimmings. After we would then sit on the front steps and talk to Mother. One night we tried to draw her out about her trip overseas and what she and Mother Stanislaus thought of Rome . . . When mother realised we were trying to draw her out she would say 'Tut tut, be gone with you! You should be in bed long ago, the three of you![42]

Less than two months later Mother Philomena died, on 24 August 1955. The Central Executive of the Holy Name Society were among the many lay groups who expressed their sympathy to the Sisters 'upon the sudden death of the Mother General, Rev. Mother Mary Philomena'.[43] For many years she had liaised with the Society in mounting an annual Corpus Christi procession in the Cathedral parish. Even though the Sisters' Rule was now based on that of the enclosed Sisters of Perpetual Adoration in Wexford, the original outgoing vision of Father Woods had been preserved:

> This Congregation has been erected for the adoration and the honour of the adorable Sacrament of the Altar, and this its members may attain by the perpetual adoration of the Blessed Sacrament in their own convents and by the care of churches and by the superintendence of pious societies of laypersons by which perpetual adoration may be kept up or additional honour and veneration given to our Blessed Lord in his great Sacrament of love.[44]

Mother Philomena, renowned for preserving the 'traditions and practices that had been handed down from the past', was faithful to that charge to the end.[45] She had achieved what many might regard as the impossible through sheer perseverance. She had led her Sisters through the confused years of the Depression and World War II to adjust to post-war demands and increasing numbers of people needing care. As she did when she pursued the rat so many years before, she never gave up. She rolled up her sleeves to serve those who waited to be fed; she dared to do both the mundane and the new—all the while trusting that Providence would provide what she could not.

Chapter 7

The deaths of Mother Maria Joseph and Mother Philomena closed an era marked by consolidation and numerical growth for the Congregation. The time was now ripe for expansion. The next twenty years would see the Sisters of Perpetual Adoration being established in other dioceses and undertaking new ministries. Under the leadership of Mother Gabriel the community would gain financial security and embark on a series of building projects. At the same time, external influences in church and society would provide fresh challenges. The response made by the Congregation to these challenges would be important for its future.

Mother Gabriel Moloney

When Mother Philomena died in August 1955, it fell to the Vicar-General, Sister Gabriel Moloney, to call a Chapter which would elect a new Mother General. A few days later Archbishop Duhig confirmed her election to this role. Her Councillors were Sisters Augustine Dobie (Vicar General), Kevin, Stanislaus and Aloysius.

When she entered the Sisters of Perpetual Adoration in 1920, Eileen Moloney had brought a background of professional education as a teacher and public servant. At the time, Mother Maria Joseph had recognised her potential and, after her final vows in 1927, had had her study accountancy in order to take on the management of the Congregation's financial affairs.[1] Since then this position of trust had given her years of access to the inner workings of Congregational leadership. To her role as Mother General, then, she now brought a lifetime of experience and wisdom. She had been involved in all the major building projects that had taken place since 1927. As Mother Philomena's assistant she knew first-hand the qualities needed to achieve one's goals.

In her new role, Mother Gabriel continued to attend to the financial matters of the Congregation. Perhaps it was a case of maintaining what she had done for years—combining various roles easily and dealing with the familiar. She was well aware of Mother Philomena's ambition for the Congregation to be established in other parts of Australia, so even suggestions for new enterprises fitted into patterns of familiarity.

Foundation in Sydney

In 1957, a request came from the Catholic Women's League in Sydney for the Sisters to take over the management of Legion House, a hostel for women needing short-term stays in the city. At the time, the president of the Catholic Women's League in Australia was Mrs Kathleen Burrow.[2] With her sister Anne, she had founded the Graham-Burrow School of Physical Education which had spread to Catholic Schools around the country.[3] Since a number of her Brisbane teachers were boarders at the Hostel for Business Women, she often stayed with the Sisters at Villa Maria. Aware of both of the Sisters' hopes for expansion, and also of the fact that the former managers of Legion House, the Poor Sisters of Mary, were withdrawing from the work, she encouraged Mother Gabriel to respond to the Sydney request.[4]

Before definite decisions could be made, negotiations had to take place between the Sisters, Archbishop Duhig and Cardinal Gilroy, since, as the Sisters of Perpetual Adoration were a diocesan congregation, canonical procedures had to be observed in order for them to be established in another diocese.[5] This done, Mother Gabriel accompanied Sisters Mary St Peter, Gerard, Gemma and Clement Thomas to Sydney to settle them into their first inter-state ministry on 21 May 1958. After twelve months, Sisters Immaculata Donnelly and Angela Turvey replaced Sisters Gerard and Gemma.[6]

Legion House was in Castlereagh Street, located close to the Central Railway Station and convenient to other city transport. It was an old, solid building. The ground floor housed the Catholic Women's League State headquarters, while the second and third floors provided bed and breakfast facilities for thirty-six women, and the top floor a six-bedroomed convent for the Sisters. There was an oratory where the Sisters could, in turn, keep vigil before the Blessed Sacrament.

While living conditions were adequate, the Sisters did feel confined, surrounded as they were by tall city buildings and dependant on only one skylight to break the gloom. Therefore, having discharged their bed-and-breakfast duties, they used to go out in the afternoons as often as they could. To their delight, on one of these expeditions soon after their arrival they found the nearby shrine of Eucharistic Adoration with exposition at the Church of the Blessed Sacrament in George Street, Haymarket. Here was another home away from home—a connection with Father Julian Woods whose life had been intertwined with St Peter Julian Eymard in France and who, like him, had founded a religious order focussed on adoration of Jesus' sacramental presence in the Eucharist.[7]

Building Again

Meanwhile, in Brisbane, the cottages that supplemented the accommodation available for the elderly and the business women in the Villa Maria Hostel and Convent were deteriorating. In Ipswich, Limestone Street, adjacent to the Hostel, was becoming busier, so that the sound of bellbirds which once greeted the Sisters when they opened the chapel windows each morning was now drowned out by the roar of traffic. So bad was it that they could not hear each other when reciting prayers. The Building Committees in both Brisbane and

Ipswich had continued their activities over the years—advertisements for garden parties, fetes and outings still featured in the weekly Catholic newspapers—and it was realised that funds would now have to be directed to actual building programs rather than just paying off debts. For Brisbane, architectural plans had already been drawn up in 1927 for the overall design of Villa Maria. The wing along St Pauls Terrace would extend to Gotha Street, and another parallel wing was envisaged for the area south of the chapel.

Before the mid-1950s, charitable organisations had raised finance for providing homes for the aged on their own initiative. The 1954 Commonwealth's Aged Persons Homes Act, however, made capital grants available by matching these with funds raised pound-for-pound in order to expand aged care facilities. Certain regulations governed acceptance of these grants, among them being an exclusive focus on the aged. For the Sisters of Perpetual Adoration, this meant that the provision of boarding for business women could no longer exist at Villa Maria.

As they pondered the implications of applying for a grant, Mother Gabriel and her Council had also to deal with the day-to-day governance of the Congregation. In 1960 they had bought a cottage in Warren Street for a chaplain to serve Villa Maria, Father Carmelo Micallef, who also served the Maltese community, himself being a recent migrant from Malta.[8] Then, at the six-yearly General Chapter held in 1961, Mother Gabriel was elected as Superior General for a second term as were the members of her previous General Council. At the time there were forty-eight Sisters living in the Congregation's three locations, thirty-nine of these being finally professed.

Over the next three years, facilities for business women were gradually phased out and cottages demolished. For Gabrielle Power-West who boarded there from 1960 to 1963, these years at Villa Maria were happy, providing 'many benefits where good contacts could be made'. At the time there were about forty boarders whose ages ranged from sixteen years to the early forties. Everyone had breakfast and evening meals in the dining room at Villa Maria, but those who lived in the cottages felt themselves privileged, since there was more freedom there.[9]

With the area along St Pauls Terrace to Gotha Street cleared of cottages, building began to complete the third phase of the overall plan for Villa Maria. By now, architect Frank Cullen, who had been responsible for the second stage of the building program, now operated as a partnership, Cullen, Fagg, Hargreaves and Mooney. Their design for the new St Stanislaus wing (so named after the foundress of the community, Mother Stanislaus Gaffney) would follow the same lines as the previous buildings and would extend the convent area to provide accommodation for thirty-eight elderly women.

Archbishop Duhig died on 10 April 1965. His episcopate had seen a huge growth in church and school building, and Villa Maria had featured in this list.[10] Back in 1940 he had expressed the hope that the Sisters might complete their building on Saint Pauls Terrace within a decade. That had not happened, but before he died he was aware that work was now proceeding. Along with the whole of the Brisbane archdiocese the Sisters of Perpetual Adoration mourned his loss. Their bereavement was particularly felt, however, because it had been due to his advocacy that their foundation was 'formally recognised by the Church'.[11] He had been their advocate through the many difficult years since 1912.

Duhig was succeeded by his coadjutor, Patrick O'Donnell. Archbishop O'Donnell's first function in his new role was to bless and open St Stanislaus wing at Villa Maria on 17 July 1965. He rejoiced that the event was happening in 'a happy and most unusual circumstance'. Due to Commonwealth and State grants and the hard work of the Building Committee, the additions, 'costing more than £100,000', had been opened 'free of debt'.[12] This, he said, should encourage the community to go ahead and complete this work. 'The Sisters of Perpetual Adoration are great builders', he said. 'Give them their heads and enough money and they will never stop building.'[13]

Mother Gabriel lived up to his expectations by applying for the necessary grants to complete the last wing of the Villa Maria complex, and work continued on this over the following year. Before actual construction could take place, however, major excavation works were necessary. The hill on which Villa Maria was built was solid rock which had to be levelled for the new building. Since it flanked the existing buildings, blasting was impossible. This meant months of chipping away with jackhammers until the ground was suitable for work to begin. At Ipswich, too, fundraising efforts were being made to build a new chapel and novitiate to replace structures inadequate for present demands. The Sisters of Perpetual Adoration were indeed 'great builders'.

Meanwhile, Archbishop O'Donnell had travelled to Rome for the closing sessions of the Second Vatican Council. While there, he received a report from Father Jeremiah Hogan SJ who had conducted a visitation of the Sisters of Perpetual Adoration on his behalf.[14] To his Vicar General, Monsignor John English, he confided that, although he was 'consoled by the absence of any grave defect in the life of the Institute' and was inspired by their 'good will and religious spirit', he was aware that urgent attention needed be given to areas of governance and community life.[15] In October 1965, too, the Decree on the Adaptation and Renewal of Religious Life (*Perfectae Caritatis*) was issued. The contents of both documents would have to be given serious consideration at the next General Chapter of the Sisters to be held in September 1967.

Preparation for Chapter 1967

During 1967, Archbishop O'Donnell gave a series of talks to all the Sisters of Perpetual Adoration to help them prepare for their Chapter. In particular, he wanted to address the canonical and pastoral irregularities he had noted in Father Hogan's report. In a letter written to the Apostolic Delegate, Archbishop Enrico, on 26 June 1967, he explained that since his return to Australia from the Vatican Council he had 'followed up with a personal visitation of the Sisters and had obtained from Propaganda approval to make certain alterations to the Constitutions to give wider representation at the General Chapter.' He now wanted 'to put this Institute on a firm canonical footing'.[16]

The 1948 text of the Constitution rightly contained instruction for the convocation of a General Chapter every six years. Details of procedures by which its membership would be decided was a matter for the Congregation's own law. The Sisters of Perpetual Adoration had a book of statutes which would normally describe such details. However, on the matter of how members would be chosen to attend the General Chapter, nothing was said. It would seem, therefore, that the Sisters were reliant on their superiors to make these decisions. The fact that very few of the Sisters actually attended Chapters was one of the 'irregularities' that Archbishop O'Donnell noted—for example, he cited only seven Sisters having been present at the 1961 Chapter.[17] With five *ex officio* members (the Mother General, the Vicar General and three General Councillors), that would have meant there were only two other Sisters drawn from the membership of the Congregation to bring their insights to this event that was recognised in Canon Law as holding 'supreme authority in the institute'.[18] For too long, authority had been vested in the few.

Mother Gabrielle

Srs Gerard, Immaculata, Angela, Dominic

Washing on the rooftop of Castlereagh Street Sr Immaculata does the ironing.

Archbishop Patrick O'Donnell

Villa Maria Brisbane, 1965.

Other matters to be addressed by the Chapter called for greater transparency and collaboration in Congregational leadership. Father Hogan's visitation had revealed that the Sisters had retained 'very little in the way of written records'. While the Constitutions required that the Mother General and Council should meet 'at regular intervals', this had not taken place, so that decisions were made autocratically. As Father Hogan had noted,

> This kind of government was more common in earlier times. At the present time the members of a community are not satisfied if they are not treated in a more adult fashion, and according to the laws of the Church and their Institute.[19]

For this 1967 Chapter, Archbishop O'Donnell determined the following:

- The number taking part in the General Chapter should be fifteen to twenty Sisters.
- All professed Sisters should elect their delegates drawn from those who had been finally professed.
- The General Chapter should deal not only with the election of offices (as had been the practice until now), but also incorporate a 'Chapter of Affairs' where decisions about local law (contained in the Statues) and changes needed in community living could be discussed.
- Proper minutes of the Chapter should be written and signed.[20]

It would be made clear that from now on the Mother General of the Congregation would carry out visitation of the Sisters at least every three years in order for Sisters to feel heard and attended to. She would also call meetings of her Council at least once per month, minutes of these meetings being kept and signed. The responsibilities of various officers should be defined and respected. In practice, it was found, Mother Gabriel had assumed a number of offices, as others had done before her. As already noted, she had retained the office of Bursar, but in addition acted as community leader (despite having appointed Sister Rosarii to this position) and even as choir-mistress. One person would no longer hold several offices.

In the report of his Visitation, Father Hogan had raised matters that needed immediate attention in the coming Chapter of Affairs. It was particularly important that decisions be made that would facilitate ongoing input into what could improve community living. For example, Father Hogan had observed that Sisters who had their sleep continually interrupted because of having to get up for night adoration or to attend to the sick elderly did not have the opportunity to rest during the day and were living under constant stress. The proper place for such matters to be raised was not the Chapter itself but at the community level where structures could be set up to remedy such situations. However, the Chapter of Affairs could encourage those who held different positions of authority to provide opportunities for feedback, dialogue and action.

At this time the thirty-five Sisters at the Brisbane Villa Maria were caring for a hundred 'boarders' and the ten at Ipswich around twenty, plus providing for the novices. The six Sisters who baked and distributed altar breads were producing over three million small breads per year plus the large hosts required for each parish throughout eastern Australia. Sisters did have ten days of vacation twice a year at their holiday house at Cleveland. However, community recreation was meagre and, given the constant hard physical work in which the Sisters were engaged, there were very few opportunities for developing wider interests and engagement in religious and secular studies. The Vatican II document *Perfectae Caritatis* required Religious to take serious heed of 'the changed conditions of our time', especially by the growth in human sciences which should inform adaptations in Religious Life.[21] Small wonder if Mother Gabriel and her Councillors felt overwhelmed as they prepared for the 1967 Chapter, given the history of how Chapters had been conducted in the past.

If they were feeling despondent, the success of another building venture would have provided a much-needed boost to morale. On 20 August 1967, the Archbishop was in Ipswich to bless and open the new Villa Maria chapel there. To replace the aging Novitiate house, a new Novitiate was also built adjoining the new chapel. On this occasion the Archbishop rejoiced in 'another step forward in the growth of the Order' and expressed his hope that it would 'spread the length and breadth of Australia'.[22] The Archbishop still had great hopes for the Sisters of Perpetual Adoration.

Mother Rosarii Ansaldo

As Mother Gabriel had already served twelve years as Mother General, a first exercise of the Chapter when it met on 25 September 1967 was to elect her replacement. This was Mother Rosarii Ansaldo.[23] Her election marked a new era, as until now, the pattern had been for the Mother General to be chosen from the previous General Council. The Sisters now recognised the need for change. For many years Mother Rosarii had served as portress at Villa Maria Brisbane and so had been the face that greeted visitors. For the past six years she had also been appointed community leader, but, as Father Hogan had noted in his report, she had been unable to exercise this role. Another new face on the General Council was Sister Philippa Barker, elected as Vicar General.[24] The other councillors, Sisters Kevin Lewis, Stanislaus Ryan and Aloysius Wallis had been on the council before.

Perfectae Caritatis had reminded Religious Congregations that a necessary step for adaptation was to touch into the Gospel sources of consecrated life and the original spirit of their founding.[25] In their discussion of this element, the Sisters gathered in Chapter defined its purpose as 'Adoration of the Blessed Sacrament'. As an extension of this aim, it saw its principle works as 'care for the aged and supplying altar breads'. Its subsidiary works were 'the giving of catechesis and caring for the sick'. In response to the requirement that the dress or habit of Religious should be 'simple and modest' and 'meet the requirements of health', another committee was formed and would report its findings after a year to a reconvened sitting of the Chapter.[26]

The decisions made during this first session of the Chapter then became the material for General Council meetings held every month. For the first time, minutes were kept of these meetings. Necessary adaptations to community living were an obvious place to start. The Archbishop had made it clear that Sisters should eliminate practices that encouraged infantilisation, such as requesting permission for basic toiletry needs or having personal letters opened by the superior. The first Council meeting dealt with these and other matters, making modifications in the Sisters' timetable to allow Sisters the opportunity to view the TV News, and cancelling the obligation for Sisters to recite the traditional long list of oral prayers after Mass in order to allow time for individual devotions. In addition, they encouraged Sisters to update themselves by attending talks on the liturgy being given in the Cathedral parish, and obtained from the Archbishop permission for the Sisters to receive Communion under both species during times of retreat.[27]

Mother Rosarii Ansaldo

St Gabriel's Wing from Gotha Street, 1968. Rounded rear of Chapel at centre, St Stanislaus Wing top.

The indebtedness of the Sisters of Perpetual Adoration to the people who formed various committees over the years to raise funds can never be over-estimated. Without them, the Sisters could not have survived. Here is one such 'Building Committee' with the following Sisters l-r: Teresa Donovan, Dympna McFadden, Cordelia Constable, Mother Rosarii Ansaldo, Mother Gabriel Moloney, Emmanuel Carroll, Cordelia Ansaldo RSM

Another area for the Council's consideration was the Chapter's description of the Congregation's subsidiary works, 'the giving of catechesis and caring for the sick'. In the early days of the Congregation, Sisters at Brisbane Villa Maria had given catechetical instruction for children in preparation for receiving the Sacraments. Once the focus had become caring for the elderly, this ministry had fallen into disuse. Paradoxically, a few weeks after the Chapter, the Council received a request by the parish priest of Ipswich who asked if the Sisters there could take Religion classes for children in the nearby State schools. The Council decided to ask nurses Sisters Philomena McAuliffe, Monica Brown and Eucharia Kingston to do a catechist course at All Hallows College to prepare for teaching catechetics.[28] These Sisters completed the course in June 1968 and were awarded a Diploma in Catechetics by the Brisbane Archdiocesan Director of Catholic Education. Soon they were setting out from Ipswich Villa Maria to the Brassall and Bremer High Schools to give weekly religion lessons. What Father Woods had written in their first rule, that the Sisters should 'seek out children or grown person who have not made their first communion and prepare them to do so', was now finding new expression in a new age.[29]

Mother Rosarii trod a delicate path as she assumed her leadership role in the Congregation, working with the Council in ways that her predecessors had not done. She would have been aware that during his 1965 visitation, Father Horgan had met with resistance from Mother Gabriel when he proposed changes that should be made: 'This is her character . . . I doubt if much improvement can be hoped for'.[30] At the same time, it is noticeable that there was mutual respect between the two leaders. Mather Rosarii made a point of including Mother Gabriel at various Congregational events, and subsequent acknowledgement of all she had done over more than forty years of service demonstrate this.

Completions

By 1968 the final stage of the building at Brisbane Villa Maria had been completed. St Gabriel's Wing, honouring the name of Mother Gabriel, was blessed and opened by Archbishop O'Donnell on 7 April. It provided forty-eight rooms for elderly women and twenty-two rooms for the Sisters. A spacious lounge laundry and a small devotional Chapel were included in the design. State and Federal grants supplemented funds raised by the Building Committee, and a Commonwealth Department of Health subsidy of £29,000 provided the furnishings. The total cost was £853,894.

Archbishop O'Donnell was exuberant in his praise on this 'happy day':

> This is a great amenity., and this fine building is an asset to the city. It is one of the great buildings, a great landmark of the city. It is something that not only the church, but the city and the state also can be proud of.[31]

In congratulating the Sisters, the State Minister for Health, Douglas Tooth, referred to his personal knowledge of their 'good work' when he was a teacher at the Spring Hill State School, directly opposite the building on St

Pauls Terrace.[32] In 1968 it was not deemed appropriate for Sisters to speak in public. Therefore, the chaplain, Father Kitts, moved the vote of thanks to all speakers on their behalf.[33] Despite the Sisters' achievements being worthy of the highest praise, the effects of patriarchy, particularly within the church, were as strong as ever.

In September 1968 the Sisters reconvened for the second sitting of General Chapter to receive the reports of the committees and to review other aspects of their lives in a post-conciliar church. The draft presented by the Constitutions committee dealing with the Nature, Objects and Works of the Congregation and the Vowed Life were approved and the committee commissioned to continue their work on the legalities involved in Formation, Authority and Government. Modifications were made to the Sisters' dress, including optional white habits and simplification of the head-dress. Because of the physical difficulties being experienced at Marian House (formerly 'Legion House') in Sydney, it was decided to look for a ministry in New South Wales more conducive to the Congregation's spirit and character. In order for the Sisters to rediscover their roots, it was decided the offer opportunities for Sisters to do intensive work in scripture, liturgy, Congregational history and biographies of Father Woods. The next Chapter to be held in five years' time would review the outcomes of this period of renewal and consider how they should be reflected in final drafts of the Constitutions. In the interim, Sister Dympna McFadden recorded her experience of these years:

> No one ever realised the ramifications involved in these first special General Chapters, and the years it was going to take to renew, adapt and update and still keep a balanced outlook and attitude on the changes involved. In our wildest dreams we could never have expected to witness such changes in our religious way of life.[34]

Transitions

Ventures into the new continued on many fronts, as the reforms of the Second Vatican Council, ongoing updates in healthcare and Chapter decisions were absorbed into the daily life of the Sisters. One of the more noticeable in the Brisbane chapel was the return of the small marble altar, no longer needed at Ipswich, which was now placed in the sanctuary to enable the celebration of Mass facing the people. Another practical undertaking was Mother Rosarii's request to Roman authorities for an indult to allow the superior of a house to open and close the tabernacle door for the purpose of exposition. In September 1970 she eventually received a letter from the Apostolic Delegate informing her that the Holy See had granted this permission. For the Sisters at Ipswich it provided a special way to celebrate the ninetieth anniversary of Congregational perpetual adoration when they took advantage of the permission on Sunday 15 August 1971.

As the Chapter had called for the Sisters to leave Marian House in Sydney, it was necessary to inform Cardinal Gilroy of this decision and of the wish to investigate possibilities for opening an aged care hostel there. The Cardinal replied graciously, so Mother Rosarii, accompanied by Mother Gabriel, made a number of trips to Sydney to follow leads in Hunters Hill and Manly. However, problems intervened, and they were led in another direction.

Villa Maria Wollongong 1969

Bishop Thomas McCabe

The Chapel, Wollongong

A long-time friend of the Sisters was Bishop McCabe of Wollongong whose mother had died at Villa Maria and who would visit the Sisters whenever he came to Brisbane.[35] On one of these occasions in September 1969 that, during a casual conversation, he turned to Mother Rosarii and asked, 'Mother would you be able to spare a few Sisters to take over Saint Francis Home for the Aged at Wollongong?'[36] Subsequent discussion revealed that the home was presently run by the Franciscan Sisters of Mercy of Luxembourg who were taking care of fifty-four elderly ladies. However, a General Chapter in Luxembourg had decided that the nine Sisters were overextended and that they must withdraw from Wollongong. Bishop McCabe was forced to find someone else to staff the home.

Sr Teresa Donovan: Reunion of Business Women Boarders in 1972.

Sr Yvonne Tobin making altar breads

Sr Dympna McFadden serves residents

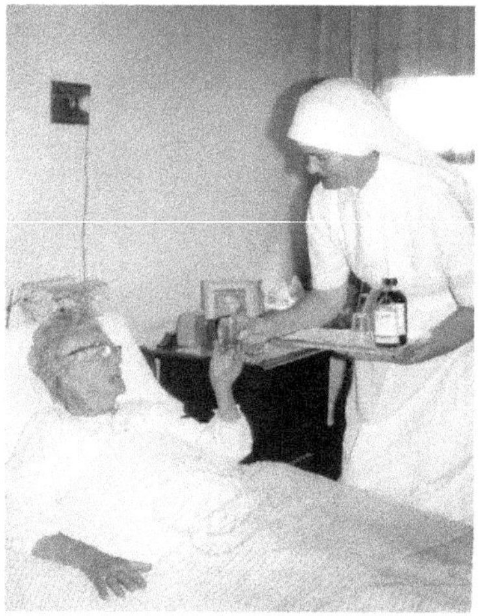

Sr Joseph Bradshaw with resident

Soon afterwards Mother Rosarii and Mother Gabriel were joined by Sister Gerard Dolan, then living at Marian House in Sydney, to inspect the Wollongong home and obtain further information. They found the home beautifully situated, with 'glorious mountains' at the back, looking out to views of the sea and coastline from the front. Six Sisters would be required to run the home, assisted by an adequate number of lay staff already employed. Over the next weeks the Sisters at Marian House 'packed up their belongings, gave everything a good cleaning and set off for a short holiday at Balmoral'.[37] With the help of Sister Rosarii's cousin who lived in Sydney, they gradually moved all their luggage to Wollongong where they were joined by Sister Philomena McAuliffe. They officially took over St Francis Home soon to be renamed 'Villa Maria', on 30 November 1969.

Transitions are never easy, and the Sisters of Perpetual Adoration, sensitively aware that the residents of the home would be grieving for the Sisters who had been caring for them, were grateful for the actions of the wider community that assured them they were welcome. Bishop McCabe took every opportunity he could to speak of the Sisters' experience in care of the aged and of their ability to create a sense of homeliness. Children who sang carols at a Christmas concert for the residents presented Sister Angela Turvey with a large box of chocolates for the Sisters.[38] A 'Younger Set' of youths who volunteered at the home doing gardening, taking residents shopping and on outings and visiting, gave the Sisters a 'Welcome to St Francis' barbecue in March 1970.[39] The Women's Auxiliary worked with the Sisters in mounting their first fete in 1971, raising a record amount of over $3,000 towards a new infirmary about to be built on the grounds of the home. What gave the Sisters greatest joy, however, was that 'the work of perpetual adoration, carried on in Brisbane since the foundation of the order by Father Tenison Woods in 1881, will now be extended interstate'.[40]

More Building

It was not until May 1972 that a government subsidy was granted for the building programme in Ipswich. For some years efforts had been made to maintain and adapt the renovated buildings of Villa Maria to the requirements of changing fire regulations, but it was now realised that demolition and rebuilding was the only answer. By the end of June the once stately home constructed in 1863 was being replaced by a brick building providing hostel accommodation for thirty-three elderly women and a seven-bed infirmary with all the latest amenities for specialised care.

This did not happen without local protest. The Ipswich Historical Society, for example, expressed regret that the 'colonial residence with wide verandahs and wrought-iron lace balustrading, decorative carved cedar staircases and wide rooms with black and white marble fireplaces' was being lost. At the same time, they acknowledged that 'plumbing and other features' posed major challenges: 'it was the Villa's turn to make way for progress'.[41]

On 23 September, 1972, Bishop McCabe laid the foundation stone for the new building planned for Wollongong. The infirmary would ensure that women in the hostel who became infirm could remain under the Sisters' care rather than having to be transferred to a hospital or convalescent home for rehabilitative and palliative treatment. Over the years the Auxiliary had raised $54,000 for the building fund.[42] The government grants would assist with the total expected cost of $390,000. A closed walkway would connect the hostel to the infirmary and the Sisters' Convent, making every part of the building accessible at all times. When finished, it would accommodate twenty-seven patients and four hostel residents.

Plans for a further building project were presented in May next year when Bishop McCabe requested that the Sisters care for retired priests. He suggested a house could be erected next to the present hostel, with provision being made for three priests. They could have the use of the Chapel and have meals delivered to their home. The General Council 'agreed that this work would bring untold blessings on the Congregation'.[43]

In 1965 Archbishop O'Donnell had said, 'The Sisters of Perpetual Adoration are great builders'. However, the stress involved in constructing large buildings was not something the Sisters would have asked for. Buildings are not only functional: they can symbolise the people who built them. It was only because the Sisters knew that to adequately serve the people, they had to dream big. Taking on another building project was only in response to the love they knew God had for the needy and for whom they had given their lives.

Ongoing adaptation

The 1967–68 Chapter had highlighted various aspects of the document *Perfectae Caritatis* to do with the 'founders' spirit and special aims', 'physical and psychological' health and the adaptation of 'obsolete laws' to present circumstances.[44] Over the years, the story of Father Woods had become less important to the Sisters, given that prominence had been given to the Wexford Rule and first-hand memory of the early foundation had faded. As part of the preparation for the Chapter, Sisters had attended a talk on Father Woods given at Banyo Seminary by historian Father Thomas Boland. They were intrigued. After the Chapter, one of the delegates from Marian House decided to find out what she could about Father Woods' final days in Sydney. She knew the address of where he died at 533 Elizabeth Street. The Marian House community was thrilled to find the place still standing, being renovated to house an Art Gallery. They were able to take photos of the rooms occupied by Father Woods and arrange for Mother Rosarii to visit.

In October 1971 the Council received an offer from Father Boland to write a book on the early days of the congregation. He asked that the Sisters should find out what they could from the older Sisters and the many people who had contact with the Congregation over the years.[45] Sister Dympna McFadden was asked to coordinate these tasks.

Examination of community practices that might need reform continued, as post-Vatican II renewal was absorbed into daily living. Because, as *Perfectae Caritatis* pointed out, the consecration of Religious Life is 'deeply rooted in that of baptism',[46] the Council invited Sisters to request this if they wished. A few did this, and others chose to adopt the feminine form of their masculine Religious name, while those who entered the Congregation from now on retained their baptismal names.

During these years many Religious Congregations experienced an exodus among their members. It has always been usual for some members to request dispensation from their vows. Before the Second Vatican Council, between 1952 and 1966, there had been seven Sisters of Perpetual Adoration who had received dispensations. However, with deeper education about the meaning of Religious Life, and, given the options now open to women and formerly not available, more numbers than usual chose to return to lay life during the social upheaval of the late 1960s and early 1970s. Among the fourteen Sisters of Perpetual Adoration who were professed from 1968 to 1973, one transferred to another Congregation and seven remained. There was still a steady inflow of young women into the novitiate, but most left before they took vows.

Yvonne Tobin entered the Sisters in 1965, just as the documents of Vatican Council II were being distributed. She had worked with the Australian Army for a number of years and had boarded with the Sisters during that time. Her keen intelligence and ability to grasp the whole picture would stand her in good stead as she worked with the committee to re-write the Constitutions soon after her profession in 1968.[47] By the time Helen Alfrey, a young teacher then living in Wollongong, entered in January 1973, the Council had replaced the long black dress postulants used to wear with a simple black skirt and white blouse.[48] With her artistic skills and perceptive mind, she, too, would soon find herself in leadership positions in the Congregation.

The seventh General Chapter of the Sisters of Perpetual Adoration was held from 25 September to 2 October 1973. Mother Rosarii was once again elected, under the new title of 'Superior General'. The former Council, Sisters Philippa Barker (Vicar General), Kevin Lewis, Stanislaus Ryan and Aloysius Wallis were also re-elected. The Congregation was on the cusp of its centenary year, 1974. Much of the Chapter's discussion revolved around what might be celebrated, especially with regard to Sisters' new appreciation of Father Woods. The work on the Constitutions was approved with some slight amendments and a committee was formed to compile a Directory and Book of Customs.

At this time there were forty-five professed Sisters in the three communities of Brisbane, Ipswich and Wollongong. In the hundred years of the Congregation's existence, eighty-five women professed as Sisters of Perpetual Adoration had directed the gaze of those whose lives they touched to the God who is always present with us. Their journey had taken many twists and turns. In one way there had been three 'foundings'—the original group of three then five women in Russell Street, the more organised group of Sisters recognised as a Diocesan Congregation by Archbishop Duhig, and now, the post-Vatican II group, responding to a changed world and having to start afresh. In each stage the Sisters had faced an uncertain future with courage. How that future would unfold as they stepped over the hundred-year threshold they did not know.

Chapter 8

The centenary of the founding of the Sisters of Perpetual Adoration was fast approaching. Preparations had begun in earnest at the end of 1973. Archbishop O'Donnell had retired in March of that year, and in May Francis Rush had been installed as Archbishop of Brisbane in his place.[1] It was appropriate that Archbishop Rush would be asked to officiate at a Thanksgiving Mass at the Cathedral as close as possible to the 15 June anniversary. The 1974 schedule required for the celebrations included discussions with the Cathedral Administrator Father Hodge about arrangements for the Mass, and attention to smaller details such as the printing of booklets and souvenir cards, engagement of choirs and the provision of refreshments. Other events with particular groups would follow the Mass. In particular, it was hoped that some of the business women who had boarded with the Sisters from the war years until 1962 would be involved in planning a reunion for the occasion.

Over the previous one hundred years, the Sisters of Perpetual Adoration had endeared themselves not only to Catholics, but to many different groups in Queensland. Therefore, an approach was made to the Queensland postal department about whether they thought an application could be made to the Australian Postal Corporation to issue a stamp to commemorate the centenary. The General Council was pleased with the answer given on 12 December 1973, offering an alternative. This was that a postmark, designed and approved by the Post Office, would be released in June 1974. The sample showed a diamond shaped square enclosing a monstrance and surrounded by the words, 'Sisters of Perpetual Adoration Brisbane 15 June 1874'.[2]

That the Sisters of Perpetual Adoration had reached their centenary was in itself a triumph, given the fact that they had received official approbation only twenty-six years earlier. Now, with forty-three professed Sisters and three novices, they could rejoice in the fact that they had not only survived uncertainties about their canonical status but had become a respected contributor to the well-being of society.

Centenary Celebrations: Wollongong

Happily, the Nursing Home at Villa Maria, Wollongong, was completed by 1974, so its opening on 2 March provided the setting for the first of the centenary celebrations. The *Illawarra Mercury* noted that the event marked 'the Order's centenary year' and described the building as 'one of the most modern of its kind on the South Coast'.[3] It was built on a round tower principle, the wards radiating from a circular ground floor corridor accommodating twenty-seven women. The interior was carpeted in shades of gold and bronze and all the wards were furnished in colours of gold, cream, cinnamon, and pale gold. An oratory opened into a large lounge room. Externally, the three-story hexagonal building provided a magnificent view of the coast. There was a convent for the Sisters on the top floor. Sister Philomena McAuliffe, a triple certificated nurse, was appointed as Matron of the complex.

Rex Connor, Federal Minister for Minerals and Energy who came from Wollongong, opened the building. The blessing was performed by Bishop McCabe who reminded the crowd:

> This Nursing Home will not only serve its patients, but we will all be helped by the continued prayers of the Sisters of Perpetual Adoration for this city and its people.[4]

The people of Wollongong were aware that the primary work of the Sisters was adoration of the Blessed Sacrament. As there were only six Sisters in this community, exposition was restricted to once a week, 9 am to 3.30 pm. The Sisters took turn about to pray each hour during that time and others, residents or people from the local parish, joined them. Even on days when there was no exposition, there was always someone praying in the oratory during the daylight hours.[5]

Tenison Woods Mountain

The next centenary celebration was the naming of Tenison Woods Mountain on 9 June. During the years of renewal since the Second Vatican Council, the Sisters had been impressed by the genius of Father Woods especially in the field of science. In 1970, when Sister Dympna McFadden visited the John Oxley Library and suggested that something should be named in honour of Julian Tenison Woods 'to make his name known to the people of Queensland and Australia', the librarian, Marjorie Walker, took things further.[6] Over the next three years, she and Sister Dympna explored various possibilities until, having obtained documents testifying to the esteem accorded to Father Woods' work, they approached the Queensland Forestry Department to put their case. When they were eventually informed that 'the highest peak of the D'Aguilar Range [forty-eight kilometres north-west of Brisbane] was still un-named to this day', they recognised this to be the solution.[7] A mountain would be named after the mountain of a man, Father Julian Tenison Woods.

With the required authorities approached and approvals given, preparations were made to hold the nomination ceremony on the mountain itself. The final notice of the naming was gazetted in the Queensland parliament on 30 March 1974. The Forestry Department printed the invitations for the occasion at their own expense. On Sunday 9 June, just prior to the centenary anniversary, a bus brought the Sisters to Tenison Woods Mountain, joining dignitaries and friends at its peak to celebrate Mass and dedicate the plaque.

Accompanied by Father Tom Boland, Monsignor Grantly Lake OBE officiated at the Mass, deputising for Archbishop Rush who was unable to be present. The dedication ceremony was led by the Queensland Minister for Lands, Wallace Rae. In his tribute to Father Woods, Mr Rae described Julian as 'one of the most picturesque personalities of Australia's early history':

> He led a strangely varied and adventurous life. He achieved distinction in many totally different spheres. He was a distinguished scientist in separate fields, a noted explorer, a writer and a missionary. But in assessing his achievements he seems to stand most prominently as a mystic and a man of God.[8]

The Villa Maria Nursing Home, Wollongong.
Opened in 1974, built on a prime location on Cliff Street

Path to the summit of Tenison Woods Mountain:
a place of peace and beauty.
Photo permission: James Stone©

Mass amidst showers on the summit of Tenison Woods Mountain. Celebrants were Msgr Lake and Fr Tom Boland. Holding umbrellas are Srs Margaret Mary and Dympna.

Launch of
Quiet Women:
Father Tom Boland, author;
Sr Helen Alfrey, illustrator;
Sr Dympna McFadden, researcher

Centenary postmark

Sisters gathered for
celebration of centenary

The air is humid and often misty on Tenison Woods Mountain. With its abundance of tropical growth and its silence broken only by the call of birds and insects, it provides a pertinent, beautiful tribute to this man who delighted in creation's wonder.

Cathedral Mass

On Friday 14 June at 7.30 pm, the Mass of Thanksgiving was held at St Stephen's Cathedral. Archbishop Rush and some fifteen other priests concelebrated. Relatives of the founders Father Julian Woods and Mother Stanislaus Gaffney came from South Australia, New South Wales, Victoria and Tasmania to join the large crowd of Sisters and friends gathered for the event. Mother Rosarii and Sister Kevin Lewis did the scripture readings and the Cathedral Boys Choir led the singing for the Mass. In his homily, Archbishop Rush gave a short history of the Congregation, marvelling at what it showed about the workings of God:

> In my view, the value of the Sisters of Perpetual Adoration to the Archdiocese of Brisbane, the Church and the community is that by the lives they lead they proclaim Christ persistently and ceaselessly . . . A Religious Congregation that has weathered the rough seas that the Sisters of Perpetual Adoration have sailed will not be intimidated easily by any rough weather that prophets of doom forecast for the Church and the world. Their life is the living Christ. They have always trusted Him and He has never failed them.[9]

Ipswich

The blessing and opening of the new hostel on Limestone Street that replaced the original house built in 1863 took the centenary celebrations to Ipswich on 20 October. Bill Hayden, Federal Minister for Social Security, opened the building, expressing his admiration for the Sisters:

> I have been enormously impressed by their dedication and respect for the human beings they are caring for. And this respect is a most important factor of success. In fact, I feel that in future years the strength and quality of our Government's work will be measured in the amount of respect gained from the people.[10]

The new $500,000 Villa Maria complex was also praised by the various dignitaries present who endorsed the Minister's remarks. Archbishop Rush thanked the State and Federal governments for grants and paid special tribute to the Building Committee who had been raising funds for many years. In congratulating the Sisters on this further celebration in their centenary year, he observed, 'The Sisters are very quiet, gentle but determined women'. As he blessed the residents of the hostel he prayed that they would be a true community of faith and love, with trust in Christ and each other.

What was true for Villa Maria in Ipswich was true also in Brisbane and Wollongong. In their care of the aged, the Sisters engendered an atmosphere of 'family'. Their hope was that each woman would feel at 'home', and comments made through the years confirmed that they achieved this aim. As Boland wrote in their centenary year:

> Villa Maria is not just another Home for the Elderly. It is a community of affection and concern for the people who come in need, even if that need is not financial. The affection and concern spring from love—love of Christ and love of all those with whom Christ's love brings the Sisters in contact.[11]

Book Launch

The final centenary celebration was the launch of the book *Quiet Women*, written by Father Tom Boland. Early in 1971 Mother Rosarii had approached him to ask if he would consider writing the history. When he indicated he would need help in gathering resources, she appointed Sister Dympna McFadden to assist him. Thanks to the research done by this woman of 'initiative, determination and amazing energy', gathering material from a variety of sources and interviewing Sisters and other people who had been part of the Congregation's story, she was able to present to Father Boland a wealth of information to facilitate the process of writing[12].

At the launch, Mother Rosarii expressed the Sisters' delight with this 'beautifully-bound, well written and thoroughly researched book'.[13] Its loose-leaf cover featured a copy of the painting by Ric Elliot of 533 Elizabeth Street Sydney, the terraced house in which Father Woods died.[14] With the depiction of two nuns on the footpath, it could re-imagine the visit of Mother Stanislaus and Sister Maria Joseph to Father Woods as he neared death in 1889, or more recently, the visit of Mother Rosarii and Sister Gerard when they rediscovered the residence in 1968.[15] A number of photos were included in the book, but most illustrations were expertly-executed black and white drawings by the former art teacher Sister Helen Alfrey, at the time a novice at Ipswich and professed in September of the centenary year.[16]

As he unfolded the story of the Sisters of Perpetual Adoration, Father Boland realised that to understand them, it was necessary 'to understand the life and spirit of Julian Tenison Woods'.[17] His inclusion of a concise yet thorough biography of Woods was a particular gift. Up to that time, the only biography available had been the work by George O'Neill SJ, *Life of the Reverend Julian Edmund Tenison Woods,* published in 1929. When Sister Dympna had produced the collection of letters Father Woods had written to the early Sisters, Boland had declared that here was 'a rich vein of precious metal for the church in Australia that has never been tapped'.[18] His reading of Julian's scientific works as well as private letters and the notes of his instructions to the first Sisters of Perpetual Adoration gave him an insight into his complex character and spirituality not highlighted in the previous publication. He appreciated the multi-faceted genius of this man whose focus on God's love gave him 'a centre of cohesion for all his visions and restless energies'.[19] Boland lit a candle that has gradually grown into a bright light. At the present time we find a steadily growing number of articles, theses and books about the life and works of Julian Tenison Woods.

Archbishop Francis Rush

Bill Hayden opens new Villa Maria hostel, Ipswich, 1974

Villa Maria Hostel Ipswich, opened October 1974.

Villa Maria Chapel, Ipswich.

The Second Century Begins

The years immediately following the centenary passed uneventfully. In 1975, the Jesuits from Toowong informed Mother Rosarii that, owning to parish commitments, they could no longer supply confessors to the Sisters at Villa Maria. Since 1894, when Father George Buckeridge had advised Archbishop Dunne to have some Sisters train with the Wexford Sisters, the Jesuits had been closely involved in the lives of the Sisters of Perpetual Adoration.[20] While some may have seen this as the regretful close of an era, it also offered another opportunity for the Congregation to be less reliant on male advisers than they had been in the past.

On 1 July 1975 the General Council received 'a request from a widow and her two daughters to join the Sisters of Perpetual Adoration'.[21] Mother Rosarii interviewed the three women and they were joyfully received as postulants on the anniversary of Father Woods' death, 7 October 1975. After spending two years in the Novitiate, Sisters Shirley, Narelle and Barbara Hickson were professed in June 1979.[22] It was not unprecedented that widows should enter religious life. In every age, they have done so, and they were often joined by their daughters. Indeed, many religious orders were founded by widows; for example, the Visitation Order was founded in 1610 by the widow Saint Jane Frances de Chantal at Annecy, France. One of the early Sisters of St Joseph was a widow, Sister Veronica Champion, whose knowledge of finance proved invaluable to Mary MacKillop. However, in the 1970s, the occurrence was rare enough to catch the attention of local and interstate Catholic newspapers. The *Catholic Leader* featured a photo of Sisters Shirley, Narelle and Barbara and an interview with the three when they made their final vows on 27 June 1983: 'We were born into love, reared in love, lived in love. Now our love can be deepened in a very special way,' said Sister Narelle.[23]

Periodic reviews of community life continued, as Sisters kept in mind the need for spiritual, psychological and physical health, as advocated by the reforms of the Second Vatican Council. With more effective consultation with the Sisters, practical suggestions could be made. Sometimes the changes were simple—replacing the flowing scapular of the habit with a simple pleat in the dress, for example, or providing electric blankets to Sisters in winter if they wanted them.[24] In Wollongong, special permission was given in October 1977 to admit a priest to the Villa Maria nursing home as he was too ill to be cared for at St Paul's, the house built next door for retired priests.[25] Little by little, small changes would shift former strongly-held, immovable convictions (such as excluding male residents), to allow for witness to God's loving presence to be demonstrated in everyday, human events.

In Ipswich, the Sisters who taught catechetics at the Bremer and Amberly High Schools were having serious difficulties with discipline in the classes. As none of them had received teacher training, it was decided to draw this ministry to a close, The parish priests were informed of this in December 1978, and trained catechists were found to take their place. There was good news for Brisbane that same month. It had long been realised that the model of having a nursing home attached to the hostel, as at Wollongong and Ipswich, was one that Brisbane should adopt. A Bonds Factory in Gotha Street had come up for sale some years before, so the General Council had bought it, letting it out as a car park for the time being to help raise funds for building. With the news in late December from the Commonwealth Department of Social Security that in-principle approval had been granted, definite plans for the nursing home on Warren Street, south of St Gabriel's Wing of the hostel, could be drawn up.

1979 General Chapter

No new matters were introduced at the General Chapter held in September 1979. The rewriting of the Constitutions and supporting documents was affirmed, as was the decision to go ahead with the building of the nursing home on Warren Street. As Mother Rosarii had already served two terms as Superior General, she was not eligible for re-election. The former Vicar-General, Sister Philippa Barker, was elected as Superior General and Mother Rosarii became Vicar General. Was this an indication that the Sisters of Perpetual Adoration would fall back into their old habit of recycling leadership? Two new Councillors did join Sister Aloysius Wallis on the General Council, Sisters Eucharia Kingston and Cordelia Constable. Both had held positions of trust before—Sister Cordelia in the foundation of Ipswich, and Sister Eucharia as Novice Mistress. While the appointment of a younger person with no former experience of leadership may have signified a willingness to promote ongoing innovation, it was important that what had been gained over the past twelve years should be strengthened without losing the Sisters' trust. Effective systems of consultation such as the House Council had been introduced. This meant that the community leader now had her own authority, and Sisters had a platform on which they could give voice to new ideas and suggestions. The members of the General Council met monthly to attend to the broader questions concerning Congregational vision and ministry. The Sisters could be assured that these features of leadership would now continue. That Sister Philippa would not curtail reform was indicated by her opting to retain the title 'Sister' instead of 'Mother'.

Over the twelve years since 1967 eleven Sisters had died and ten Sisters had left the Congregation. For a small group, this was a large and sudden depletion of numbers. With the centenary of continuous perpetual adoration approaching in 1981, the Sisters decided to mount a 'campaign' to promote membership. They would place advertisements in the Catholic newspapers in Queensland, New South Wales and Victoria, and would appoint some younger Sisters to go to Youth Camps and to country parishes to make the Congregation known.[26] While there is no record as to whether this latter resolution was put into effect, the advertisements continued to appear in the *Catholic Leader* each week for the next ten years. In addition, the House Council of Villa Maria, Brisbane, decided to spend half an hour each day praying together for vocations and to 'go without snacks one day a week', offering this action as another form of prayer.[27]

Warren Street Nursing Home

Before the plans for the new nursing home at Brisbane Villa Maria could go ahead, it was necessary to move the chaplain's residence, St Isadore's. Eventually this house was purchased and transported to an outer suburb north of Brisbane. The Bonds building that had been temporarily used as a car park was demolished and in March 1980 the land was cleared for building to begin. For many years the strip of land that ran south of St Gabriel's Wing between Warren and Gotha streets had been used by the hostel as an area for drying clothes. The Sisters had applied to the city council to buy the land, but while queries were being made about its ownership, the Sisters could use it by default. Despite newspaper advertisements no owner came forward, so the land was able to be purchased. An overpass connecting the proposed nursing home and the hostel was then incorporated into the plan.

On 26 April 1981 Archbishop Rush officiated at the blessing of 'the modern and well-equipped nursing home' extending from Warren Street through to the parallel Gotha Street. Built to accommodate fifty women, the five-level home was simple in design and afforded full patient care including occupational therapy provided by the Red Cross. Its total cost of $1.9 million was partly funded by the Federal and State Government grants of $638,000. The Federal Minister for Finance, Senator Margaret Guilfoyle, was to have opened the home but was unable to do so because of an airline dispute that prevented her from travelling.[28] In her place, Queensland Senator John MacGibbon conducted the opening.[29]

In his speech, Archbishop Rush accounted for the magnificent buildings now extending from St Pauls Terrace by recalling the history of the Sisters of Perpetual Adoration:

> From the start, [the Sisters] were quiet, determined, strong-willed women. One of the secrets of their success has been the strength of all their Mothers-General, from Mother Stanislaus to Sister Philippa. Their leaders have guided them valiantly, often against appalling odds.[30]

In 1968, at the opening of St Gabriel's Wing of Villa Maria, the chaplain, Father Kitts, had moved the vote of thanks on the Sisters' behalf. Now, in 1981, 'the Superior General of the Sisters of Perpetual Adoration (Sister Philippa) addressed the gathering'.[31] Not only the Sisters, but the Church to an extent, and society in general, had come a long way towards gender equality.

The occasion may have been counted a success by the fact that the appeal raised over $8,000 that day. But what the Sisters remembered most was that it was both a happy neighbourhood and an ecumenical affair. On the day of the opening 500 people surged out into Warren Street which was cordoned off, creating a festive atmosphere. The local Salvation Army provided the music not only for the hymns sung during the dedication ceremony but also as background as the crowd mingled, sharing refreshments provided by the Sisters.[32] Once again, they were seen as part of the Spring Hill community.

Centenary of Perpetual Adoration

For one hundred years, since 15 August 1881, the Sisters of Perpetual Adoration had kept watch before the Blessed Sacrament in the Brisbane chapel for twenty-four hours a day. Even when there were as few as ten Sisters in the house, they had rostered themselves for one-hour shifts during the day and two-hour shifts at night to pray in adoration and in intercession for the needs of society.

To celebrate this centenary on 15 August 1981, the General Council decided to hold a 'Day of Thanksgiving', beginning with Mass in the morning and ending at 3 pm with a Holy Hour—that is, an hour of communal meditation with exposition of the Blessed Sacrament—and Benediction, the ceremony where all present are blessed with the Eucharistic Host exposed in the monstrance. The general public were invited to share in the day by visiting the chapel for some time. Special invitations were given to the Hostel residents and to friends and relatives of the Sisters. Beforehand, the TV Channel 2 had televised Sisters and other people at prayer in the chapel and the broadcast was shown during the evening news of 15 August.

While Father Woods had stipulated in the first rule that the Sisters should 'consider themselves principally bound to the perpetual adoration and more in their own convents than anywhere else', he had also charged them to encourage other expressions by which 'honour and veneration [are] given to our Blessed Lord in the great Sacrament of love'.[33] Traditionally, one of the ways the Sisters had done this was by taking part in public celebrations of the feast of Corpus Christi such as the Eucharistic processions held since 1912, initially through the city streets and, later at the Brisbane Exhibition Grounds. In 1977, however, the procession was no longer held, so each year the Sisters extended an open invitation to their chapel to celebrate the feast with a Holy Hour. In Ipswich, Villa Maria became the centre where the parish held its 'major celebrations' of Corpus Christi, with Exposition of the Blessed Sacrament, Benediction and other Eucharistic devotions.[34]

After the 1981 centenary, some Brisbane Sisters raised concern that the public face of the Sisters had more to do now with care of the aged than with their primary purpose of adoration. In response, it was decided to hold a Holy Hour each month to which everyone was invited and to place a permanent advertisement for this in the *Catholic Leader*. They also resolved to ask the Director of Vocations for the Brisbane Archdiocese, Father William Morris, to bring Youth Groups to the chapel occasionally for a Holy Hour.[35] How effective these invitations were can only be surmised, as no records of direct responses were kept.

1985 General Chapter

In preparation for the 1985 General Chapter, the members of the Council surveyed the happenings of the past six years. Regarding the primary aim of adoration, they recorded that the Brisbane house was the only community that was able to continue adoration without interruption. The Sisters in the other communities of Ipswich and Wollongong had a half-hour roster for adoration each day and as much of adoration at night as was possible. Even though Sisters were 'fewer and frailer', the Brisbane community had determined to continue their schedule 'with a greater trust in the Providence of God'.[36]

Since the last Chapter a number of women had inquired about the lives of the Sisters. Of six who entered, four had been professed. Three Sisters had left the Congregation and three had died, including Mother Gabriel Moloney whose death on 17 September 1983 had caught the attention of a large number of people. The *Catholic Leader* had acknowledged the great contribution Mother Gabriel had made to the welfare of elderly women in Queensland and celebrated her many roles as a Sister of Perpetual Adoration:

A gifted person who could put her hand to practically anything, she proved an asset to the struggling community in the 1920s in her ability to sew, for sewing was their 'bread and butter' at that time. Her musical talent was recognised. She had been taught the violin and played that at Benediction. Then she taught herself to play the organ, and was organist for many years.

Sisters Shirley, Narelle and Barbara Hickson

Sr Emmanuel Carroll packing altar breads

Sr Elizabeth Bargenquast displays her expertise.

Srs Eucharia Kingston, Yvonne Tobin, Kevin Lewis, Clement Thomas, Elizabeth Bargenquast

Sr Philippa Barker

Villa Maria Nursing Home,
from Gotha Street

Former St Isadore's Presbytery, Warren Street.

Opening of Villa Maria Nursing Home, Warren Street, 1984

The article went on to note that, besides her responsibilities as Bursar (a post she had held from 1927 until 1973), Mother Gabriel was Mistress of Novices from 1943 to 1950, Vicar General from 1950 to 1955 and Mother General from 1955 to 1967. Her long and full life of ninety-one years had come 'to a close in the convent she loved, with her Sisters around her'.[37]

Of the secondary aims of the Congregation, Care of the Aged was causing most concern. The Sisters in Brisbane, Ipswich and Wollongong were feeling the stress of maintaining the ever-growing requirements of government legislation. For example, when the Sisters undertook the building of the new Villa Maria nursing home in Brisbane with approval for twenty-five nursing home and twenty-five temporary hostel beds, they had understood that 'Federal Government approval would be given for the reclassification of the hostel beds to nursing home beds when the demand warranted this'. However, with demand now at crisis level where at least five elderly women per week were being turned away, this approval was being withheld. The Sisters were subsidising nursing care for a number of women in their hostel accommodation, but without proper funding they could not continue to do so. The Commonwealth Department of Community Services which controlled the allocation of nursing care beds gave no hope of their applications succeeding. In October 1985, Sister Philippa Barker had reported to the *Catholic Leader*:

> Some of our residents do not have immediate relatives to turn to. Nor do they wish to be sent away from Villa Maria to another nursing home—some of our ladies have been with us for twenty-five years—this is their home. In an outside nursing-home they miss the chapel where they can find peace, they miss the Sisters and they miss their friends from the hostel.[38]

The Sisters gathered for the Chapter re-elected Sister Philippa Barker as Superior General. Three new Councillors—Sisters Angela Turvey, Yvonne Tobin and Jean Duncan—joined Mother Rosarii on the General Council.[39] Externally the Sisters' lives looked much the same as they had thirty years before, for their dress and interactions with others had changed little. Internally, however, with openness to wider representation on Council and improved structures of communication, the reforms of the Second Vatican Council encouraging Sisters to trust each other had taken root.

Papal Visit

The visit of Pope John Paul II to Australia in 1986 had direct implications for the Sisters of Perpetual Adoration. Primarily, it meant that the demand for altar breads would increase enormously. Sisters Emmanuel Carroll and Yvonne Tobin now carried out the apostolate of making altar breads[40] Four lay women were employed to help them with the work of sorting, weighing and packaging the breads for postage. Modern machinery helped facilitate the baking and cutting of the average monthly output of 510,000 small breads, 13,000 large and 250 extra-large breads, with increases occurring for seasonal feasts such as Christmas and Easter.

Father John Lennon, the financial administrator of the Brisbane Archdiocese, was appointed by Archbishop Rush as State Director of the Papal visit. His request to the Sisters of Perpetual Adoration was that they should provide two Sisters who, with others, would serve as sacristans for the Mass to be celebrated at the Queen Elizabeth II Stadium, Brisbane.[41] Part of their duties would be to fill 400 ciboria with 150 hosts in each. Sisters Margaret Mary Allport and Anthony Ordish were assigned this task.[42] The Sisters of Perpetual Adoration also responded to the appeal for the loan of vestments and sacred vessels for use at the Mass. The O'Brien family of Defiance Flour from Toowoomba offered to provide the flour for the baking of the altar breads, and the Sisters arranged for them to receive a letter of recognition from the organisers of the Papal visit.

After the Brisbane event, attended by over 70,000 people, the General Council reflected on the experience of the pilgrimage of the Pope to Australia. Sister Philippa focused on a homily given in Sydney to Religious where the Pope had pointed out that while the government has rightly taken responsibility for health care, social welfare and education, these traditional apostolates of Religious needed their attention now more than ever. In the light of rapid secularisation taking place in Australian society (as in other parts of the world), the contribution of Religious must give witness to the 'Gospel message of salvation in Christ Jesus': 'care also involves the spiritual'.[43]

Anniversary of Father Woods' Death

On 3 August 1987 Father Tom Boland visited the Sisters and suggested they join with the Sisters of St Joseph who were preparing for the centenary of Julian Woods' death in October 1989. The first meeting between the two Congregations in Brisbane was held the next month.

While many Queensland Sisters of the Sisters of Perpetual Adoration and the Sisters of St Joseph knew each other personally, some even being related, it was true that for many years there were almost no formal contacts between the two Congregations. Some recent efforts had improved this situation. In 1974, the Sisters of Perpetual Adoration had distributed to all groups of Sisters of St Joseph copies of the *Memoirs* of Father Woods that had been entrusted to them by Anne Bulger to whom he had dictated his story.[44] The 1979 publications of biographies of Father Woods by Josephite Sisters Margaret Press from Perthville, New South Wales, and Isabel Hepburn from Whanganui, New Zealand, had enlarged on what Father Boland had written in *Quiet Women*.[45] From 1986 to 1988 Sister Jan Tranter RSJ from Lochinvar had visited Villa Maria in Brisbane during research for her Master's thesis and had interviewed Sisters of Perpetual Adoration for their memories of what older Sisters had told them about Father Woods.[46] Sister Dympna McFadden RPA had pursued information about Father Woods' last days in Sydney and had grown in admiration of the former Sister of St Joseph Sister Ignatius O'Brien (Gertrude Abbott) who cared for him and who had founded St Margaret's Maternity Hospital in Sydney. When author Suzy Baldwin advertised for nominations of lesser-known but significant figures in Australian history for her book *Unsung Heroes & Heroines of Australia*, Sister Dympna had put forward the name of Gertude Abbott. In October 1988 the book was launched in Brisbane at Government House and Sister Dympna was presented with a copy of the work by the Governor Sir Walter Campbell.[47] All of these happenings had raised awareness of the founding links between the Sisters of Perpetual Adoration and the Sisters of St Joseph.

The committee preparing for the celebration of Father Woods' anniversary met over many months during 1988 and succeeded in producing a rich plan for 1989. Leading up to the celebration, the Sisters would listen to a set of tapes on 'refounding' which advocated getting into the mind of the founder and the story of the founding into order to recontextualise it into a different world.[48] As part of this process, Sister Philippa arranged for Sister Jan Tranter to give a series of reflections on Julian Woods to the Sisters of Perpetual Adoration in Brisbane, Ipswich and Wollongong during 1989. The main celebration of the centenary would be a Mass for the Sisters of both Congregations to be held on Tenison Woods Mountain on 7 October, the actual anniversary of Julian Woods' death. Father Tom Boland would preside at the Mass. On 28 October there would be a 'People's Day' to be held at Corpus Christi College at Nundah.[49] Here the celebration would highlight a display of the life and works of Father Woods. A symposium on Father Woods would form part of the proceedings.

Two events coincided with the centenary year of Julian Woods' death. The first was the unexpected death of Mother Rosarii Ansaldo on 18 July. Small in stature, she had been a 'big' presence. Like Moses (and Miriam, as some scripture scholars now assert) who led the Israelites to Israel, she had, through kindness and courage, led the Sisters to the post-Vatican II world. Two months after her death, Mrs Pat Lucas (81 years) wrote to the Readers' Letters section of the *Catholic Leader* that the residents at Villa Maria were still missing her:

> We have lost 'Our Mother'—Mother Rosarii, 67 [years of age]. Although years younger than the majority of us who live here, we looked to her for our comfort and that little personal word she gave to us all. Her prayer every morning set us on our day . . . I called her *The Little Sparrow*—if you didn't catch her when she came out of the lift, she was gone over to the chapel to do her perpetual adoration. She never spared herself in any way for Villa Maria, not only for the business side of the administration, but no menial task was too hard for her to do. If any of our ladies were sent to hospital, she always found the time to visit them all and give them the little word of comfort.[50]

Inevitably, Mother Rosarii's death left a huge gap; the members of the General Council missed her enormously. In her place they elected Sister Emmanuel Carroll to serve as an interim councillor until the next Chapter to be held in 1991.

The second happening was the dedication of the restored and extended St Stephen's Cathedral, Brisbane. There had been delays in completing the work, but eventually the ceremony was held on 4 December 1989. The Sisters of Perpetual Adoration considered the history of St Stephen's to be linked with their own. Father John Lennon, now acting as the Appeal Director for the project, thanked the various groups of Religious for their donations to the work at St Stephen's, citing the Sisters of Perpetual Adoration who 'wanted to be identified with the project because their Congregation was founded only a month after the original opening of St Stephen's in 1874'.[51] He did not add that Father Woods had purposely asked the founding group not to draw attention to their presence until after the opening: 'The opening of the Cathedral at Brisbane will not take place until 17 May, and I do not care about your going until that is all over and the people settle down again.'[52] As part of reconstructing their own history, the Sisters had made a pilgrimage to the Cathedral site in their preparing for Father Woods' centenary of death.

The planned celebrations at Tenison Woods Mountain and at Nundah were joyful occasions and did much to foster friendships among the two groups of Sisters. The *Catholic Leader* reported on their celebrations of the 'accomplishments and genius of Fr Tenison Woods', citing Sister Evelyn Pickering RSJ:

> No-one would be foolhardy enough to deny that he was well above the ordinary. Who else has combined, as he did, the qualities and skills of priest, scientist and founder not only of one religious institute but of a half-dozen?[53]

At the symposium held at Nundah on 28 October, Brother Peter Anderson CFC gave the occasional address on 'Julian Tenison Woods: Bush Scientist & Geologist'. As a scientist himself, he said he felt honoured to have his name associated with 'an Australian of the stature of Julian Tenison Woods, priest and scientist'. Most of all, he marvelled at Julian's 'mystical insights into the unity of all that is, and [his] passionate desire to share this with all'.[54] The stance of the mystic is one of openness to 'communion with the Divine'—another way of describing 'adoration'. It was this stance, passed on in the legacy that Julian Woods left them, that the Sisters of Perpetual Adoration could celebrate in the centenary of his entry into eternal life.

Chapter 9

For the Sisters of Perpetual Adoration the last decade of the twentieth century dawned with more concern about government policies regarding small nursing homes. The 'greying population' of Australia was growing. Government reviews to cope with new demands, innovations in health care and rationalisation of resources led to 'remarkable growth' in some areas and 'a state of ferment' in others.[1] Both extremes were being felt by the Sisters of Perpetual Adoration. In mid-1990, with government restrictions on small nursing homes, the Ipswich Infirmary had to close. Eight beds then became available to the Brisbane nursing home and residents were transferred on 15 October. With each review came extra expenses. In Brisbane, a new physiotherapy room had to be equipped with the necessary items; the recreational officer was provided with an office and the nursing staff a lecture and in-service room. Incidentals, such as advances in medical knowledge of diabetes and other conditions, required the employment of chefs to accommodate special diets and, for the safety of staff, safety equipment for moving patients had to be purchased.

In 1987, the Lutheran Church south of the Warren Street nursing home had come up for sale and the Sisters of Perpetual Adoration had purchased it. Since then they had let it out to a charitable group Teen Challenge.[2] In February 1990, Teen Challenge informed the Sisters they no longer required use of the building for day programs but asked if they could use it temporarily for the storage of furniture. This permission was given, but owing to the building's position in Fortitude Valley, squatters and vandalism soon became a problem. Various attempts were made to obtain other tenants such as a St Vincent de Paul Day Centre. However, these were not successful, and even though an amateur theatre company did use the space for some time, the building was gradually falling into disrepair. Both this building and problems connected with health care would play a prominent part in the decisions of the General Council as the decade unfolded.

1991 General Chapter

The General Chapter was held at Villa Maria in September 1991. Sister Yvonne Tobin was elected as Superior General, and the General Council was made up of Sisters Angela Turvey (Vicar General), Philippa Barker, Jean Duncan and Helen Alfrey. The Chapter of Affairs was delayed until June 1992 to allow time to present proposals that needed approval from this assembly. The number of Sisters was decreasing rapidly, and at least two of the 'younger' ones were in poor health. There was a need to get professional advice about setting up a 'retirement' scheme for the Sisters so that adequate provision was made for them when they could no longer manage the hard, physical work that they had carried out in the past.[3] The Sisters of Perpetual Adoration from Wexford had written to the General Council in July 1990 telling them that they now had a group of lay people on the roster to assist with adoration. This was a step that the Sisters in Brisbane would need to take. By this time the nursing home in Brisbane was run entirely by lay staff. The Council could see that it would be necessary in the near future to extend this trend to employ lay managers for the hostels in Brisbane, Ipswich and Wollongong. In order to make decisions about these matters, Chapter delegates needed to have access to the best information available.

At the Chapter of Affairs next year, the final version of the Constitutions that Sister Yvonne had been working on for a number of years was at last approved. Approvals were given too for the General Council to take whatever steps were necessary to put these proposals into effect. Archbishop Rush had retired on 3 December 1991 so it was to his successor, Archbishop John Bathersby, that Sister Yvonne had to report about the Chapter proceedings.[4] One of the incidental outcomes of the Chapter for the Sisters was the Council's decision that they would have one day off per week—previously it had been one day off per month.[5] Another was that the night shifts for adoration in Brisbane were changed from one to one and a half hours. This allowed Sisters to have unbroken sleep every second night.[6]

Establishment of Co-Adorers

For some time a few lay people had been joining the Sisters in adoration on a regular basis. Michael Lynch, for example, was particularly taken by the words written around the archway above the chapel door at Villa Maria: 'Could you not watch one hour with me?' After dinner at around 8 pm, he would ring the doorbell of Villa Maria and one of the Sisters—'usually Sister Teresa'—would let him into the chapel lit only by the altar candles. There he joined Sisters Cordelia and Michael who were kneeling before the exposed Eucharist. He found that after his day's work as a guidance officer, the spending of an hour or so in quiet prayer helped him in life.[7]

When Sister Emmanuel was charged by the Council to take forward the Chapter's hope that the Sisters' primary aim of Adoration might continue despite depleting membership, she spoke with Michael and several others about the possibility of forming a 'Eucharistic Confraternity' to promote adoration of the Blessed Sacrament. It would take some years of conversation about this before a sufficient number of people could be found who would make such a commitment. Other efforts were made by Sisters to nurture the spiritual life of hostel residents and to invite the wider public to take part in events provided for this purpose. Invitations were placed in the *Catholic Leader* for a yearly Retreat Day and Anointing Mass at Brisbane Villa Maria.[8] Because the Sisters could no longer count on the services of a priest from the Cathedral parish for such events, the Sisters purchased a unit at 53 St Pauls Terrace to house a chaplain in the future.[9]

In Ipswich, a Prayer Centre was established with accommodation being provided at Villa Maria for lay people who wished to spend a day or two in private prayer and directed meditation.[10] The Sisters there also arranged for a Marist Brother to give a series of scripture lectures to residents and others in the parish.[11] In Wollongong the Sisters had 'taken up the idea [of a Eucharistic Confraternity] enthusiastically'.[12] Here a number of lay people and a priest living in a nearby parish had agreed to become part of the roster for adoration.[13] From 25 March 1995, daily adoration from noon until 6 pm had been maintained.

On 6 June 1997 Archbishop Bathersby gave his permission for 'Co-Adorers' to be rostered for perpetual adoration at Villa Maria, Brisbane. By now there were about fifty people who had agreed to became part of the movement. The General Council decided to commence this new arrangement on Friday, 12 September, with one night of adoration per week being covered by them and two Sisters being on call should there be problems.[14] The information given by the Wexford Sisters in one sentence back in July 1990 had begun a journey lasting seven years.

Altar Breads

The 1991 election of Sister Yvonne Tobin as Superior General of the Congregation meant that she had to devote herself full-time to the role and could no longer work in producing altar breads as she had done previously. Sister Emmanuel continued this ministry and was joined by other Sisters who, in turn, found their health could not sustain the physical demands required. The Council therefore decided that this ministry would have to be handed on to someone else. They found that the Benedictine Sisters at Rockhampton could look after the northern dioceses of Queensland and Ozenham Industries would supply New South Wales and the Brisbane Archdiocese through Christian Supplies.[15]

On 9 June 1994 Archbishop Bathersby was informed that, after seventy-two years, the altar bread production at Villa Maria would cease on 14 September. While it was a decision that had to be made it caused heartache to the Sisters, as its association with their primary purpose was obvious. Through this ministry the Sisters of Perpetual Adoration had become a household name in most parishes throughout Queensland, at least in the minds of priests. Sister Yvonne wrote to the Sisters at the time and referred to the many 'thank you letters' that had been received:

> Those Sisters who actually participated can really appreciate the back-breaking work and tedious cutting and sorting that went in to producing the quality breads which have been supplied over the years. Giving up the altar breads is the direct result of the lack of vocations to our Congregation . . . Let us pray for each other.[16]

In one way the Sisters continued their production of altar breads, albeit by proxy—in August, the General Council had informed the Patriarchal Vicar of the Chaldean Catholic Church in Australia that the Sisters of Perpetual Adoration would donate their altar bread machinery to the Daughters of Our Lady Immaculate in Baghdad.[17]

Lay Management

The transfer of health care to lay managers did not happen easily. Brisbane Villa Maria now had 130 people in hostel accommodation and thirty-three in the nursing home. In December 1992 a government grant had been given for the upgrading of the hostel. Even before the upgrading began, an atmosphere of disruption prevailed, exacerbated by poor communication and unsuitability of the lay supervisor. Large financial losses were also causing problems. Industrial action over 'mishandling of a termination of employment' followed but was eventually solved.[18] At the end of November 1993, Sister Narelle Hickson was appointed Hostel Supervisor and an Advisory Board was set up. Later, this would become a Management Committee comprising the Sisters in leadership and experienced lay personnel.

Ipswich Villa Maria, too, was experiencing financial losses. With the close of the infirmary, it was difficult to maintain ongoing services in the hostel with the same efficiency as previously. However, when Mrs Robyn Gugenberger, Sister Yvonne's sibling, was appointed part-time manager in 1996 to assist Sister Helen Alfrey, new structures were put in place and improvements made.[19]

In June 1995 negotiations had taken place at Villa Maria Wollongong to purchase eight beds, which, if granted, would require the Sisters to give up their convent space on the top floor of the hexagonal nursing home. However, there were other complications. Although the design of the building was pleasing to the eye and had many advantages, the government's more rigorous requirements for fire safety were proving very difficult to fulfill. Furthermore, the home itself was not meeting financial costs. While visiting Wollongong, Sister Yvonne, who had an extraordinary ability to recognise who might best solve problems, happened to meet two professional advisers from Catholic Healthcare Australia, and decided they were 'just the people we need to guide us through this time'.[20] Catholic Healthcare was then engaged in a consultancy capacity to help change managerial practices and restructure staffing in the three aged care centres. It was the Sisters' wish that they should retain the apostolate with the aged, 'especially the financially disadvantaged and those whom society rejects'.[21]

Amidst all this turmoil, the inner life of the Congregation had to go on. According to the Constitutions approved by Archbishop Bathersby after the 1991 Chapter, the stipulation that the General Chapter should occur every six years had been changed. The date was flexible, being one that was 'designated' by the Superior General, with the Sisters being notified six months ahead.[22] Sister Yvonne decided, that in order to maintain focus on the reforms being called for in community and ministries, she would call for a Chapter of Election in July 1996 and the Chapter of Affairs a year later. The election, held on 4 July 1996, returned her as Superior General. Her Council members were the same as previously—Sisters Angela Turvey (Vicar General), Philippa Barker, Jean Duncan and Helen Alfrey.

Meanwhile, Robyn Gugenberger became manager of both Ipswich and Brisbane and Carol Nowak was appointed administrator of Ipswich. Government changes in requirements for healthcare, however, were 'imposing a heavy managerial and administrative burden'.[23] In Brisbane, the upgrading of the hostel was being held up by the threat of the building being heritage-listed. Legal advice was sought, and in September the solicitor advised:

> If we objected to the listing of Saint Pauls Terrace Fortitude Valley as heritage, our objection would most likely fail. We will endeavour to restrict the listing to the external portion of the building if we cannot avoid being listed.[24]

If the Sisters were expecting a period of calm in order to give full attention to the matters that would be brought up at their next sitting of Chapter, it was not to be.

Sr Yvonne Tobin

Archbishop John Bathersby

Robyn Gugenberger

Former Lutheran Church, Warren Street

Villa Maria chapel reaches its arms out over the city.

Coping with Depletion

The Chapter of Affairs was held on 5 and 6 November 1997. In her report to Archbishop Bathersby, Sister Yvonne gave her opinion that, while she could rejoice at the Sisters' spirit during the Chapter, they were now at a 'crossroads': 'If we do not take new directions, our Congregation will become extinct (in my opinion).' New directions would not change what the Congregation did—it was the *how* they did it that was changing.[25]

It was obvious that the main instigator of change was the decreasing number of Sisters. In January 1997 Sister Raphael Mizzi from the Sisters of St Joseph had begun the process of transference to the Sisters of Perpetual Adoration.[26] However, since the last Chapter, only one other person had joined the Sisters as a novice and she did not stay. In 1997 alone there had been three deaths, and the number of Sisters in the Congregation had fallen to twenty-eight with an average age of seventy years.

According to the Constitutions approved at the 1991 Chapter, the term of office fixed for the Superior General, General Councillors and Local Superiors had been six years. However, many of the Sisters were now too old to undertake the demanding work of administration. As there were no longer enough Sisters now able to fill vacant positions, the 1997 Chapter requested the Archbishop that these items in the Constitutions be left open to allow for future adjustments.

On 9 October 1997 the Sisters had been withdrawn from Ipswich and the running of Villa Maria there was left entirely to lay management. A farewell Mass, led by Bishop Putney, Auxiliary Bishop of Brisbane, was held the week before at St Mary's Church, Ipswich, in recognition of the Sisters' service to the parish.[27] Sister Helen Alfrey, having now become part of the Brisbane community, travelled to Ipswich for a day each week to give pastoral care to residents and to provide staff formation in spirituality and ethics.

At Brisbane Villa Maria, community prayer times and hours of adoration were able to be adjusted, as more lay people joined the adoration roster. At a Mass in September 1998, Bishop Michael Putney congratulated the Co-Adorers who now numbered more than a hundred.[28] To all appearances, life was going on as usual at Villa Maria. Lay staff had been employed to attend to domestic duties where Sisters needed help; volunteers continued to provide small outings and treats for residents; Christmas parties, concerts and other entertainment were given as they always had been. A lay administrator was engaged at the hostel, thus relieving Sister Narelle Hickson to take on the position of Treasurer General for the Congregation.[29] On 11 September 1998, Robyn Gugenberger was appointed manager of the Brisbane Villa Maria site in addition to that in Ipswich.

However, it seemed that as soon as one problem was solved, another arose. Rising building standards for government healthcare were now presenting difficulties that demanded immediate attention. While the move to have the heritage listing of Brisbane's Villa Maria apply only to its external structure had succeeded, the building was old and renovations would be expensive. In the economic climate of the day, the nursing home was too small to be viable. The nursing home at Wollongong had already failed to gain accreditation, and while interior deficiencies could be addressed, the building's structure could not.

Solutions

After thorough research of various options, three major decisions were taken to address the situation. First, on 11 September 1998, the Brisbane nursing home was closed and, with approval from the Commonwealth Department of Health and Family Services, the thirty-five beds were transferred to the nursing home run by the Canossian Sisters at Oxley in the south-western suburbs.[30] Sister Helen Alfrey remembered the transition as having been 'handled very smoothly'. The women in the nursing home had plenty of time to find another place between the nursing home closing and the beds being transferred, and the staff were able to gain other positions.[31]

Forty years previously, the conditions for Commonwealth funding for aged care had meant that the Villa Maria Hostel had had to cease allowing business women to board there. Now, in 1998, a similar situation presented itself. In order for the hostel to be feasible, its interior would have to be upgraded and the whole complex be refurbished exclusively for aged care. Until now the Sisters' convent had occupied the top floor of St Gabriel's Wing. The Sisters' property advisers, John McAuliffe and Laurie Rogencamp, saw that it would be an advantage to revamp the vacant nursing home on Warren Street as a convent, thus allowing the renovations of the hostel to go ahead unencumbered.[32] Accordingly, both works proceeded. Stage One of the $5m. upgrade of Villa Maria was able to be funded with the help of the already-allocated Commonwealth grant, while the Sisters' holiday homes in Toowoomba and Cleveland were sold to help pay for the transformation of the nursing home into a convent.

Meanwhile, the buildings at Wollongong were at the end of their economic life. Again, consultation involving meetings upon meetings came to one conclusion—it would be necessary to relocate and build a completely new home. Further research informed the General Council that the most urgent need for aged care in Wollongong was for those suffering from dementia, so it was decided to make this the focus of the new venture. The Bishop of Wollongong, Philip Wilson, was informed of the move and a request for an indult to sell the property on Cliff Road was forwarded to the Vatican.[33]

On 8 November 1999 the deposit was paid on a large piece of land on the Old Pacific Highway at Unanderra, about ten minutes' drive by car from the centre of Wollongong. The General Council was relieved that there was no adverse publicity when the property at Cliff Road was put up for sale.[34] A loan was obtained from the Brisbane Archdiocesan Development Fund and by 2001 the building of the new facility at Unanderra could go ahead.[35]

With lay administrators now employed for each of the three aged care facilities, Robyn Gugenberger had been appointed in September 2000 as general manager for Brisbane, Ipswich and Wollongong. Thus she could oversee proceedings at the Unanderra site and ensure that, from the start, it absorbed the vision and values of the Sisters of Perpetual Adoration. The Advisory Board for Villa Maria Aged Care, of which Robyn was now a member, recommended to the General Council that the three facilities should be incorporated separately to protect the Sisters against public risk claims and this was done.

Villa Maria Convent and Chapel

By 8 March 2000, the conversion of the Brisbane nursing home had been completed, and the Sisters packed their personal possessions into boxes ready to move to the new Villa Maria Convent, 123 Warren Street. However, if the St Pauls Terrace complex was being funded exclusively for aged care, the Sisters, as did the public in general, had to respect the buildings as they would the private homes of the residents. Therefore, access to the chapel at its centre would not be available to the Sisters twenty-four hours per day as it had been in the past. In designing the new convent, the Sisters had incorporated a small oratory where they could gather for prayer. For people who wished to attend week-day Mass and especially for Co-Adorers, a larger chapel was necessary.

In January 1999, the General Council had made inquiries with the Queensland Heritage Council about the status of the former Bethlehem Lutheran Church, 115 Warren Street, immediately south of the convent. They were informed that it was a place of local rather than of state significance.[36] The church had been constructed mostly of second-hand materials in 1929. Additions had been made in the 1960s and served the congregation in a variety of ways until its amalgamation with St Andrew's Lutheran Church on Wickham Terrace in 1976. When the Sisters of Perpetual Adoration bought the property in 1990, the St Andrew's congregation had used the sale funds to purchase a new pipe organ, dedicating it as the Bethlehem Memorial Organ.[37]

Now negotiations began with Archbishop Bathersby, the Brisbane City Council, Church liturgists and architects about the possibility of demolishing the old church and building a chapel able to be used by the Sisters, Co-Adorers and the general public for daily Mass and 24-hour adoration. What resulted was the plan by the architectural firm McKerrell Lynch for a magnificent contemporary building with rich symbolism throughout that would provide for the city of Brisbane yet another landmark.

When the Lutheran church was demolished, the original foundation stone was found, so the Sisters presented it to the St Andrew's congregation who gratefully placed it beside the Bethlehem Memorial Organ. The foundation stone of the new chapel was laid by Archbishop Bathersby on 22 June 2000. The year 2000 had been named by Pope John Paul II as the Great Jubilee and dedicated to 'the Holy Trinity and the Eucharist', marking the second millennium of the birth of Jesus Christ. Therefore, said Sister Yvonne, the building project was being named 'Eucharist 2000'. She went on to describe her hopes for the project:

> The chapel would be an easily accessible haven, attractive to people wanting to spend time in quiet prayer. Secure undercover parking would be provided, prompted by the Sisters' vision for their prayer apostolate and their welcoming of generous Co-Adorers. A nearby library and reading room for the Co-Adorers should assist their quest to deepen their prayer life.[38]

Once again, Sister Yvonne's ability to find the 'right' people came to the fore. She happened to see examples of stained glass windows executed by Sister Margaret Broadbent RSM from the Mercy Art and Creativity

Centre at Black Rock, Melbourne, and quickly made contact.[39] There, she met Gael O'Leary who did sculpture in bronze. Discussion with the two women produced ideas for the interior furnishings of the chapel.[40] A photograph in a travel book of a font in the gardens of a monastery overseas had led Sister Yvonne to decide it would be 'just the thing' for the quiet space separating the convent from the chapel:

> I have always delighted in the reading from the Prophet Ezekiel . . . seeing the picture of the water flowing from the temple as a symbol of the graces which flow from the many prayers in our Chapels. Imagine the endless abundance of graces which will flow from the prayers in this new Chapel.[41]

Contrasting with the abstract, colourful design of the stained-glass windows depicting Creation along the southern side and the scalloped windows piercing the bronze-gold of the chapel walls, the clear glass wall of the north side would look out onto a pool whose waters rippled over rounded stones. In the centre would stand a font filled with water reflecting the light around it and surmounted by two doves. These would be a reminder of baptism into the living water of Christ, whose reflection we are and whose Spirit calls us to mission.

Ongoing conversations with the architect enabled the integration of these ideas into a unified whole. When Archbishop Bathersby blessed and opened the Chapel of the Risen Christ on 24 March 2001 he spoke of what its symbolism meant to him:

> This is built not only to be a place of prayer and worship for the Sisters, as they go about their unique apostolate of adoration in support of the mission of the Church, but it is built to reach out and embrace the city that surrounds it. It is to provide a linkage between the religious life of the Sisters and the lay vocation of those whose primary role is to transform the world by using their own particular God-given charisms.[42]

On the day of the opening, another 'linkage' was celebrated by representatives from St Andrew's Lutheran congregation who attended the opening and rejoiced that the site was once again being used for the worship of God. The concept of 'linkage' is also noted in an article for the Australian Architecture Association, which speaks not only of architectural links but the links of purpose and spirit:

> Across a city block in Spring Hill, Brisbane, is a series of buildings that stitch together Romanesque, modern, and post-modern, culminating in a devotional church: the Villa Maria Centre of Perpetual Adoration. Few religious buildings speak so broadly of the transformation in religious life over the twentieth century, all the while maintaining its foundational principles. The remarkable Villa Maria Chapel of the Risen Christ . . . is the latest building in almost 140 years of Catholic worship and community service on this site . . . It exemplifies the transformation of liturgical processes throughout the twentieth century as expressed architecturally, but also the continuation of religious life, all within the one precinct.

The Risen Christ

Lectern frontage:
the boy Jesus
and Mary

The Tabernacle, rich in symbolism

Sisters entertaining residents

Sr Gemma Lincoln
dressed as 'bride'

Sr Margaret Mary Allport

Srs Helen Alfrey, Elizabeth Bargenquast, Emmanuel Carroll, Raphael Mizzi

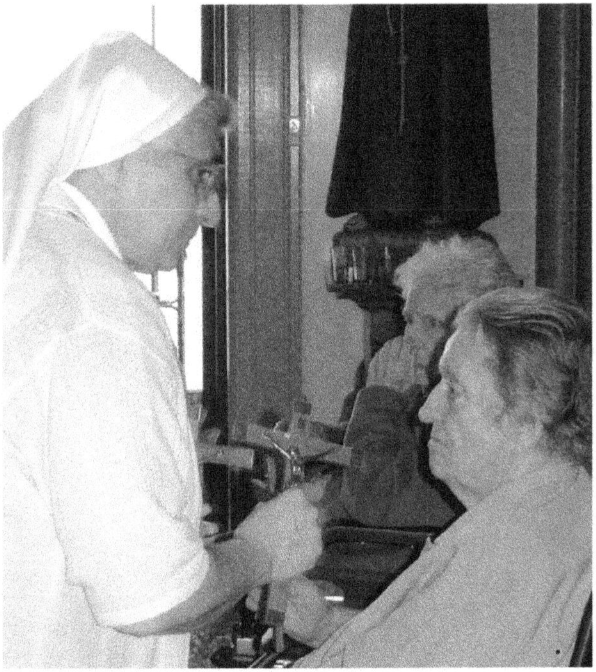

Sr Raphael Mizzi gives Communion to residents

Sr Jean Cain rsj

Srs Yvonne Tobin and Helen Alfrey with John McAuliffe from the Advisory Committee.

The article then focuses on the new chapel, highlighting the feminine, rounded design of the brickwork and the 'slender stained-glass windows', contrasting with cubic crosses that 'maintains its liturgical symbolism at the very edges of its abstraction'. The contrast might be likened to an oasis in the desert: 'Residing on a busy street in the centre of Brisbane, it is remarkable how quiet the interior of this comparably loud building is—a place for quiet, constant contemplation.'[43]

A booklet to explain concepts behind the artwork in the chapel was produced to prompt further contemplation about the continual work of God in salvation history. The design of the tabernacle is of a tent, recalling the Tent (or Tabernacle) of Meeting, the portable tent set up each time the Israelites, led by Moses, stopped on their desert journey from Egypt to Canaan.[44] In it was housed the Ark of the Covenant, a box containing the stone commandments given to Moses and therefore symbolising the place where God met in covenant with the Israelites. It also contained a jar of manna, the bread given in the desert. Parallels between the symbolism of this earthly dwelling of God and the connected reality of Eucharist are obvious. In front of the tabernacle is a small, wreath-shaped holder into which the Eucharistic Host can be placed and, illuminated by a soft light, exposed.

Similarly, the symbolism of other artworks leads beyond the depiction to their meaning. The large figure of the risen Christ, near-naked as in death, stands out, free and triumphant, against the cut of the cross open to the daylight pouring down on the altar. On the front of the lectern is a bronze relief of Mary and the young boy Jesus who reads from Scripture. Jan Tranter RSJ explains:

> Mary, mother of the Word, has her hand on the shoulder of Jesus as if protecting and/or presenting him at the Synagogue. (The artist told me she used artists' licence to have Mary [in this role], not Joseph).[45]

A Byzantine icon of Mary with the child Jesus in a circle of light at her bosom, is positioned near the tabernacle. With arms outstretched in the praying position and facing the worshipper, she is the new tabernacle presenting the Word of God who brings forth creation.[46] At the entrance to the chapel is a bronze statue of the Holy Family journeying to Egypt. As worshippers enter this sacred space, they are invited to open themselves more fully to God who is with us on our life journey.

A former Archbishop had once described the Sisters of Perpetual Adoration as 'good builders'. This last of the buildings sweeping down from St Paul's Terrace gave further confirmation of that statement. What it also did was to give an indication of what the Eucharistic presence meant to the Sisters—its intimacy and its mission. The former large chapel has always been at the heart of Villa Maria Hostel, enclosed at its centre. This new chapel, in the elliptical shape of its roofline and in its intention, stretched out beyond the confines of Villa Maria to the city. Not everyone grasped this gesture, so there were those who criticised the 'modernity' of the chapel. There are always those who find change difficult, especially when they perceive the change as attacking a pillar of belief rather than as inviting that belief to become wider and deeper. On the other hand, as the new chapel settled into its surroundings, people in general found its accessibility welcoming and have expressed their appreciation of the 'stillness, silence and peace' that they experience in this 'sacred space'.[47]

2001 General Chapter

At the next Chapter, on 27 September 2001, Sister Philippa Barker was elected as Superior General. Sisters Helen Alfrey (Vicar General), Yvonne Tobin, Narelle Hickson and Raphael Mizzi were elected as Councillors. At the completion of the three-year canonical process of transferring from the Sisters of St Joseph to the Sisters of Perpetual Adoration, Sister Raphael had made her final profession on 5 February 2000. When asked how she felt when she was elected so soon after profession, she had replied nonchalantly, 'Well, there weren't many Sisters to choose from'.

That, indeed, was the case. In taking account the profile of their twenty-three Sisters, the Chapter recommended that 'the Superior General and Council consider realistically the future of our Congregation'. Practically, it was obvious that measures would have to be taken regarding the Sisters' daily life. Therefore, the Chapter made the following statement to be added to their Statutes:

> If perpetual adoration for the Sisters is no longer possible, the Superior General and Council may determine, in the spirit of the constitutions, what needs to be done in the circumstances.

A further decision was made to spread responsibility for governance by forming different Steering Committees who would assist the Superior General and Council in applying the Congregation's charism and underlying theology to 'how it meets needs in today's Church'; to promote vocations and attend to the formation of candidates; and to promote Eucharistic adoration and the possibility of affiliation of Co-Adorers.[48]

Immediately after the Chapter, Sister Philippa Barker, acting on the mandate to 'look realistically' at the Congregation's future, made contact with Sister June Flynn, president of the Federation of the Sisters of St Joseph, to broach possibilities of connecting with them.[49] Another immediate response was the Sisters' invitation to Co-Adorers to share the recitation of Divine Office. At the recommendation of Archbishop Bathersby, the General Council consulted the archdiocesan Vicar for Religious and Canon Lawyer Sister Patricia Scully RSC.[50] They arranged to meet with her once a month to look at options for their future.

The Steering Committee concerned with vocations decided first of all to listen and get feedback from young people. For example, on 27 February 2002 they invited members of the Youth Evangelisation Team to visit Villa Maria convent.[51] Thirty-eight young people spent the morning with the Sisters who were impressed by their commitment as they shared their stories of devoting a year of their lives to go out to parishes to evangelise youth. In turn, Sisters shared their vocation story. Morning tea followed, and then some time together in prayer in the chapel.[52] However, such gatherings did not develop further and were given up after a time.

Wollongong Unanderra

For the Sisters in Wollongong, the year 2000 had a particular significance in that, on 11 June, Bishop Wilson had inaugurated a Eucharistic Congress for the diocese. In writing of the event, Father Mark De Battista noted that the Congress, titled 'Bread for New Life' and spanning two weeks, was 'the first such congress in Australia held outside a capital city'. Coinciding with the International Eucharistic Congress in Rome, it involved thousands of primary and secondary school children from across the diocese and various gatherings of adults. Bishop Michael Putney from Brisbane gave an address to a gathering of three thousand people on the 'Themes of the Jubilee 2000 and the Eucharistic Congress' in which he emphasised that the primary purpose of the liturgy was adoration of God. A highlight of the congress was the celebration of Mass in two of the Eastern Catholic Rites derived from the Byzantine tradition, the Melkite and Ukrainian Rites 'handed down from the time of Saint John Chrysostom'.[53] The Congress ended on the feast of Corpus Christi with Benediction and the reading of a message from Pope John Paul II, expressing his delight that the Eucharistic events of both the diocese of Rome and of Wollongong united them as one.

While the building of Villa Maria Unanderra occupied most of the next year, the three Sisters at Cliff Road were uncertain about their future. They had expressed the hope to the General Council that they would remain in Wollongong to be a 'presence' there and travel to Unanderra to give pastoral care to the residents. After much discussion with the new bishop Peter Ingham and the General Council, it was decided that the Sisters might rent a house near the Cathedral from where they could promote Eucharistic devotion.[54] These arrangements would be reviewed after a time, while the pastoral care of the Unanderra residents would be provided locally. By 15 December 2001 Villa Maria Unanderra was completed, and the eighty-six residents were relocated from Cliff Road to the new facility.

Confirming New Directions

The end of 2001 saw the new shape of aged care on the three sites of Villa Maria proceeding with confidence. A new Advisory Board was set up which would meet bi-monthly and report to the Superior General. Its members represented an appropriate field of competencies—Chair Laurie Rogencamp (solicitor), John McAuliffe (property advisor), Les Jones (accountant), Michael Kennedy (doctor), Brother Brian Sweeney FMS (Canon Lawyer) and Sisters Helen Alfrey (Vicar General), Yvonne Tobin (Administrator of Villa Maria Aged Care Centres) and Narelle Hickson (Treasurer General). Robyn Gugenberger, as manager of the three sites, chose administrators and staff wisely. The 'family feel' that had always been a mark of Villa Maria Aged Care was strong, and those Sisters who could continue serving in the Brisbane hostel were able to give assurance to residents that all was well.

In the past, the Sisters of Perpetual Adoration had felt secure in their place in society. They had been able to go about their ministries of adoration and care of the aged knowing they were loved by people in their neighbourhood and supported by the clergy of an hierarchical church. Since the 1960s, all had changed. At first, the Sisters of Perpetual Adoration had been slow to adjust to a more egalitarian image of society and church. Gradually, they had put in place some structures that encouraged shared responsibility among their own members. However, theirs was a culture that was built on hard work and unquestioning trust in authority. Few Sisters had had opportunities for higher education in theology or to obtain professional qualifications. During the 1990s huge steps had been taken. The Sisters were coping with enormous advances in health care, and those who had given outstanding service in a less regulated world were left behind. Those in leadership acted wisely and quickly in setting up advisory committees to ensure the continuance of this ministry, but it meant the Sisters were now involved only at a nominal level.

There was a similar pattern happening with regard to the Sisters' primary purpose: adoration of the Blessed Sacrament and its promotion. The schedule of community prayer and recreation, rostered time for adoration and physical work in caring for the aged left little opportunity for other activities. While some Sisters had occasionally attended courses for adults in biblical studies which would have enriched them personally, this had not led to a community effort to reinterpret how adoration might be expressed in a theologically updated church. The engagement of lay Co-Adorers simply prolonged what had been the customary way.

The building of the new chapel in Warren Street was a bold, creative move. In a way it symbolised all that the Sisters of Perpetual Adoration wanted to be—a sign of our time enabling all to recognise that the praise of God is life lived fully, reaching out to others and centred on the mystery of Jesus, the gift of Love among us. However, in order to engage in dialogue with the young and with society in general, one must learn its language, and this in turn demands effort, time and energy. The Sisters could only offer what they had—a space that affords possibilities for silence and peace. They did this with grace and generosity.

Chapter 10

The passing of the twentieth century marked a peak of achievement for the Sisters of Perpetual Adoration. They had successfully negotiated the complications of advances in the care of the aged and the necessary adjustments this involved for the management of the facilities at Brisbane, Ipswich and Wollongong. Furthermore, the building of the chapel on Warren Street, the invitation to Co-Adorers to share the Sisters' mission and the establishment of committees to enable Sisters' participation in decisions for their future looked like a new beginning. The first years of the third millennium, however, would pose the sobering question as to whether these achievements could be sustained, given the dwindling numbers of the Sisters, the uncertainties associated with dependence on lay volunteers for the adoration roster, and the ongoing professional demands of healthcare.

Aged Care

Villa Maria Unanderra was blessed and opened on 17 March 2002 by the Bishop of Wollongong, Peter Ingham. Constructed by Carmada & Cantrill Pty Ltd, this single-storey, award-winning building featured six cottage-like areas with each room looking out onto pretty gardens and, more importantly, communal spaces from where passing traffic and people going to the nearby shopping centre could be observed.[1] This encouraged conversation among the residents, even those suffering from dementia. It was obvious that the relocation would be a success.

From 2002, the senior management of the three aged care sites held quarterly meetings and relevant issues were reported to the Health Care Advisory Board. The Sisters had obtained the services of Father Michael Rego SM in 2001 as chaplain for the Brisbane and Ipswich sites of Villa Maria.[2] Each week he and Sister Helen Alfrey drove to Ipswich to spend the day there giving whatever pastoral and spiritual help was needed. However, there was concern about the feasibility of Villa Maria Ipswich: it was obvious that it would soon have to relocate in order to expand, so a search began for a greenfield site in order to do so.

At the same time, research was being conducted about the future of Villa Maria Brisbane. Discussions were held with the Brisbane City Council about possibilities for St Gabriel's Wing currently being renovated. For example, could there be a partnership in their housing project for inner city living for disadvantaged aged? Could this proposal for St Gabriel's Wing then be subsidised by letting out two-bedroom apartments in St Stanislaus' Wing for the rich? The Sisters could then be involved in providing spiritual and pastoral care for both groups. Such questions had no immediate answer but could provide indications for the eventual shape the hostel might take.

The Sisters had sold properties acquired over the years in order to help fund the first stage of the refurbishment. However, the total renovation of the interior of Villa Maria Brisbane was a major undertaking, requiring application for loans and permission from the Vatican Congregation for Institutions of Consecrated Life for extraordinary expenditure. At least thirteen million dollars would be needed to accommodate contemporary expectations for hostel and aged care facilities. In April 2003 Sister Philippa received the approval from Rome and Archbishop Bathersby gave his formal authorisation for planning to go ahead.[3]

In May 2005, with the future of the aged care apostolate still uncertain, the General Council entered into discussions with the Sisters of St Joseph who conducted an aged care facility at Nundah.[4] Would they be interested in combining with the Sisters of Perpetual Adoration in their mission to the aged? By August a number of meetings had been held and Sister Margaret Cleary RSJ had joined the Aged Care Advisory Board. However, the Sisters of St Joseph were likewise struggling with the question of how best to deal with aged care. They had planned a national meeting of Leadership Teams to discuss the matter on 28 August of that year, and the Congregational Leader, Sister Katrina Brill RSJ, invited the Sisters of Perpetual Adoration to join them. Sister Yvonne Tobin and Robyn Gugenberger attended, but again no clear path was indicated.

The first stage of the Villa Maria Brisbane upgrade was now completed. On 30 August 2005 the fifty residents who had been temporarily housed in St Stanislaus' Wing, moved in. A certification inspection was conducted within a month and, after some adjustments had been made to fire safety provisions, the facility was given full approval. The 2004 mission statement of the Senior Management of the aged care centres could be put into action: 'To provide care to the aged in accordance with Christian values by promoting a holistic approach to care in an environment that meets the needs of residents and staff and welcomes family and friends.'[5]

The Sisters of Perpetual Adoration were not the only religious congregation facing problems with decreasing membership and the future of ministries such as health and aged care, education and social welfare. Since the early 1990s a recurring topic for discussion at the yearly assembly run by the Australian Conference of Religious Institutes (ACLRI) had been evolving governance structures whereby lay people could be authorised by Church authorities to conduct services that were previously the responsibility of Religious. According to canon law 116.1, Public Juridic Persons (PJPs) are established by Church law to perform specific functions in the Church's name. Dioceses and parishes are examples of a PJP. Up to recent times Religious Congregations were the PJPs entrusted with many works of mercy conducted on behalf of the Church. The 1994 approval of Catholic Healthcare by the Bishops of the Sydney Province was the first lay-led entity in Australia to be commissioned as a PJP.[6] Like Religious Congregations who minister in New South Wales, it is registered as company limited by guarantee under the Corporations Act. It is governed by a Board which is assisted by various committees and advisory bodies to carry out its mission.

In 2005 Sister Yvonne Tobin attended an ACLRI-sponsored conference dealing with the transference of ministries to lay leadership. There she met up with guest speaker Maureen Cleary, a consultant whose primary focus was to advise boards of non-profit organisations in matters of governance and management. Again, for Sister Yvonne, here was 'just the person' to help the Sisters of Perpetual Adoration hand over their involvement in aged care. Maureen was subsequently engaged and a process of discernment followed, involving the General Council, the Sisters' communities and the Health Care Advisory Board and management of the Villa Maria homes followed. By 17 March 2006 a clearer sense of direction for the future was emerging. Maureen led a special meeting with the Sisters to inform them that it may be necessary to divest themselves of the ministry of aged care because of their inability to continue governance of these works. The focus was on the need for the Sisters to keep raising questions for clarification and on how the realities of communal grieving might be embraced.[7]

During the following months interviews were held with Catholic Health (NSW) and Southern Cross Homes to gauge the extent of their interest in the Villa Maria aged care facilities. At the end of August, Archbishop Bathersby attended a presentation made by them and let it be known to the General Council that he was impressed by that of Catholic Healthcare.[8] As General Chapter was approaching, no further action was taken for the present. Sister Philippa asked the Villa Maria Health Care Advisory Board to continue in its present role of overseeing the management of aged care while the General Council would seek further advice on the matter.

The Community

For as long as their health allowed, the Sisters maintained the roster for adoration of the Blessed Sacrament and provided pastoral care to the residents of the Ipswich and Brisbane hostels. However, despite the generosity of co-adorers, it became obvious by September 2002 that night adoration would have to be curtailed. From 16 September, 24-hour adoration ceased except for Friday nights. On the other days the roster was set to commence at 6 am and end at 7 pm.[9]

Coming to terms with depletion was not easy for the community. While over the past decade there had been at least five women who had joined them on a 'Come and See' basis for a while, none had stayed. Comments recorded in the notes of community meetings around this time betray puzzlement and anxiety:

> If God is happy with us the way we are living in community the Holy Spirit will inspire the vocations. A joyful faith-filled community will attract vocations.[10]

> If we are patient and pray hard we will get good vocations very soon. A lot of the young Filipino girls are saying to me that adoration is what they want. [11]
> Most congregations are now only getting vocations from other cultures. We need to place ourselves in God's hands and be welcoming. We have to pray and be willing to meet others halfway or even more.[12]

Along with a concern over falling numbers, there were other signs that brought joy and encouragement. In 2003 Sister Yvonne Tobin's dream of installing a sculpture of the Byzantine mosaic, 'The Chalice of Living Water' by the chapel, came to reality. The General Council approved the finance needed, and Sister Yvonne commissioned local sculptor Dr Rhyl Hinwood to do the work. Rhyl was a well-known artist, having produced artworks for the Great Court of the University of Queensland, St Stephen's Cathedral and, in 1987, the prestigious ceramic Australian Coat of Arms for the House of Representatives Chamber in Parliament House, Canberra.[13] The World Community for Christian Meditation had adopted the representation of the mosaic as their logo, so the Sisters were familiar with image of the chalice from which the two doves drink the Water of Life. When the recently-consecrated Auxiliary Bishop, Brian Finnigan, blessed Rhyl Hinwood's sculpture on 22 February 2004, he emphasised that, as a Eucharistic symbol, it recalls both baptism (which is why it was featured in the baptisteries of early Christian churches) and the assurance of eternal life.[14]

In the past, very few Sisters had had opportunity for further theological or professional education. As if making up for lost time, the Sisters now took on a plethora of courses to enrich their appreciation of liturgy, Eucharist, Scripture and spirituality. They obtained materials for the Little Rock Scriptures courses in which a commentary on a biblical text is prayerfully read each day and, at the end of the week, reflections and insights are shared with the whole group.[15] In 2003 a number of Sisters attended lectures on liturgy given at the Cathedral parish by Father Ken Howell.[16] The community hosted a Christian Meditation group that met at the convent each week.[17] The opportunity for personal development was offered for Sisters to gain insights into personal feelings and interactions when Sister Lucy Tierney RSJ was invited to give individual instruction on the Enneagram.[18] During 2005 and 2006 Sister Carmel Pilcher RSJ gave presentations on the theology of the Eucharist. The General Council noted, 'There was a very positive response from the Sisters.'[19] When Sisters Margaret Schiemer RSJ from Perthville and Mary Cresp RSJ from Adelaide were invited by the General Council to lead the Sisters' annual six-day retreat in November 2005, yet another new space was opened, and with it, challenge.[20] Up to now, their retreats had been conducted by priests. To trust the ability of Sisters to give a retreat was a leap. They did so with grace.

The first years of the new century set before the Sisters of Perpetual Adoration a rich, spiritual fare that had taken many other Religious thirty-five years to absorb.[21] Was it too much too late? While we might surmise in hindsight, it is true that individuals and groups depend on circumstances in their past in order to take the next step. There is no record of Sisters having attended lectures on the theology of the Second Vatican Council during the 1960s and 1970s. Given their schedule of work and prayer, they would hardly have had time to do so. Their library contains many publications encouraging devotional spirituality but very few dealing with the documents of Vatican II. Certainly, Archbishop O'Donnell and Father Jeremiah

Hogan SJ had encouraged the Mother General, Mother Gabriel Moloney, to attend to the reforms called for by the Decree on the Adaptation and Renewal of Religious Life (*Perfectae Caritatis*).[22] Changes made in response were mainly practical, concerned with internal practices rather than with theological and liturgical education. Mother Rosarii Ansaldo, leading the Congregation at a time that was critical for the embedding of attitudinal change after the Second Vatican Council, had brought a freshness and sense of freedom to the Sisters. However, with the retired and tradition-minded Mother Gabriel still wielding much influence among the Sisters, it is possible that she may have held back from seeming to branch out too far.

Given this background, the Sisters of Perpetual Adoration brought to the new millennium a generosity of spirit that in the past created a culture of hard, physical work, utter devotion to their tradition of adoration and reliance on figures of authority. Now, with that same generosity, they allowed the new to be part of their communal lives but, with a certain wariness and the wisdom of senior years, chose what helped at an individual level and let the rest 'be'.

'The Chalice of Living Water' beside the Villa Maria Chapel

Assembling for General Chapter 2006 in which all Sisters took part: Srs Raphael Mizzi, Jean Duncan, Philippa Barker, Bishop Brian Finnigan (Archbishop's deputy), Br Brian Sweeney FMS (Canonical advisor), Sr Helen Alfrey.

Leadership Team,
Srs Yvonne Tobin, Mary Cresp
Philippa Barker, Helen Alfrey

Coreen Small
Administrative
Assistant

Governance

At the same time as the General Council had to attend to major decisions about care of the aged and the welfare of the community of Sisters, it also had to remember that its prime responsibility was the overall governance of the Congregation. A year after their 2001 General Chapter, Sister Philippa Barker had written to the Sisters asking them to attend a meeting where they would review the decisions made at the Chapter and to draw up a timeline for their application.[23] Questions about the future of 24-hour adoration at Brisbane and about whether the Sisters should remain at Wollongong had been left by the Chapter for the General Council to decide. In October 2002 the decision was made to recall the community of Sisters from Wollongong to Brisbane.[24] By July 2003 the rented house in Wollongong was closed. Even though that meant two extra Sisters for the adoration roster, it became obvious that not even the 24-hour adoration held on Fridays at Brisbane could be maintained and so it ceased. The Sisters made the chapel available to other groups who might want to hold particular events such as the Filipino community who had 40-hour exposition once a month and who led the singing at Sunday Mass in the hostel.[25]

The most important mandate of the 2001 Chapter was for the General Council to 'look realistically' at the Congregation's future. Regular meetings with the Vicar for Religious, Sister Patricia Scully, had raised various options, the most appealing of which was some kind of union with the Federation of the Sisters of St Joseph. At a community meeting on 14 November 2003, Sister Patricia suggested possibilities for how the two groups of Sisters could get to know each other. They could visit each other, invite Josephite Sisters to holiday with them, hold joint community meetings whose agendas would include the sharing of the vision and spirituality handed down by their common founder Julian Tenison Woods. Documents of both groups could be examined to compare similarities of history, spirituality and purpose. A gentle interactive retreat could be conducted by Sisters from the Federation.[26]

Sister Philippa followed through with the recommendations. Subsequent communication with the Federation of the Sisters of St Joseph led to their Executive Officer, Sister Jean Cain RSJ, being appointed as consultant to the Sisters of Perpetual Adoration to help forge closer bonds.[27] In an email on 24 April 2004, Sister Jean indicated that the Sisters of St Joseph would encourage visits between the two groups and would include the Sisters of Perpetual Adoration in their communication. She invited them to contribute a page to the annual Federation Newsletter and informed Sister Philippa that she had assigned Sister Jan Tranter from Lochinvar to prepare a paper comparing the constitutions that Julian Tenison Woods wrote for the Sisters of St Joseph and the Sisters of Perpetual Adoration.[28]

However, the Sisters of St Joseph were themselves uncertain about their own futures. Sister Philippa had attended the meeting of the Federation of the Sisters of St Joseph at Goulburn on 18–20 April and five days later gave a report of this to the Sisters of the Brisbane community. She informed them that Sister Kerrie Cusack, Congregational Leader of the Goulburn Sisters of St Joseph, had been elected as president of the Federation. Having noted the presence of Sister Mary Cresp, 'former leader of the brown Josephites' at the meeting, she commented:

> I'm not sure when these two congregations, the Central and Federation Josephites began drawing closer to each other. Perhaps it goes as far back as Mary MacKillop's Beatification. I am sure it is slowly moving towards greater sharing, as Sr Mary Cresp has been overseas looking into the various Josephite communities. I'm not exactly sure of the reason for this, but it points to linking with the spirit behind their foundation.[29]

Sister Philippa was certainly intuitive! As yet unclear even to themselves, the path that the Sisters of St Joseph were taking would eventually lead to permanent links being made.[30]

On 26–28 July 2004 Bishop Finnigan conducted a visitation of the Sisters on behalf of Archbishop Bathersby. Sister Monica Stallard RSM assisted him. The Sisters had many questions about options open to them and these were gathered to present to Sister Patricia Scully. Indications were that the Sisters felt comfortable pursuing closer relationships with the Federation of the Sisters of St Joseph.

Having received this report, the Archbishop asked the General Council to give him a definitive decision by May 2005 about whether they would join the Federation. The Council expressed their concern to the Archbishop that much more had to be done before they could make such an enormous move. Ultimately, however, the decision was taken out of their hands when, in February 2005 Sister Kerrie Cusack, as president of the Federation of Sisters of St Joseph, informed Archbishop Bathersby that they were not in a position to admit the Sisters of Perpetual Adoration into the Federation as they were too uncertain about their own future. They were happy to continue conversations with the Sisters and would invite them to their meetings when appropriate but not at a membership level.[31]

Sister Jean Cain continued to liaise between the Sisters of Perpetual Adoration and the Federation of the Sisters of St Joseph and to work with Sister Patricia Scully about options for the future. Among these was the possibility that the Archbishop might need to appoint a canonical superior at the end of Sister Philippa's current term as Superior General. A meeting was held with the Sisters to introduce this idea. In a letter dated 9 September 2005, Sister Philippa advised the Archbishop that 'the majority of the Sisters' accepted this possibility.[32]

The next steps did not proceed without controversy. Having been assured by the Congregation for Institutes of Consecrated Life that to appoint a canonical superior was 'the right decision for him to make', Archbishop Bathersby informed the Sisters through Bishop Finnegan that he now intended to write to the Federation of the Sisters of St Joseph to name someone whom he would then appoint to the position.[33] The General Council was shocked. The Archbishop had neither consulted with them nor indicated whether the Sisters would have a say in the matter. At their bidding, Bishop Finnigan, who had been asked to 'monitor the progress for the appointment of a canonical superior', was then able to negotiate an agreement that the Archbishop should obtain a list of nominees not only from the Federation of the Sisters of Joseph but also from the Sisters of St Joseph of the Sacred Heart, and that the Sisters themselves should then indicate to him which nominee they would wish him to appoint.[34] In April 2006, the General Council took it on themselves to meet with the Leadership Teams of all six groups of Sisters of St Joseph and speak with them about the qualities they would be looking for in someone who would potentially take on the role of canonical superior.

Sisters of Perpetual Adoration, 7 October 2006
with Sister Mary Cresp and Bishop Brian Finnigan (centre).
(Back Row: Sisters Angela Turvey, Xavier Woods, Regina Greenhalgh, Yvonne Tobin, Elizabeth Bargenquast, Emmanuel Carroll, Margaret Mary Allport, Narelle Hickson, Philomena McAuliffe, Barbara Hickson, Helen Alfrey.
Middle Row: Raphael Mizzi, Evangelist Quinn, Jean Duncan, Philippa Barker, Aloysius Wallis, Shirley Hickson,
Front Row: Leonard McDonald, Gemma Lincoln, Dympna McFadden.

Meanwhile, preparations were under way for the Sisters' General Chapter to be held in September 2006. Sister Lauretta Baker of the Sisters of St Joseph Lochinvar was to be facilitator, and she and Sister Jean Cain met with the Sisters at regular intervals to answer questions and familiarise them with the process that would be used. It was expected that the canonical superior would have been approved by the Archbishop by then and that she would attend this Chapter.

By August, nominations from the Sisters of St Joseph had been received by the Archbishop and the General Council. The Sisters entered 'a process of discernment' on 16 and 17 August to choose their preference. The next day, the General Council met with Archbishop Bathersby to inform him 'that the Sisters had chosen Sister Mary Cresp RSJ as their new congregational leader'. Before the appointment could be official, 'satisfactory Terms of Agreement' had to be drawn up between the Sisters of St Joseph and the Archbishop. It was agreed that Sister Mary would take up her office at a ceremony to be held on 7 October, the anniversary of Father Julian Woods' death.[35]

At their General Chapter on 4–6 September 2006 the Sisters adapted their Constitutions and Statutes to suit their now changed situation. The final meeting of the General Council of the Sisters of Perpetual Adoration took place on 27 September. Earlier that year, Sister Yvonne had contacted Sister Berice Livermore to ask her advice about establishing a schedule for the ongoing support of the Sisters, quite separate from financial arrangements for the health care ministry.[36] Sister Berice would play an important role in ensuring that Sisters in their 'retirement' years were well provided for. All was now ready for a new phase in the history of the Sisters of Perpetual Adoration to begin.

Canonical Leadership

Bishop Finnigan presided at the Mass and commissioning of Sister Mary Cresp RSJ as canonical Congregational Leader of the Sisters of Perpetual Adoration on 7 October 2006. It was a happy occasion where Sister Christine Rowan RSJ, on behalf of the Sisters of St Joseph, missioned Sister Mary to serve the Sisters of Perpetual Adoration under the terms stipulated in the Memorandum of Understanding:

> She will govern the Congregation according to Canon Law, the Constitutions of the Sisters of Perpetual Adoration of the Most Blessed Sacrament and the directions of the Archbishop. She will report regularly to the Archbishop through his appointed delegates.[37]

The *Catholic Leader* reported on the event, noting Bishop Finnegan's comment that 'although such arrangements are not uncommon for small congregations overseas, they are rare in Australia'. It also pointed out: 'Sr Cresp will continue to be a member of her South Australian Josephite Province, but will live part-time in Brisbane, working with elected councillors Srs Yvonne Tobin, Helen Alfrey and Philippa Barker'.[38]

Immediately, the new General Council started work. Having met with Archbishop Bathersby and discussed with him his wish to have an Advisory Committee established to keep him informed about the

Sisters' financial welfare, they met with Vicar General Father Peter Meneely to draw up terms of reference for the said committee.[39] Its main focus would be negotiations that would take place as the Sisters chose another provider for their aged care facilities.[40] Within two months the committee was formed, four members being appointed by the Sisters and four by the Archdiocese with Father Meneely its Chair. Sister Mary McDonald SGS acted as liaison between the committee and the Archbishop.[41]

Because Sister Mary Cresp's assignment was on a part-time basis, the General Council agreed to appoint Sister Yvonne as her assistant. When Sister Mary was absent from Brisbane, she would keep in touch with her daily either by phone or email.

The Future of Aged Care

According to the Memorandum of Understanding set up between the Archbishop and the Sisters of St Joseph, one of the first duties Sister Mary Cresp was to attend to was to 'follow up the management of Aged Care conducted by the Sisters'. By February 2007 the Health Care Advisory Committee had met and had set out a plan whereby the Sisters' ministry of aged care could be handed on. One of their first tasks was to have valuations carried out for the three properties at Brisbane, Ipswich and Unanderra. Another was to approach all Catholic providers of health care in Queensland to gauge their interest in acquiring the Villa Maria facilities. Seven criteria were stipulated:

1. That the Villa Maria Centres would remain under the governance and management of another Catholic aged care provider.
2. That their Mission would continue. [See 2004 Mission Statement above].
3. That the work and history of the Sisters would continue to be celebrated and remembered in the Villa Maria Centres.
4. That the involvement of the Sisters in visiting and pastoral care at the Centres would continue.
5. That the Sisters' needs for residential aged care could be ensured.
6. That the provider could obtain the three Centres in one transaction.
7. That through the sale of the Centres the Sisters could fund the ongoing financial needs of the Congregation.[42]

All providers replied that they were not interested at the time or would have difficulty managing the three sites. Catholic Healthcare was based in New South Wales, but, as they had previously worked with the Sisters of Perpetual Adoration, they submitted an expression of interest and was the only body that met the criteria. In June 2007 the committee duly handed their recommendation to Archbishop Bathersby that the submission of Catholic Healthcare should be accepted under the condition that they should buy the Villa Maria sites at Ipswich and Unanderra and lease the Brisbane site for 99 years.

Before final permission could be granted, Archbishop Bathersby had to approve the status of Catholic Healthcare as a Public Juridic Person and give his permission for them to minister in the archdiocese. While they already had recognition in the Wollongong diocese, Bishop Ingham had to agree to the transfer of the ministry. Since the sale or leasing of the properties would constitute alienation, to do this the Sisters would have to obtain the consent of the Archbishop and an indult from the Vatican.

Meeting after meeting followed in the next months. Sisters Mary, Yvonne, Helen and Robyn Gugenberger held frequent discussions with management personnel of Catholic Healthcare to ensure the progress of transfer. Archbishop Bathersby needed to be certain that no concerns, financial or canonical, remained in order for him to give the necessary permissions. It was agreed that all funds obtained from the sale of the properties would provide for the Sisters' upkeep, care and ongoing ministries into the future. After ten years, once property payments to the Sisters of Perpetual Adoration had been completed, Villa Maria Brisbane and its lease arrangements would be transferred to the archdiocese.

During these months, too, the Sisters helped prepare staff for the handover. To inform them of their background story and the spirit underlying their ministry, Sister Mary Cresp wrote a short history, *Villa Maria: The Sisters of Perpetual Adoration and Care of the Aged*. This was published and a copy given to each staff member at Brisbane, Ipswich and Unanderra.[43]

With approval being given for the alienation of properties by the Vatican on 19 October, all was clear for the process of transfer to begin. A ceremony of handover was held at Unanderra on 15 November, 2007, with Bishop Ingham presiding. Archbishop Bathersby officiated at the ceremony held at Villa Maria Brisbane on Sunday 2 December, 2007. A similar ceremony was held at Ipswich the next day. Mayoress Cheryl Bowers attended, as did the parish priest, Father Peter Casey. The *Catholic Leader* reported:

> One of Queensland's oldest religious orders, the Sisters of Perpetual Adoration, has handed over the running of the Villa Maria Centres for the Aged to Catholic Healthcare . . . Transition ceremonies were held at each Villa Maria Centre to mark the occasion. Residents, resident families, staff, dignitaries and representatives from the Sisters and Catholic Healthcare attended the ceremonies. At each service the Sisters presented a statue of the Holy Family to Catholic Healthcare as a symbol of their tradition of hospitality, care and 'family feel' at the Villa Maria Centre. Sr Cresp said . . . 'We have confidence that the mission of the Sisters will be ably carried into the future by Catholic Healthcare—it will continue to bring Christ's love to the aged, to uphold their dignity and integrate them into the life of the wider community of care.'[44]

Community and Ministry

While some Sisters would continue to serve in pastoral care at Villa Maria Brisbane, the community could now put more effort into their main focus, Adoration of the Blessed Sacrament. In February 2007 Pope Benedict XVI wrote his Apostolic Exhortation *Sacramentum Caritatis* (The Sacrament of Love). In various ways, the Sisters were able to put points made in this reflection into practice.

Former Cliff Street sign

Bishop Peter Ingham

Villa Maria, Unanderra. Photo permission: Catholic Healthcare Unanderra

During the ceremony of transferring the Care of the Aged to Catholic Healthcare, the Sisters of Perpetual Adoration presented each facility with a statue of the Holy Family.

Transfer of Care of the Aged to Catholic Healthcare, December 2007: Srs Yvonne Tobin, Elizabeth Bargenquast, Evangelist Quinn, Emmanuel Carroll, Angela Turvey, Helen Alfrey, Leonard McDonald, Philippa Barker, Mary Cresp

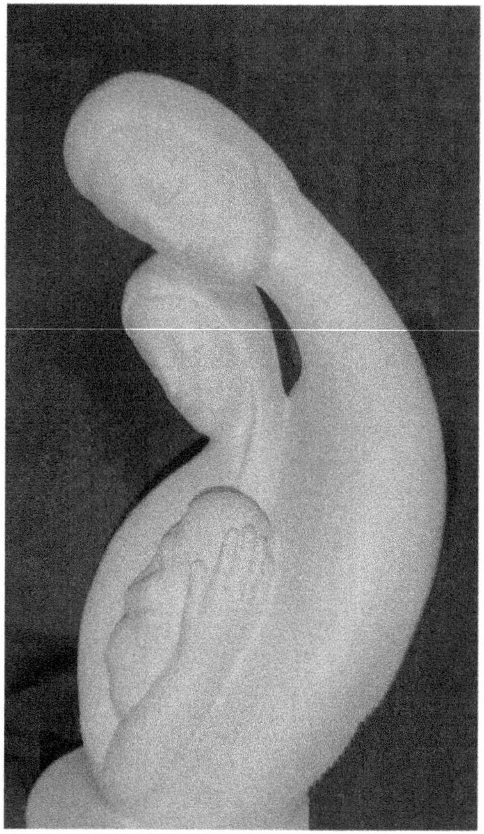

Symbol of entrusting the heritage during the ceremony of transfer

Paragraph 68 of the exhortation states: 'The personal relationship which the individual believer establishes with Jesus present in the Eucharist constantly points beyond itself to the whole communion of the Church and nourishes a fuller sense of membership in the Body of Christ.' For some time, especially with the input that Sister Carmel Pilcher had given to them, some Sisters had suggested they might go further than offering Co-Adorers and others opportunities to pray. Already, several groups were using the facilities, such as the Christian Meditation group and the Holy Family Alliance who conducted their 40-hours devotion in the chapel. This could be extended so that the chapel and sections of the lower areas of the convent could become an inner-city spirituality centre where spiritual direction could be offered, people invited to join the recitation of the Divine Office and lunch-time lectures given, as happens in many monasteries and churches in Europe.[45]

The sub-editor of the *Catholic Leader*, Peter Bugden, paid tribute to this decision:

> Changing times have caught up with one of Queensland's oldest religious orders, but its members must be admired for the way they are facing the challenge . . . Most importantly for the Sisters, they are moving on full of faith and hope to new challenges, open to God's will. They are looking ahead to the possibility of establishing a spirituality centre for the heart of the city. Their faith in the face of change is an example to us all.[46]

In February 2007 Sister Yvonne Tobin began Spiritual Direction training with Ministry Education, Milton. During the year, she and Sister Ann Fleming RSJ conducted research and by December put forward a plan for the Sisters of Perpetual Adoration and the Queensland Sisters of St Joseph to establish a co-ministry of spirituality with its centre at the Warren Street precinct. Meetings followed with the Provincial Sister Margaret Robertson RSJ and her council, and a Memorandum of Understanding was drawn up.[47] A support group of two Sisters from each Congregation was formed and Spiritual Directors from different Congregations were invited to use the facilities, whose close proximity to the city offered advantages for those seeking spiritual direction during lunch time or after work. The Archbishop was informed of this venture and was very affirming. At Evening Prayer on 1 August 2008 Sisters Ann Fleming and Yvonne Tobin were commissioned to coordinate the co-ministry by Sister Mary Cresp for the Sisters of Perpetual Adoration and Sister Moya Campbell, now the Provincial of the Queensland Sisters of St Joseph.[48]

Subsequently, approaches were made to Father Ken Howell to have the Cathedral parish use the facilities at Villa Maria Convent for liturgical instruction, such as the training of readers and Eucharistic ministers.[49] Even though nothing came of these proposals, the Inner-city Spirituality Centre did flourish, being used various prayer groups and for the giving of retreats and spiritual direction.

In his Apostolic Exhortation, Pope Benedict had pointed out: 'Missionary outreach is an essential part of the eucharistic form of the Christian life.'[50] While some of the Sisters could carry missionary outreach to the Villa Maria Hostel, others found there were opportunities in the wider neighbourhood. For example, Sister Regina Greenhalgh had worked at a radio station before she joined the Sisters, so one day as she was passing a local community station nearby she called in and inquired if they needed anyone to do some volunteer work. She had an audition and the manager told her, 'You have a good voice for radio'. For the next five years she read the stock market report once a week from the *Financial Review*.[51] Towards the end of 2008 Father Jim Smith was looking for volunteers to be part of his psychiatric pastoral care team in Fortitude Valley.[52] Sister Xavier Woods was interested, so she did the required courses and served on the team once a week for some years. As for the first Sisters of Perpetual Adoration, her visiting of people who struggled became a sign of the presence of Christ among us.

A communal response to mission was occasioned by Mary Gavin from 'Always People' asking the Sisters of Perpetual Adoration to assist a small indigenous Congregation in Vietnam by offering scholarships to their members to study in Australia.[53] Like all Religious Congregations, the Sisters received hundreds of requests each year. In their yearly budget, the General Council set aside a substantial amount and distributed it according to need. However, this project was larger than usual. Eventually, since the Sisters of Perpetual Adoration were not able to be primarily responsible for such a large project, the Council entered into partnership with the Sisters of St Joseph to respond to this request. Conversations between Sister Mary Cresp, the Josephite Congregational Leader Sister Katrina Brill, Sister Catherine Trinh RSJ and the Leader of the Miraculous Medal Sisters in Vietnam led to the decision that culturally, it would not be suitable for Sisters to come to Australia (as well as visa difficulties posed by the Department of Home Affairs in Canberra). Instead, two scholarships to a Philippines University were offered.[54]

In 2008 two Sisters from the Brisbane community, Sisters Shirley Hickson and Margaret Mary Allport, died. The frailty of the Sisters was obvious. To provide the community superior and general councillor Sister Helen Alfrey with extra support, Coreen Small had been employed to assist in convent management by overseeing supplies.[55] Now Sister Mary McDonald SGS was engaged on a part-time basis to facilitate a process of grieving with the Sisters and, taking into account their health needs, to help them make adjustments to their timetable. This was not an easy task, as the Sisters came from a lifetime of strict discipline. For instance, they worried that people who came to weekday Mass on their way to work would be inconvenienced if the time of Mass was changed from 7 am to 7.30 am.

Sister Philippa Barker was combining her role on the General Council with organising the Sisters' archives. As she had not had training for this, Sister Margaret McKenna RSJ and Coreen Small spent time with her each month to help.[56] It was Sister Philippa who suggested that Sister Mary Cresp should use the resources of the archives 'to write something on Julian Tenison Woods' for the Congregation's 135th anniversary on 15 June 2009, coinciding with the celebrations of the 150th anniversary of the Archdiocese of Brisbane.[57] The *Catholic Leader* described the event:

> The Sisters of Perpetual Adoration in Brisbane celebrated their 135th anniversary on June 15. A large crowd of friends and family gathered at Villa Maria, Fortitude Valley, for a Mass and morning tea . . . In his homily, Auxiliary Bishop Brian Finnigan noted the significant part the Sisters had played in the history of both the State of Queensland and the Catholic Church in this city . . . A book—*Prayer-Chats*

with Julian: The Integration of Spirituality, Theology and Ecology in the Life of Julian Tenison Woods—was launched at the celebration. Josephite Sister Margaret McKenna commended author Sister Mary Cresp for her research and engaging style of writing in her book. Much of the material for the book came from the archives of the Sisters of Perpetual Adoration.[58]

Governance for the Future

At their General Chapter in September 2006, the Sisters of Perpetual Adoration had charged its leadership with pursuing possibilities for their future. Previously, Sister Patricia Scully had explained to the Sisters that they had options of amalgamation or merger with another Congregation: union, where two Congregations come together to form a new group: forming links with another Congregation in a relationship called aggregation: or, finally, dissolution.[59] These options had been shelved as the Sisters investigated what might arise in their discussions with the Federation of the Sisters of St Joseph and with the decision of the Archbishop to appoint a canonical Congregational Leader. Now it was time to look again at the paths open to the Sisters of Perpetual Adoration.

To help with administration, the General Council extended Coreen Small's employment in November 2007 to appoint her as Assistant to the Leadership of the Sisters of Perpetual Adoration. This role included clerical duties, overseeing observance of workplace health and safety regulations and attending to financial systems and reports. Over the years the Sisters had come to know and trust Coreen. Her respect for them meant she never interfered with their lives, and yet the service she gave was invaluable.

During 2008 a series of community meetings with the Sisters was held to ensure they understood what the options for future governance might mean. In a merger, or fusion, the Sisters of Perpetual Adoration would be absorbed into another Congregation, thus losing their name and identity. In union, two Congregations would cease to be, and instead they would come together to start a new Congregation. With aggregation, each Congregation would share resources and mission but remain autonomous. Governance would be provided by the Congregation to whom the other is aggregated.[60]

Sister Mary Cresp had been receiving advice on these matters from a canon lawyer friend, Sister Margaret Modde OSF from Rochester in the United States, and also from Sister Sharon Holland IHM who was working at the Congregation for Institutes of Consecrated Life at the Vatican.[61] As the Archbishop had expressed his wish that he be 'kept informed of all matters pertaining to the Congregation', she met with him regularly about the options she had discussed with the Sisters.[62] In February 2008 she gave him a copy of a paper she had written, 'New Structures and Functions of Government'. This had been discussed with the community and distributed to the Josephite Province Leadership Team.[63]

The Sisters themselves had suggested that, since both the Sisters of St Joseph and the Sisters of Perpetual Adoration had been co-founded by Father Julian Tenison Woods, they should look to link in some way with them. Therefore, they proposed that they should meet up with the Sisters of St Joseph at Nundah to both enjoy social time together and share ideas with them on possibilities for the future.

Meetings and social events followed. By September 2008, Sisters from both groups had read the Constitutions of the other's congregation and had familiarised themselves with the main points of congregational history. Different scenarios were considered on what relationships might exist between the two congregations. It was time now to involve the Congregational Leadership Team from Sydney. From 3 October 2008 Sisters Anne Derwin (Congregational Leader of the Sisters of St Joseph) and Annette Arnold (General Councillor) met regularly at gatherings of the two groups held at the Province Centre of the Sisters of St Joseph in Nundah.[64]

In February 2009, canon-lawyer Father Frank Morrisey OMI from Ottawa in Canada, visited Sydney and generously gave of his time to meet with Sisters Anne Derwin and General Councillors, Moya Campbell (Queensland Provincial of the Sisters of St Joseph), Patricia Scully (Queensland Vicar for Religious), Mary Cresp, Yvonne Tobin and Helen Alfrey.[65] Sister Patricia Scully expressed the hope that the Sisters of St Joseph 'might take on responsibility for the Sisters of Perpetual Adoration'.[66] From then on Father Morrisey was in constant communication with the General Council of both Congregations.

Over the next months an intensive process of phasing into communal decisions and protocol were carried out. Sister Mary interviewed each Sister to make sure they were clear about what was happening. On 6 May 2009 the community voted for their preference of aggregation with the Sisters of St Joseph, and the next day the General Council of the Sisters of Perpetual Adoration drew up a letter of petition to the Archbishop for the Sisters' reflection and comment.[67] Legal matters such as responsibilities for the patrimony of the Sisters of Perpetual Adoration and Sisters' personal wills had to be attended to. Later, in accordance with Canon 123, the Sisters would be making their communal will with regard to what would happen if or when the Sisters of Perpetual Adoration ceased to exist.[68] Discussions with Sisters Anne Derwin and Moya Campbell surfaced three areas of consideration after aggregation:

- Welfare of the Sisters would be attended to by a community leader appointed by the Queensland Provincial.
- Support for the Sisters' ministries of adoration and outreach would come under the administration of the Queensland Province in conversation with the community.
- Finance and property management would be handled by a leadership team put in place by the Sisters of Perpetual Adoration which would report back to the Queensland Provincial. To ensure the independence of the Sisters of Perpetual Adoration, a finance committee would be formed and include two representatives of the Sisters of Perpetual Adoration, one delegate from the Sisters of St Joseph and other financial advisers.[69]

On 10 June 2009 Sisters Mary Cresp and Yvonne Tobin delivered the letter of petition to Archbishop Bathersby requesting aggregation with the Sisters of St Joseph of the Sacred Heart. He was also given an outline of structural plans to be put in place so that he could be assured that the welfare of the Sisters was guaranteed. Meetings and workshops with Sisters from both Congregations continued. A letter from Archbishop

Bathersby to Sister Anne Derwin on 16 July confirmed his acceptance of the petition and entrusted the care and governance of the Sisters of Perpetual Adoration to the Sisters of St Joseph of the Sacred Heart. He concluded: 'Therefore, with this letter and in a spirit of deep gratitude and confidence, I appoint you as Congregational Leader of the Sisters of Perpetual Adoration to take effect from 7 October 2009.'[70]

Signing the Aggregation papers during the ceremony at St Stephen's Cathedral,
7 October 2009
Srs Mary Cresp, Helen Alfrey, Yvonne Tobin, Philippa Barker, Anne Derwin

At farewell for Sr Mary Cresp, 24 March 2010
Back: Srs Ann Fleming rsj, Lyn Stabler rsj, Moya Campbell rsj (Queensland Provincial), Mary Cresp rsj. Xavier Woods.
Middle: Elizabeth Bargenquast, Regina Greenhalgh, Helen Alfrey, Yvonne Tobin, Narelle Hickson, Emmanuel Carroll, Angela Turvey.
Front: Raphael Mizzi, Philippa Barker, Aloysius Wallis, Leonard McDonald, Evangelist Quinn, Philomena McAuliffe.

During the 'beautiful and powerful ceremony' of aggregation at St Stephen's Cathedral on 7 October, Archbishop Bathersby 'appointed the Australian Congregational Leader of the Sisters of St Joseph Sr Anne Derwin (and her successors) as the Congregational Leader of the Sisters of Perpetual Adoration for as long as both orders are agreeable.' It was apt that this happened on the anniversary of the death of Julian Tenison Woods, the co-founder of both Congregations. The *Catholic Leader* reported:

> The two orders lived together in South Brisbane for a short time initially until the Sisters of Perpetual Adoration found their own premises. Sr Cresp said the order 'has now come the full circle as the lives of both Congregations become intertwined once again.'[71]

After Aggregation

For the next five months, Sister Mary Cresp and the General Council worked with Sister Moya Campbell in a process of transition to the new system of governance. For the Sisters, life seemed to go on as usual. A new group of lay people, the 'Perpetual Adoration Association', had asked permission from the General Council to form a roster for 24-hour adoration, so an agreement was prepared and signed concerning the availability of car parks and swipe cards for night access to the chapel.[72] Meanwhile, the Sisters and Co-Adorers kept their own roster of adoration according to the restricted hours they were able to manage. The Queensland Sisters of St Joseph included short biographies of the Sisters of Perpetual Adoration in their 2010 monthly newsletters, 'Cross Country'. Refurbishment of St Francis Xavier's Cathedral, Wollongong, was being planned, so the Sisters who had ministered there were asked to write their Villa Maria memories to be displayed in the Cathedral on the completion of its renovation.[73] The Sisters were assured they were not forgotten.

On 9 February 2010, Terms of Reference were drawn up for the Finance Committee of the Sisters of Perpetual Adoration. Meeting at least four times a year, the committee would manage the financial affairs of the Congregation and assign moneys connected with the areas concerned with the Sisters' life and ministry.

Sister Mary Cresp RSJ completed her service to the Sisters of Perpetual Adoration on 24 March 2010. Her farewell was marked by a prayer and tree-planting ceremony in the Sisters' garden, with gifts given and speeches made at a dinner in her honour.

Sister Helen Alfrey continued her role as Community Leader for the Sisters until Sister Therese Wilson RSJ was appointed in mid-2011. Sister Therese considered her time at Villa Maria to be 'happy' and 'blessed'—a 'privilege'.[74] Thanks to the structures already put in place and 'the assistance given her by Coreen Small', she quickly adapted to her pastoral role, receiving companionship and inspiration from the lives of the eighteen Sisters in the community.

In August 2010 Sister Emmanuel Carroll died, leaving the legacy of the small group of Co-Adorers she had formed during the 1990s. A year later, Sister Dympna McFadden died at the Canossa Nursing Home where she had lived for the past eight years. Without the research she had done for Father Tom Boland's book, *Quiet Women*, much of the history of the Sisters of Perpetual Adoration would have been lost.

Sister Philippa Barker died on 11 May 2013. She was a woman of deep prayer, kindness, vision, flexibility, wit and great strength of character. In her three terms as Congregational Leader, she had carried her Congregation forward with courage during what were traumatic times for the Sisters. Sister Gemma Lincoln, so loved in her role as pastoral carer at the Villa Maria Hostel, died in August. Sister Leonard McDonald, a woman of great faith and quiet common sense, died in October. The Congregation of the Sisters of Perpetual Adoration was nearing the time of its fulfillment.

Yet the spirit lived on. In 2011, a new ecumenical ministry began at the Villa Maria Inner-city Spirituality Centre for those living with a life-threatening illness. The facilitators were Spiritual Directors Sister Denise Brosnan RSJ and David Betts (who died in August 2013). The group is now called the 'Circle of Friends' and is open to all. Sister Denise says that, before she died, Sister Phillipa told her that the group was doing the work of the Sisters of Perpetual Adoration.[75]

The 140th anniversary of the founding of the Sisters of Perpetual Adoration occurred on 15 June 2014. Their number by now had depleted to just thirteen. Despite this, since they had entrusted their legacy to the Sisters of St Joseph, it would continue to grow and develop through the wise use of the resources they had placed into their care.

In his last letter to his friend William Archer, Julian Woods had written in 1889: 'Though severely ill, somehow or other it is with hopeful confidence that I say *Resurgam*.'[76] In editing Julian's letters in 1983, Sister Anne Player RSJ had explained, 'Written in Greek, this quote is part of 2 Cor. 6:9 which reads in full, "as unknown and yet well known: as dying, and behold we live: as chastened and not killed".'[77] Over the 140 years of their presence in Brisbane and beyond, the Sisters of Perpetual Adoration and their works and mission had been unknown to many, so much so that when Father Tom Boland had written their story in 1974 he had called them *Quiet Women*. Yet through them the lives of untold thousands were touched, whether through the unknown effect of intercessory prayer, through their example of patience and forbearance in the face of impossible odds, or through their practical ministry such as care of the aged or the supply of altar breads to become 'the bread of life'.[78]

The Sisters of Perpetual Adoration might well say '*Resurgam*'. Their lives, spent in adoration before the presence of Christ among us, demonstrate the meaning of life itself (Jn 6:35). As creatures, it is God in whom 'we live and move and have our being' (Acts 17:28). Adoration is the stance of the creature before its creator. It is the hope of '*Resurgam*' that gives meaning to life and looks forward to the future.

POSTSCRIPT

Since 2014, eight Sisters of Perpetual Adoration have died: Sisters Evangelist Quinn (2015), Jean Duncan (2016), Angela Turvey (2016), Aloysius Wallis (2017), Regina Greenhalgh (2018), Philomena McAuliffe (2020), Yvonne Tobin (2022) and Barbara Hickson (2023).

In 2015 Sister Marie Dowling from the Queensland Sisters of St Joseph replaced Sister Therese Wilson as Community Leader, and arrangements with the Congregational Leadership changed so that she liaises directly with the Congregational Leader (Sister Monica Cavanagh RSJ) in Sydney.

A portrait of Father Julian Tenison Woods and Catherine Gaffney (Mother Stanislaus), co-founders of the Sisters of Perpetual Adoration, was unveiled at a special celebration at Villa Maria on 7 October 1916. The artist, Jan Williamson, has won many awards in both Australia and overseas.[79]

The Finance Committee of the Sisters of Perpetual Adoration was replaced in 2020 with the Sisters of Perpetual Adoration Trust with Sister Berice Livermore RSM as chair. It provides accommodation and board to the Sisters of Perpetual Adoration. In addition, it ensures financial and physical resources to support adoration in the Convent Chapel and other ministries in accord with the spirit of the Congregation: for example, the giving of retreats and providing accommodation for the same at the Villa Maria Convent.

On 15 June 2024 the Sisters celebrated the sesquicentenary. Archbishop Mark Coleridge, Bishop Brian Finnigan, Sisters Monica Cavanagh, Mary Cresp, Marie Dowling and many Queensland Sisters of St Joseph joined in prayer and celebration with Sisters Helen Alfrey, Elizabeth Bargenquast, Narelle Hickson, Raphael Mizzi and Xavier Woods, thanking God for the blessing the Sisters of Perpetual Adoration have been over the past 150 years.

Archbishop Mark Coleridge

Sisters of Perpetual Adoration Finance Committee 2015 (later replaced with a Board of Trust)
Back: Les Jones, Coreen Small, Chris Townsend, Sr Berice Livermore rsm (Chair)
Front: Srs Marie Dowling rsj, Josephine Dubiel rsj.

Community 2012 with Fr David Nugent:
Back : Srs Therese Wilson rsj (Community Leader), Xavier Woods, Elizabeth Bargenquast, Helen Alfrey, Regina Greenhalgh, Judith Steer rsj.
Front: Philippa Barker, Aloysius Wallis, Evangelist Quinn, Raphael Mizzi,.

Community 2014 with Archbishop Mark Coleridge
Back: Srs Yvonne Tobin, Marie Dowling rsj (Community Leader), Xavier Woods, Raphael Mizzi, Elizabeth Bargenquast.
Front: Helen Alfrey, Aloysius Wallis, Philomena McAuliffe.

150 Years: Sesquicentenary 15 June 2024

Back: Srs Narelle Hickson, Mary Cresp rsj, Elizabeth Bagenquast, Raphael Mizzi, Monica Cavanagh rsj (Congregational Leader),
Front: Srs Xavier Woods (holding Pope's blessing), Helen Alfrey.

Epilogue

If you go to the Villa Maria Chapel at 123 Warren Street in Brisbane at any time during daylight hours today, you will always find a number of people praying before the exposed Blessed Sacrament. Moreover, Pope Francis is often cited as encouraging the practice of this way of worship. 'Immersing oneself in silent Eucharistic adoration is the secret to knowing the Lord', he said when commenting on St Paul's letter to the Ephesians (3:14–23):

> To waste time—if I may say it—before the Lord, before the mystery of Jesus Christ. To adore, there in the silence, in the silence of adoration. He is the Lord, and I adore Him.[1]

One might ask, 'Does Pope Francis approach Eucharistic adoration with the same understanding that would have characterised the first Sisters of Perpetual Adoration in the 19th century?' We have had the Second Vatican Council since then, and liturgical reforms have been carried out to more accurately signify developments in that understanding. How is worship of Christ outside the celebration of the Eucharist to be carried out today?

The Constitution on the Sacred Liturgy, *Sacrosanctum Concilium*, was the first decree to be issued by the Second Vatican Council in 1963. It followed years of research in which Scripture scholars, liturgists, historians and theologians unearthed ancient scripts and archaeologic evidence of how the Eucharist was understood and celebrated in the early Church. Some reforms in liturgical practice had already taken place before the Council. The 1943 encyclical of Pope Pius XII, *Mystici Corpus Christi* ('The Mystical Body of Christ') had led to a fresh awareness of the presence of Christ in his members. In the 1950s there were attempts to encourage the participation of the faithful in offering the Mass instead of just being 'onlookers'. The 'Dialogue Mass' was introduced where the Epistle and Gospel were read in the vernacular and some of the Latin responses were made by the whole assembly. In 1955, Pope Pius XII restored the ancient rites of the Holy Week Triduum, including the Easter vigil. In doing so, he highlighted the central place that the remembrance of the life, death and resurrection of Christ holds in Catholic Christianity.

This prior work enabled the members of the Second Vatican Council to put in place the 'restorations' needed to align liturgical celebrations with primitive practice.[2] In particular, the document said, those gathered for the celebration of the Eucharist 'should not be there as strangers or spectators'.[3] In the celebration of the Eucharist, or 'Mass', there was to be 'full and active participation of the faithful', since it was to the whole Church that Jesus 'entrusted' the 'memorial of his death and resurrection—a sacrament of love, a sign of unity, a bond of charity, a paschal banquet in which Christ is consumed, the mind is filled with grace, and a pledge of future glory is given to us'.[4]

Pope Paul VI followed up the Constitution on the Sacred Liturgy with his encyclical on the Eucharist, *Mysterium Fidei*.[5] In this work he situates the reforms proffered by the Council within those made along the course of history, including those made by the Council of Trent which retrieved what was then known about worship in the Early Church and by Pope Pius X who in 1905 encouraged frequent, even daily Communion.[6] Pope Paul also comments on the worship of the Sacramental presence of Christ beyond the celebration of the Eucharist:

> It is not just while the Sacrifice is being offered and the Sacrament is being confected, but also after the Sacrifice has been offered and the Sacrament confected—while the Eucharist is reserved in churches or oratories—that Christ is truly Emmanuel, which means 'God with us'. For He is in the midst of us day and night; He dwells in us with the fullness of grace and of truth. He . . . comforts the sorrowful, strengthens the weak and stirs up all those who draw near to Him to imitate Him . . . Anyone who has a special devotion to the sacred Eucharist and who tries to repay Christ's infinite love for us with an eager and unselfish love of his own, will experience and fully understand . . . just how worthwhile it is to carry on a conversation with Christ, for there is nothing more consoling here on earth, nothing more efficacious for progress along the paths of holiness.[7]

Many of those who come to the Villa Maria chapel today find they bring the same attitudes of faith to adoration of the exposed Blessed Sacrament as they do when they gather for the liturgy of the Mass. Their adoration is an extension of the Mass. 'In adoration we are conscious of the presence of God with us', says Heather Joseph. She is on the day-time roster now, but when there was night adoration in the chapel, she used to be rostered for the 4–5 am 'shift'.[8] Doctor Michael Kennedy who, in retirement, spends time in adoration every day, found when was going through a very difficult time in his life that time spent in 'the company of Jesus who suffered' gave him strength:

> Coming to the Villa Maria chapel sustained me. I could get above knee-jerk reactions. Adoration gave me the chance to tap into my deepest self. Decisions could be made at a higher level in the reality of Love.[9]

There are those who, knowing that the presence of God is in the whole of life, challenge the idea that adoration of the Blessed Sacrament outside of Mass is anything 'special'. 'I find the presence of God in the beauty of nature', they will say. 'I don't need to go to a church to find God.' Pope Paul VI does not deny this when speaking of the Eucharistic presence: 'This presence is called "real" not to exclude the idea that the others are "real" too,' he says. However, referring to the immediate presence of Christ in the Eucharist rather than its extension in nature, he explains that the Eucharist indicates 'presence par excellence, because it is substantial and through it Christ becomes present whole and entire, God and man.'[10]

One of the valuable insights of the Second Vatican Council is that, within Church doctrine, 'there exists an order or "hierarchy" of truths, since they vary in their relation to the foundation of the Christian faith.'[11] Pope John Paul II names the core of the hierarchy of truths in this way:

> The truth that God is Love constitutes as it were the apex of all that has been revealed . . . This truth illumines the whole content of divine revelation.[12]

Christian belief is that God who is Love, the Creator of all, is fully revealed in Jesus Christ. It is through the incarnation, life, death and resurrection of Christ that the Father is revealed and the Spirit given to enable humanity to be made one with God and each other in his Body the Church.[13] This doctrine held by the church in Scripture, Tradition and official church teaching, forms the central premise to which all others are related and from which all flow.[14] The liturgy of the Eucharist is directly linked to these central mysteries, since in that liturgy, the act of Christ's revelation of the Father's love in his death and resurrection is made present through the power of the Spirit.

Devotions are practices that individuals and groups might perform to express their beliefs, but in themselves they are not doctrine. They are like the lace around a doily—they need to be related to the central truth but the practice itself is not obligatory for belief. If it does not reflect what is at the heart of Gospel belief, it is not valid. Devotions such as the Rosary, which is a way of meditating on the incarnation, life, death and resurrection of Jesus Christ, relate to the central truth of Christian faith of who Jesus is 'for us and our salvation.'[15]

There is a difference, however, with the various Eucharistic devotions that are separate from its liturgical celebration. Certainly, individuals may choose or not choose to adopt devotional practices to honour the presence of Christ in the Eucharist apart from the Mass. Nevertheless, it is to be remembered that these are not just 'lace on the doily'—they are a direct extension of the liturgy that celebrates the central tenets of Christian belief: 'The celebration of the Eucharist in the sacrifice of the Mass is truly the origin and goal of the worship which is shown to the Eucharist outside of Mass.'[16]

Don Barrett, now a resident of the Villa Maria Nursing Home in Brisbane, has always admired the 'practicality of the Sisters of Perpetual Adoration', having joined them at morning Mass and adoration ('meditation') in the chapel for many years. He is grateful for the prayerful setting of the chapel: 'For example, the stained-glass windows are an inspiring sight, especially at night', he says. Nevertheless, he wonders if, in the past, 'opportunities for the catechesis of adults who come there' may have been 'lost'.[17] Michael Lynch knew from the time he was a child what 'adoration of Jesus present in the Blessed Sacrament' was about. He was one of the first Villa Maria Co-Adorers enrolled by Sister Emmanuel Carroll in the 1990s. Thirty years later he still takes his turn on the roster of adoration there. One thing he has noticed is that numbers of young people often 'drop in' to the chapel: 'They sit on the floor and just spend the time quietly.'[18] Do they come with an awareness of the presence of Christ there and of the deeper meanings of the Eucharist? We do not know. Is it the peace that draws them, away from the noise of city traffic and hurry? Even if that is the case, they choose the chapel over the peaceful gardens that are in the vicinity.

Pope Francis often refers to silence as a gift that we need and for which we should be grateful. In his 2015 encyclical *Laudate 'Si*, he reminds us that creation is 'a continuing revelation of the divine': '[F]or the believer, to contemplate creation is to hear a message, to listen to a paradoxical and silent voice.'[19] When speaking of the relationship between husband and wife in his 2016 Post-Synodal Apostolic Exhortation he writes: '[F]or where love is concerned, silence is always more eloquent than words.'[20] How apt, therefore, is the silence associated with adoration of the Blessed Sacrament. Relationships are formed when one's heart is open to the other. When speaking about the silence of St Joseph in the Scriptures, Pope Francis points out: 'Profoundness of the heart grows with silence . . . which leaves space for wisdom, reflection and the Holy Spirit'. The silence of Villa Maria Chapel during these hours of adoration provides the setting for God's Spirit to speak to those who 'sit and wait'—no matter what their level of theological education nor their conscious intention. Pope Francis continues, quoting St John of the Cross: 'The Father spoke a Word, and it was his Son—and it always speaks in eternal silence, and in silence it must be heard by the soul.'[21]

To adore the presence of Christ in the Blessed Sacrament outside the celebration of Mass is not a passive exercise. There are two things to consider. First, as Elizabeth Harrington points out:

> [A]doration of the Blessed Sacrament is a part of, and continuation of, the Eucharistic action itself. Our sense of mystery and awe at God's great gift of our redemption through the paschal mystery prompts such reverence and worship. Adoration expresses our belief in the real presence and is a response to that presence.[22]

Second, just as the presence of Christ in the reserved Sacrament relates to the Eucharistic celebration, so, too, does the adorer who took part in that celebration now brings that same self to the action of adoration. St Augustine explained that when we receive the 'food of life' in Communion, this food actually changes us into the likeness of Christ.[23] In his famous Sermon 272 he said:

> If you, therefore, are Christ's body and members, it is your own mystery that is placed on the Lord's table! It is your own mystery that you are receiving! You are saying 'Amen' to what you are: your response is a personal signature, affirming your faith. When you hear 'The body of Christ', you reply 'Amen.' Be a member of Christ's body, then, so that your 'Amen' may ring true![24]

Being the Body of Christ calls us to act as Christ does. Pope Francis reminds us that while we kneel 'before the Tabernacle', we do so with 'arms always open wide to [our] brothers and sisters'.[25] Just as the Sisters of Perpetual Adoration found the presence of Christ in service to the aged and those who were poor, adorers today cannot be passive onlookers but, growing into Christ, their love must reach out to others. As Pope Benedict XVI said, 'the worship of God in our lives cannot be relegated to something private and individual, but tends by its nature to permeate every aspect of our existence.'[26]

Adoration of the Blessed Sacrament outside the celebration of the Eucharist is a devotion that serves the world of today. It fosters and expresses personal love of Jesus; it affords us the setting and possibility to get in touch with our inner selves, and it can help us immerse ourselves more deeply into the paschal mystery of Christ which we have celebrated in the Eucharist and which we express in service of others. Ronald Rolheiser, in a meditation on adoration, quotes Gerhard Lohfink (1934–2024), a prominent German theologian:

> For him, the highest form of prayer is adoration. But what does it mean to 'adore' God and why is that the highest form of prayer? Lohfink answers: 'In adoration we ask nothing more of God. When I *lament* before God it is usually my own suffering that is the starting point. Even when I *petition* God, the occasion is often my own problem. I need something from God. And even when I *thank* God, unfortunately I am usually thankful for something I have received. But when I *adore*, I let go of myself and look only to God.'[27]

With all who have gone before us since Jesus, in his life, death and resurrection, revealed for us the face of God and who today calls us into discipleship, we respond, 'Come, let us adore!'

Notes

Prologue

1 Colin Buchanan, *Justin Martyr on Baptism and Eucharist: Texts in Translation with Introduction and Commentary* (London: SCM Canterbury Press, 2007), 49.
2 Buchanan, *Justin Martyr on Baptism and Eucharist,* 49.
3 Paul Bradshaw, *Early Christian Worship* (Collegeville Minnesota: Liturgical Press, 1996), 64.
4 John H McKenna CM, 'Theology of Adoration' in *Vincentiana,* 49/1 (2005): 84.
5 Exposition of the Blessed Sacrament is a way of honouring the presence of Christ, the consecrated host is being displayed in a container called a Monstrance, thus exposing it to the view of the faithful as they pray. Benediction is a ceremony where the Blessed Sacrament is exposed, and where, after prayers and hymns of praise, worshippers are blessed with the monstrance. People who make Visits to the Blessed Sacrament simply pray before the reserved Sacrament in the Tabernacle, 'visiting' as one would to a friend. The Forty Hours Devotion is a period of forty hours during which worshippers pray continuously before the exposed Sacrament.
6 The Feast of Corpus Christi is a special feastday honouring the presence of Christ in the Eucharist and translated into English as the 'Solemnity of the Most Holy Body and Blood of Christ'. It is celebrated by Catholics of the Latin (western) Rite and in some Orthodox, Anglican and Lutheran churches.
7 Timothy P O'Malley, 'Medieval Assent: Communion of Body and Soul as an Ascending Model for Liturgy', <https://adoremus.org/2021/01/medieval-assent-communion-of-body-and-soul-as-an-ascending-model-for-liturgy/> accessed 1 September 2024.
8 Council of Trent, Session 13, Chapter 1. <https://www.ewtn.com/catholicism/library/thirteenth-session-of-the-council-of-trent-1479> accessed 3 September 2024.
9 Council of Trent, Session 13, Chapter V.
10 Jansenism owes its name to the Flemish bishop of Ypres, Cornelius Jansen (1587–1638), the author of its foundational text, *Augustinus,* which was based on an erroneous interpretation of Augustine's teaching on Original Sin and was published posthumously in Leuven in 1640.
11 Damian Cash, *The Road to Emmaus: A History of the Blessed Sacrament Congregation in Australia* (Kew East, Vic: The Congregation of the Blessed Sacrament in Australia, 2007), 7.

12 Oratorians are priests who, after the example of St Philip Neri, form communities for particular apostolic service. They are not a religious order but have over the years formed a confederation with other groups of Oratorians.
13 The devotion of the Niine First Fridays had its origin in the apparitions of Christ holding his heart as an expression of God's love to Margaret Mary Alacoque at Paray-le-Monial, France, in 1673–1675, the aftermath of the European Wars of Religion.
14 The Society of Mary was approved as a religious congregation by Rome in 1836, with Jean-Claude Colin as its Superior-General.
15 John A Hardon, *With Us Today: On the Real Presence of Jesus Christ in the Eucharist* (Ave Maria, Florida: Sapientia Press, 2001), 141.
16 Julian Woods, *A Guide to Confession and First Communion* (Sydney: Louis Gille & Co, 1875), 32.
17 Woods, *A Guide . . . Communion,* 15.
18 Woods, *A Guide . . . Communion,* 15–16.
19 Jan Tranter RSJ. Her paper prepared for presentation at World Youth Day 2008 at Mary MacKillop Place, North Sydney shows that of the first 25 Sisters of Perpetual Adoration (1874–1902), 20 were either born in Ireland or had Irish-born parents.
20 James Quinn (1819–1881) was born in County Clare in Ireland. After studies for the priesthood at the Irish College in Rome, he was ordained in 1845. He was appointed Bishop of Brisbane in 1859 and arrived in Australia two years later.
21 David Walker, 'The French Influence', in *Australasian Catholic Record*, 55/1 (1978): 35.

Chapter One

1 The Feast of the Sacred Heart was fixed by Pope Pius IX in 1856 as nineteen days after Pentecost. The Sisters of Perpetual Adoration commemorate their founding day on 15 June, a strong oral tradition naming that day as the Feast of the Sacred Heart. However, in 1874 the Feast of the Sacred Heart was on Friday, 12 June. It could well be that the 12 June was the day when the three women arrived in Brisbane. In that case they would have stayed with the Sisters of St Joseph until they moved to their own premises.
2 Sister Clare was born Mary Wright in Portland, Victoria, on 10 January 1844. She entered the Sisters of St Joseph in Adelaide on 1 July 1867 and left the Institute in 1881.
3 Even though Anne's details including her birth date are unrecorded, her age was given as 65 years when she died on 30 July 1906. Sisters of Charity of Australia, Congregational Archives, Potts Point NSW.
4 Hugh M Laracy, *Marists and Melanesians A History of Catholic Missions in the Solomon Islands* (Canberra: Australian National University Press, 1976), 30. Angelo Ambrosoli was ordained in 1851. He left Milan in 1852 as a missionary of The Pontifical Institute for Foreign Missions, stationed on Rook Island in eastern Papua. In August 1855 Ambrosoli and his missionary companions returned to Sydney due to lack of success and illness. He convalesced with the Sisters of Charity from April to June 1856 and in August 1856, became chaplain to the Benedictine Sisters at Subiaco. In 1876, Father Ambrosoli returned to Potts Point to serve as chaplain to the Sisters of Charity and also as St Vincent's College chaplain, where he remained until the end of his life. He died at St Vincent's Convent on 11 May 1891. Sisters of Charity of Australia, Congregational Archives, Potts Point NSW.
5 There is one surviving letter between Father Woods and Father Ambrosoli inserted in a collection, 'Transcribed letters of Father Julian Woods and the first Sisters of Perpetual Adoration 1872–1896', 2A, Sisters of Perpetual Adoration Archives, Brisbane (SPAA). Here, Father Woods writes 'a few lines to ask your prayers' for his mission work in Queensland and for guidance in making decisions about his future.
6 Dympna McFadden RPA, 'Australia's Eucharistic Adorers, Brisbane, 1873–1974', typed manuscript, SPAA. The Gaffney family struggled financially and suffered from some anti-Catholic prejudice in the district. However, because Hugh was able to supplement the education his children received at the local government school with his own learning, most of the family went on to succeed very well in adulthood.

7 Transcribed letters of Father Julian Woods and the first Sisters of Perpetual Adoration 1872–1896, SPAA.

8 Julian Edmund Tenison Woods was born in Southwark, London, on 15 November, 1832. His parents came from Ireland—his mother, Henrietta St Eloy Tenison, the daughter of an Anglican clergyman, and his father, James Dominic, barrister and parliamentary reporter for *The Times*, originally from Cork. One of seven surviving children, Julian's upbringing was typical of the Victorian middle class. He attended schools for short periods but was otherwise tutored at home. Although the boys were baptised Catholics, there was no open display of religion in the family since the effects of the Emancipation Act of 1829 were barely being felt at the time. After his mother's death in 1847, Julian came under the influence of Father Frederick Oakeley and took on the practice of the Catholic faith in earnest, leading to studies for the priesthood—see Prologue.

9 The Catholic diocese of Brisbane was established in 1859, the same year that Queensland become a colony. It was made an archdiocese in 1887 with Robert Dunne its first archbishop. William O'Shea, in 'Building a Diocese: James Quinn, Bishop of Brisbane, 1859–1881' in *Good Shepherds 1859–2009: The Catholic Bishops of Brisbane* (Brisbane, Brisbane Archdiocesan Archives, 2009), 1–28, gives the following details: Bishop James Quinn (1819–1881) was born at Rathbawn, County Kildare in Ireland. He arrived in Australia in 1861, having been appointed as Bishop of the new diocese of Brisbane in 1859.

10 Transcribed letters . . ., 13 May 1873.

11 Mary MacKillop had been born in Melbourne of Scottish immigrants in Melbourne on 15 January, 1842. In 1861 she was governess to the children of Margaret and Alexander Cameron of Penola, and it was here that she heard Julian Woods describe his hopes for an order of Sisters whose way of life would enable them to serve those who would otherwise never have an education, given poor circumstances and geographic isolation.

12 Julian Eymard (1811–1868) left the Marist Fathers to found the Congregation of the Blessed Sacrament in 1856. Two years later he and Marguerite Guillot established the Servants of the Blessed Sacrament, a contemplative congregation for women. He was canonised by Pope John XIII in 1962.

13 Anne Bulger (comp.), *Memoirs of Reverend J E Tenison Woods*, dictated by Julian Woods. Anne was a former Sister of St Joseph who lived with the group who cared for Fr Woods at Elizabeth Street, Sydney, during the years of his infirmity 1887–1889.

14 Transcribed letters . . . 13 January 1873

15 Transcribed letters . . . 13 May 1873.

16 Transcribed letters . . . undated, 1873.

17 Transcribed letters . . . 14 July 1873.

18 In these early days of Queensland settlement, housing was scarce. Added to that was a certain prejudice. Julian Woods had explained the situation in a letter to the women on 3 December 1873: 'My great difficulty here is to find a house. You know Brisbane is a small place with a rapidly increasing population, and houses are not to be had. There was one near here vacant last week and the man kept me waiting for four or five days as he did not want to let it for nuns, and then when he got another tenant, he threw me over.' (Transcribed letters, SPAA).

19 Julian wrote this rule while he was giving a mission at Mackay in Queensland in February 1873.

20 'Practices', SPAA.

21 Transcribed letters . . . 23 June 1874. TM Boland, on page 45 of his book *Quiet Women* (Deception Bay, Qld: Refulgence Publishers, 1974), suggests the woman was Mrs Young, a woman who had cared for Julian during one of his bouts of illness. However, the friendship did not last, which might explain the lack of follow-up in this instance.

22 Bridget was born in Ireland on 1 February 1859 and had come to Queensland with her parents, Thomas Lillis and Margaret Maloney. They had settled on a farm at Gympie.

23 John Stuart and Deborah Beach married in 1851. John died on 17 January 1877 and is buried in the Toowong Cemetery. Ancestry.com.

24 Reminisces of Miss Ellen Gertrude Connolly, SPAA. Cited by TP Boland, *Quiet Women*, 86.

25 McFadden, 'Australia's Eucharistic Adorers'.
26 This name—the House of Mary—was a common name for the houses of the Marist Fathers to whom Julian had belonged and one that aptly expressed his devotion to Mary, the mother of Jesus.
27 In a letter to the three women in Sydney on 3 June 1873, Father Woods suggested that they should 'practise' the rule he was sending them, 'or at least learn it until Sister M. Ignatius should come to Brisbane with me. . . . I hardly think I shall be able to be with you until at least the middle of July or perhaps a little later, but there is no great hurry as we can't do much until Sister M. Ignatius arrives from Adelaide.'.
28 George O'Neill, *Life of the Reverend Julian Edmund Tenison Woods* (Sydney: Pellegrini & Co, 1929), 371.
29 Transcribed letters . . . 13 May 1873
30 Transcribed letters . . . 24 August 1878.
31 Mary MacKillop to Sister Josephine McMullen, 11 June 1877, St Joseph's Archives, Kensington, South Australia (SJASA).
32 Minutes of Council Meeting, Sisters of St Joseph, 2 April, 1879. SJASA. Mary Anne Fox was born in Dublin on 14 April 1844, the daughter of Patrick and Catherine. She was professed as a Sister of St Joseph in Adelaide in October 1870 and left on 4 June, 1879.
33 'Section 2: 'Of the Houses', *Rules and Constitutions of the Congregation of the Blessed Sacrament,* composed by Julian Woods, 1873, SPAA.
34 Anne Lafferty was admitted to the Sisters of Charity on 2 February 1882. She was professed on 10 July 1884 and took the name Sister Mary Bonaventure. She died on 30 July 1906. Ellen Connolly was admitted to the Sisters of Charity on 24 February 1881. She was professed on 14 July 1883 and took the name Sister Mary de Pazzi. She died on 24 October 1925. Sisters of Charity of Australia, Congregational Archives, Potts Point NSW.
35 McFadden, 'Australia's Eucharistic Adorers'.
36 Transcribed letters . . . 26 August 1880.
37 Transcribed letters . . . 28 August 1880
38 These were Emily Francis (Sister Gabriel), and Bridget Donoghue (Sister Michael). Both were to die young—Sister Gabriel on 9 Jun 1888 and Sister Michael 27 May 1892

Chapter Two

1 Dympna McFadden RPA, 'Australia's Eucharistic Adorers, Brisbane, 1873–1974', typed manuscript, Sisters of Perpetual Adoration Archives, Brisbane (SPAA).
2 McFadden, 'Australia's Eucharistic Adorers'.
3 Reminiscences of Sister Josephine Leavy, SPAA and Brisbane Archdiocesan Archives (BAA). Sister Josephine, (Mary Leavy) was born in Ireland on 15 August 1861. Her family settled in Townsville, Queensland, and she entered the Sisters of Perpetual Adoration on 6 May 1882. Evidently she was telling this 1881 story as it had been handed on to her by the first Sisters. She died on 24 March 1955
4 McFadden, 'Australia's Eucharistic Adorers'.
5 Transcribed letters of Father Julian Woods and the first Sisters of Perpetual Adoration 1872–1896, SPAA.
6 Bridget McGrath was born in Tipperary, Ireland in December 1853. She died on 15 November 1937.
7 It was well-known that Bishop Quinn was overbearing in his dealings with the Sisters of St Joseph and the Sisters of Mercy at that time. Indeed, Mary MacKillop had withdrawn the Sisters of St Joseph from Queensland in 1879, as the Bishop would not compromise in his ideas about the funding of schools and the Sisters' own governance, both of which clashed with their rule,
8 Transcribed letters . . . 1 October 1881.
9 Transcribed letters . . . 27 November 1881.

10 Neil Byrne, in 'What is Becoming of the People? Robert Dunne, Archbishop of Brisbane, 1882–1917' in *Good Shepherds 1859–2009: The Catholic Bishops of Brisbane* (Brisbane: Brisbane Archdiocesan Archives, 2009), 29–49, gives the following details: Robert Dunne (1826–1917) was born in Lismore, County Waterford in Ireland. He was ordained at the age of 24 and arrived in Brisbane in December 1864.
11 Transcribed letters . . . 17 April 1882.
12 McFadden, 'Australia's Eucharistic Adorers'.
13 Transcribed letters . . . 4 March 1882.
14 See note 3.
15 The only detail about Sister Clare (Bridget Hayes) written in the Register of Professions of the Sisters of Perpetual Adoration is that she died on 21 April 1883. In Father Tom Boland's book *Quiet Women* (Deception Bay Qld: Refulgence Publishers, 1974), 51, we learn that she had been advised by Father Woods in Tasmania of his intention to found the Sisters and had come to Brisbane in 1873 but had only joined the group seven years later. Similarly, the only detail in the Profession Register about 'Miss Oliver' (Sister Mary Clare) who entered in May after the death of Bridget Hayes, is that she died on 12 May 1891.
16 Reminiscences of Sister Josephine Leavy, SPAA, BAA.
17 McFadden, 'Australia's Eucharistic Adorers'.
18 McFadden, 'Australia's Eucharistic Adorers'. Sir Charles Lilley (1827–1897) was elected for Fortitude Valley to Queensland's first Legislative Assembly. He was Queensland's fourth premier 1868–1871. His wife, Sarah (1841–1902) was well-known as a philanthropist and suffragist.
19 Canon 589 states that a diocesan religious congregation is one that is approved by a local bishop and is answerable to him. A religious congregation that is of pontifical rite is one that is approved by the Vatican. Any group who wishes to establish a religious congregation must get diocesan approval first of all. When and if the group becomes stabilised and has sufficient numbers (generally over 40), they may, if they wish, apply for pontifical approval. Mary MacKillop did this for the Sisters of St Joseph.
20 Neil Byrne, in 'What is Becoming of the People', 35, says that Bishop-elect Dunne arrived back in Brisbane in March 1882. In his biography *Robert Dunne: Archbishop of Brisbane 1830–1917* (St Lucia: University of Queensland Press, 1991): 129, Byrne says that previous to this, Dunne was hesitant about accepting the appointment and that he spent a time of retreat at the seminary in Bathurst to decide. Julian Woods was in Bathurst at the same time and, claims the author, 'Dunne's conversations with Woods may have caused him to reconsider the Brisbane mitre, for Woods was able to provide the first really unbiased account of the ecclesiastical climate of the north.'
21 Mother Philomena Callaghan RPA, 'Sisters of Perpetual Adoration, "Villa Maria", Brisbane', 1952, SPPA. Sister Philomena entered the Sisters of Perpetual Adoration on 15 August 1906. She served as Mother General from 1932–38 and 1944–55. She died 24 August 1955.
22 Transcribed letters . . . 28 November 1882.
23 Frederick Aloysius Weld (1823–1891), born in England, was Governor of Tasmania from 1875 to 1880, so Julian would have known him then. Weld held various government posts for the United Kingdom in Oceania and South East Asia, and offered his invitation to Julian while he was Governor of the Straits Settlements and living at Government House, Singapore. See T. S. Loch, 'Sir Frederick Aloysius Weld (1823–1891)', *Australian Dictionary of Biography*, <https://adb.anu.edu.au/biography/weld-sir-frederick-aloysius-4829> accessed 25 June 2024.
24 Transcribed letters . . . 20 March 1885.
25 Transcribed letters . . . 14 December 1883.
26 Transcribed letters . . . 15 October 1884.
27 Transcribed letters . . . 14 December 1883.

28 Transcribed letters . . . 16 January, 1886.
29 Transcribed letters . . . 20 March 1885.
30 Transcribed letters . . . 20 March 1885.
31 The Northern Territory was part of South Australia from 1863 to 1911, when it was transferred to the control of the Federal Government. A Catholic Mission had been established in Darwin in 1882 by four Jesuits.
32 In her book *Song of Seasons* (Wollongong: Sisters of Perpetual Adoration, 1996), 169, Carmel Doherty RPA notes that Julian telegraphed his 'Report on Geology and Mineralogy of Northen Territory' and that the press described this as 'the longest telegram ever transmitted via the overland line'—the work comprising more than 21,000 words.
33 Jan Tranter RSJ, 'Memories of Fr Julian Tenison Woods, shared at Villa Maria, Brisbane, a century after the founder's death': Interview with Sr Dympna McFarlane quoting Sr Josephine Leavy, SPAA.
34 Tranter, 'Memories of Fr Julian Tenison Woods . . .'.
35 Sarah Meagher (Sister Maria Joseph) was born in Ireland on 15 April 1861. With their parents, Daniel and Annie, the family migrated to Australia in 1883. Sarah died 7 July 1955.
36 Annie Shannahan (Sister Mary Baptist) was born in County Tipperary, Ireland, on 5 May 1862. She died on 7 October 1919.
37 Book of Instructions, 'The Month of St Joseph', incorrectly dated 29.2.87 (the year was not a leap-year), SSPA.
38 Julian Woods, letter to Sarah Woods, 15 March 1887, SSPA.
39 Anticipating his arrival, the group had moved to a 13-roomed house at 533 Elizabeth Street, Paddington, Sydney, setting aside three rooms comfortably furnished for Father Woods.
40 As the Catholic population of the diocese was now large, as was the city of Brisbane itself, the diocese was proclaimed an archdiocese on 10 May 1887. Consequently, Bishop Dunne was now Archbishop.
41 McFadden, 'Australia's Eucharistic Adorers'.
42 Transcribed letters . . . 30 May 1887.
43 Transcribed letters . . . 19 July 1887.
44 Transcribed letters . . . 17 October 1887.
45 Transcribed letters . . . 29 June 1887.
46 *Memoirs of Reverend J E Tenison-Woods*, dictated to Miss Anne Bulger, SPAA.
47 Terry died on 30 June 1887 and his funeral took place on 4 July.
48 Anne Player RSJ editor, *The Archer Letters: Letters of Julian Tenison Woods to William Henry Archer*, (North Goulburn: Sisters of St Joseph, 1983): Letter no. 30, 3 January 1888. William Henry Archer (1825–1909) was born in London. He migrated to Australia and served as a politician and public servant in Melbourne. He and Julian were friends and corresponded for many years on personal, scientific and religious matters.
49 Transcribed letters . . . Undated, 1888.
50 McFadden, 'Australia's Eucharistic Adorers'.
51 George O'Neill, *Life of the Reverend Julian Edmund Tenison Woods* (Sydney, Pellegrini & Co, 1929), 388.
52 McFadden, 'Australia's Eucharistic Adorers'.
53 Transcribed letters . . . 26 April 1889.
54 Mary Dinan was born in County Clare in Ireland on 13 May 1865, daughter of William and Mary. She died on 16 July 1939.
55 Byrne, 'What is Becoming of the People?', 44.
56 Joseph Canali was born in Rome, Italy on 15 December 1841 and died in Brisbane on 15 August 1915.
57 *Catholic Leader* 21 August 2015.
58 See Note 59.

59 The term '*ad limina*' is used for the regular visits that a bishop must make to Rome (at present, every five years, according to Canon 399) where he prays at the tombs of Sts Peter and Paul and meets with the Pope and other Vatican officials to give a detailed report on the state of the diocese.

60 It is not surprising that Father Woods' Constitution was not accepted by Rome, as it was almost the same as what he had written for the Sisters of St Joseph. When Mary MacKillop took this Constitution to Rome in 1873 it had been re-written by the Roman authorities.

61 Edmund Vaughan (1827–1908), born in Herefordshire, England, was the uncle of Cardinal Roger Vaughan who was Archbishop of Sydney from 1877 to 1883.

62 George Buckeridge SJ was born in Dublin in January 1842. In 1886 he came to Melbourne, giving retreats to different groups all over Australia. He died at 'Manresa', Norwood (suburb of Adelaide) on 30 October 1904.

63 Archives list, 'Jesuit Priests Known to the Community', SPAA. The top slope of Fortitude Valley is Spring Hill where the Sisters of Perpetual Adoration are located.

64 Archives list, 'Jesuit Priests Known to the Community'.

65 Mary McNulty (Sister Juliana) was born in County Donegal, Ireland, on 3 June 1868. She entered the Sisters of Perpetual Adoration on 17 January 1893, and died on 10 February 1939. Catherine Breen (Sister Michael) was born in Tasmania, and was a sister of Sarah (Sister Mary Joseph), one of the founding members of the group whom Father Woods had sent from Tasmania. Sister Michael entered in July 1893 and died on 2 August 1907.

Chapter Three

1 The Dominican Sisters of North Adelaide were invited to establish a community in the diocese of Adelaide with the approval of Bishop Reynolds. Six sisters arrived in Adelaide in 1883. They intended to open a hospital, but when this did not eventuate, they opened a school for girls instead—St Dominic's Girls Priory College which still operates on the North Adelaide site. See Stephanie Burley and Katherine Teague (editors), *Chapel, Cloister and Classroom: Reflections on the Dominican Sisters at North Adelaide* (Adelaide: Lutheran Publishing House, 1993), 14–15.

2 The Poor Servants of the Mother of God were founded in London in 1869. Tom Boland, *Quiet Women* (Deception Bay Qld: Refulgence Publishers, 1974): 281, has the travellers staying with the Poor Servants of the Mother of God in England on their way to Dublin. However, Dympna McFadden RPA, 'History of the Foundation of the Sisters of Perpetual Adoration 1874' SPAA, says that it was on their return trip that they stayed with the Sisters, this time in Rome. Both circumstances could be the case.

3 Since 2019, because of falling number, the Sisters of Perpetual Adoration of Wexford have relocated to smaller accommodation at the St John of God convent. The Bride Street convent now provides accommodation for international students.

4 'Transcribed letters of Father Julian Woods and the first Sisters of Perpetual Adoration 1872–1896', Sisters of Perpetual Adoration Archives (SPAA).

5 *Rules and Constitutions of the Congregation of the Blessed Sacrament*, 1873, V. 'Of Employments', SPAA.

6 *Rules and Constitutions* . . . I. 'Objects of the Congregation'.

7 *Rules and Constitutions* . . . II. 'Of the House'.

8 *Rules and Constitutions* . . . XII. 'Of Novices'.

9 *Constitutions of the Congregation of the Perpetual Adoration of the Most Blessed Sacrament,* Wexford, Diocese of Ferns, Chapter IX. 'Concerning the Vows and Aids Towards Their Observance', SPAA.

10 The Poor Servants of the Mother of God opened the Mater Dei convent in Rome in 1886. It was closed in 2023.

11 Sisters' Reminiscences, collected by Dympna McFadden RPA, 1973, SPAA.

12 Sisters' Reminiscences.

13 Margaret Mary was born in County Limerick in Ireland on 13 August 1868. She died in Brisbane on 21 April 1953.
14 Sisters' Reminiscences.
15 Reminiscences of Sister Josephine Leavy, SPAA and Brisbane Archdiocesan Archives (BAA).
16 Bridget Meagher (Sister Berchmans) was born in County Tipperary on 16 December 1877, daughter to John (farmer) and Mary (nee Ryan). She entered on 13 January 1898 and died on 8 March 1963.
17 Dympna McFadden RPA, 'Australia's Eucharistic Adorers, Brisbane, 1873–1974', SPAA.
18 Thomas L Dunphy CSsR, *An Australian Mustard Seed: The Sisters of Perpetual Adoration*, (publication details not given on the booklet).
19 'Reminiscences of Father William McGoldrick' SPAA. According to an article in the Toowoomba Diocesan publication *Horizons* Feb 17, 2017, Fr McGoldrick (1889–1975) served at St Stephen's Cathedral after his ordination in 1912. In 1923 he went to China with the Columban Fathers and returned to Australia in 1951. Cunnamulla is a town about 750 kilometres west of Brisbane.
20 Mother Philomena Callaghan RPA, 'Sisters of Perpetual Adoration, "Villa Maria", Brisbane', SPAA.
21 Mother Stanislaus' Diary, SPAA.
22 Dympna McFadden RPA, 'History of the Foundation of the Sisters of Perpetual Adoration 1874', Typed manuscript 1990, SPAA.
23 Dympna McFadden RPA, 'Interview with Mrs Nancy Tiernan, 1973', SPAA.
24 Dympna McFadden RPA, 'Interview with Father Frank Masterson, 1964', SPAA. Sister Dympna writes, 'These notes were written in August 1964. Father was almost 85 years of age, with a mind as clear as a bell.'
25 William Maher, an Irish emigrant, first established himself as a baker in Wickham Street Fortitude Valley in 1877. He was very successful, by 1886 supplying the needs of the Brisbane General Hospital and the Blind, Deaf and Dumb Institute. He was made a Justice of the Peace in 1898. <https://heritage.brisbane.qld.gov.au/heritage-places/762#:~:text=Maher%20rose%20to%20the%20top,the%20peace%20in%20the%20Valley> accessed 2 May 2024.
26 Dympna McFadden RPA, 'History of the Foundation of the Sisters of Perpetual Adoration 1874' and 'Interview with Father Frank Masterson', SPAA.
27 *Age*, 1 July 1899, 9, Brisbane Archdiocesan Archives. BAA.
28 An Edward J. Corbett, solicitor, who had his office in the Australian Chambers, Queen Street at this time and it is likely that he was the 'Mr Corbett' who was so good to the Sisters of Perpetual Adoration. He remained a true trusted friend until his death when the Sisters learned he had left his home and possessions to them.
29 McFadden, 'History of the Foundation . . . '.
30 Anthony Innocent Keenan CFC, 'My Recollections of Villa Maria, St Paul's Terrace, Brisbane', SPAA.
31 McFadden, 'History of the Foundation . . .'.
32 Jan Tranter RSJ, Interview with Fr Tom Cruice CSsR (1912–2013), a grandson of William Maher. The *Age* reports the donation of the 'handsome marble altar' in its 18 February 1905 edition, 6.
33 McFadden, 'History of the Foundation . . .'.
34 McFadden, 'History of the Foundation . . .'.
35 Mother Philomena Callaghan RPA, 'Sisters of Perpetual Adoration, "Villa Maria", Brisbane', SPAA.
36 The word Loretto (or Loreto) is associated with a 13th-century legend which has angels transporting the childhood home of Mary from Nazareth to Loreto in Ancona Province, Italy.
37 Victoria Park (its Turrbal name Barrambin) is a heritage-listed park located in Spring Hill/Herston, Brisbane. Prior to colonisation, it was a traditional meeting place for cultural gathering of the indigenous peoples.
38 Reminiscences of Father Frank Masterson, 1964, SPAA.
39 Reminiscences of Sister Josephine Leavy, SPAA.
40 *Age*, 28 May 1904, 7.
41 *Age*, 27 November 1909, 10.

42 Julian Woods, Letter to the Sisters 19 March 1885, 'Transcribed letters of Father Julian Woods and the first Sisters of Perpetual Adoration 1872–1896', SPAA.
43 Mother Stanislaus' talk, 'Feast of Mother's Presentation, 21st November 1891'. SPAA.
44 'Antonnia' was the name given to another cottage the Sisters had purchased.
45 *Age*, 22 November 1913, 10.
46 Dympna McFadden RPA, 'Mother Mary Stanislaus (Gaffney)', collation of memories from various Sisters, 1976, SPAA.
47 McFadden, 'Mother Mary Stanislaus (Gaffney)'.
48 Boland, *Quiet Women*, 91.

Chapter Four

1 Sisters' Reminiscences, collected by Dympna McFarlane RPA, 1973, Sisters of Perpetual Adoration Archives (SPAA).
2 T. P. Boland, 'Irish and Australia: James Duhig, Archbishop of Brisbane, 1917–65' in *Good Shepherds 1859–2009: The Catholic Bishops of Brisbane*, (Brisbane: Brisbane Archdiocesan Archives, 2009), 49–71, gives the following details: Archbishop James Duhig, 1871–1965, was born in Ireland. Before being appointed coadjutor bishop of Brisbane he was Bishop of the Rockhampton diocese in Queensland, his consecration taking place in 1905 when he was only thirty-four years old.
3 The *Curé d'Ars* was a nintenth century French priest, Jean Marie Vianney (1786–1859) who struggled to obtain the education required to be ordained priest but who, while serving as pastor (*curé*) of the parish of Ars, France, became renowned for his holiness, humility and care of the poor. He was canonised in 1925.
4 James Byrne was born in Ireland in 1870 and after ordination volunteered for the Brisbane Archdiocese. In 1929 he was consecrated as the first Bishop of Toowoomba. He died in 1938.
5 *Age*, 21 August 1915, 8, Brisbane Archdiocesan Archives (BAA). Cited by Patrick Tynan, *The Apostle of Brisbane: A Biography of Fr Joseph Augustine Canali* (Toowoomba: Church Activists' Press, 1992), 110.
6 *Age*, 4 November 1916, 7. Catherine Mary Fitzgibbon was born in Ireland and migrated to Queensland with her family in 1853. She married Joseph Bragg in 1864.
7 *Age*, 1 December 1917, 9.
8 Dympna McFadden RPA, 'Interview with Father Frank Masterson, 1964', SPAA.
9 *Age*, 5 October 1918, 5.
10 Reminiscences of Rev W McGoldrick, SPAA.
11 'Jesuit Priests Known to the Community', SPAA. Richard Murphy was born in Ireland in 1875. He was the first parish priest of Toowong, Brisbane. He died in Sydney in 1957, Jesuit Archives, Melbourne (JAM)
12 'Jesuit Priests Known to the Community'. John Roney was born in Ireland in 1856. He died in Sydney in 1931, JAM.
13 *Age*, 29 July 1916, 6. Robert Little was born in Canada in 1885. He died in Brisbane in 1933, JAM.
14 Reminiscences of Rev W McGoldrick. 'Exposition' refers to the placing of the Host consecrated during Mass into a Monstrance, a vessel with a glass opening which allows the Host to be exposed for adoration by the congregation.
15 Thomas L Dunphy CSsR, *An Australian Mustard Seed: The Sisters of Perpetual Adoration,* BAA.
16 Archbishop Duhig to Mother Maria Joseph, 20 December 1920, SPAA.
17 Archbishop Bonaventura Cerretti (1872–1933) was born in Italy and became the first Apostolic Delegate to Australia in 1914.
18 Archbishop Bartolomeo Cattaneo (1866–1943) was born in Italy and served as Apostolic Delegate to Australia from 1917 to 1933.
19 Archbishop Cattaneo to Father John Roney SJ, 13 January 2921, SPAA.
20 William Lockington was born in Ireland in 1871, He died in Brisbane in 1948, JAM. He had given a retreat to the Sisters of Perpetual Adoration in June 1919 (*Age*, 28 June 1919, 1) and at the end of July 1921 (*Age*, 23 July 1921, 1).

21 Ellen Callaghan was born at Mount Walker, Queensland in 1879 and entered the Sisters of Perpetual Adoration in 1906, taking the religious name of Philomena. She was elected as Mother General in 1932.She died in 1955.
22 Mother Philomena Callaghan RPA, 'Sisters of Perpetual Adoration, "Villa Maria", Brisbane', SPAA.
23 Anthony Innocent Keenan CFC, 'My Recollections of Villa Maria, St Paul's Terrace, Brisbane', SPAA.
24 Joseph Gates SJ was born in Ireland in 1889 and died in Sydney in 1947, JAM.
25 Joseph Gates SJ, 'The Sisters of Perpetual Adoration, Brisbane', undated typed manuscript, SPAA.
26 In his book *Quiet Women* (Deception Bay Qld: Refulgence Publishers, 1974), 304, Thomas Boland names this priest as Father Dorrigan, Parish Priest of South Brisbane. But as Father Dorrigan had died in 1919, this could not have been the case. The lead article in the *Age*, 26 July 1919, 1, gives the account of the death of Father Francis Dorrigan, St Mary's, South Brisbane, and states that the Sisters of Perpetual Adoration visited him during his last illness.
27 Philippa Barker RPA, 'The Story of the Sisters of Perpetual Adoration', 2008, SPAA.
28 T. P Boland, 'Irish and Australian: James Duhig, Archbishop of Brisbane, 1917–65', 57.
29 The architectural firm 'Hennessy and Hennessy' was established in Sydney in 1912. During Archbishop Duhig's administration of the Brisbane Archdiocese, they were responsible for the erection of many significant Church buildings.
30 Dympna McFadden RPA, 'History of the Foundation of the Sisters of Perpetual Adoration 1874', 1990, SPAA
31 *Age*, 12 February 1921, 5
32 Barker, 'The Story of the Sisters of Perpetual Adoration'.
33 Dympna McFadden RPA, 'Australia's Eucharistic Adorers, Brisbane, 1873–1974', SPAA.
34 *Age*, 21 November 1925, 7.
35 *Age*, 14 July 1923, 8.
36 *Age*, 27 September 1923, 7.
37 Sister Mary Teresa (Jean Inverarity) was born in Tasmania in 1889. She died on 10 April 1927. Sisters make temporary profession for up to six years before their Final Profession.
38 Excerpt typed from *The Age*, 15 April 1927, page not recorded, SPAA. Original edition now extant.
39 *Age*, 27 August 1927, 1.
40 *Age*, 10 September1927, 7.
41 *Age*, 23 June 1928, 5.
42 *Catholic Advocate,* 7 June 1928, 26, SPAA.
43 *Age*, 9 June 1928, 1.
44 Mother Philomena Callaghan RPA, 'Sisters of Perpetual Adoration, "Villa Maria", Brisbane', SPAA.
45 Gates, 'The Sisters of Perpetual Adoration, Brisbane'.

Chapter Five

1 Carmel Black, 'Depression Era' in *Queensland Historical Atlas*, <https://www.qhatlas.com.au/content/era> accessed 5 July 2024.
2 Appeal Letter, 1933, Sisters of Perpetual Adoration Archives (SPAA).
3 Dympna McFadden RPA, 'Reminiscences of the Early Sisters', SPAA. Sister Mary Paul (Mary Baggot) entered the Sisters of Perpetual Adoration in 1915 and died in 1938.
4 Thomas L Dunphy CSsR, *An Australian Mustard Seed: The Sisters of Perpetual Adoration*, 4–6.
5 'Reminiscence of Villa Maria', author unknown, SPAA.
6 McFadden, 'Reminiscences of the Early Sisters'.
7 Dympna McFadden RPA, 'Resumé of 100 years', 1974, SPAA.
8 Sister Philomena (Callaghan) to Mr Blake, 22 March 1928, SPAA.

9 Mother Philomena Callaghan RPA, 'Sisters of Perpetual Adoration, "Villa Maria", Brisbane', SPAA.
10 *Catholic Leader,* 28 July 1932.
11 McFadden, 'Reminiscences of the Early Sisters'. Bridget McGrath was born in Ireland and migrated to Australia with her family. She entered the Sisters of Perpetual Adoration in 1881 (see Chapter 1) and died on 15 November 1937.
12 McFadden, 'Reminiscences of the Early Sisters'.
13 Samuel Hunter was born in Belfast, Ireland, on 29 April 1901. After serving as a priest on the African missions he came to Brisbane in 1935. He died on 25 September 1970 after many years of service in the Brisbane Archdiocese.
14 Dympna McFadden RPA, 'Australia's Eucharistic Adorers, Brisbane, 1874–1974', SPAA.
15 Archbishop Giovanni Panico was appointed Apostolic Delegate to Australasia in November 1935. He played an important role in the pastoral care and repatriation of Italian Prisoners of War in Australia. After thirteen years of service in Australia, he was appointed papal nuncio to Peru in October 1948.
16 The section of Leichhardt Street along the ridge of Spring Hill had been officially renamed St Paul's Terrace in the mid-1930s. St Paul's Presbyterian Church, opened in 1889, was a prominent architectural feature of the area.
17 *Catholic Leader,* 15 August 1940, SPAA.
18 *Catholic Leader,* 15 August 1940.
19 McFadden, 'Resumé of 100 years'.
20 *Catholic Leader,* 3 August 1944, 11. Mrs Marian Moore (nee Walker), widow of James Moore, migrated from Newfoundland, Canada, to Brisbane in 1901.She died at Villa Maria on 30 July 1944.
21 *Brisbane Truth,* 23 Jan 1944, 19, <http://nla.gov.au/nla.news-article203756261> accessed 2 June 2024
22 Dympna McFadden RPA, 'Collation of Memories from Various Sisters: Sister Mary John (Lillis)', 1976, SPAA.
23 *Catholic Leader,* 20 May 1943, 10.
24 Archbishop Duhig to Mother Maria Joseph, 15 June 1943, SPAA.
25 McFadden, 'Resumé of 100 years'.
26 McFadden, 'Australia's Eucharistic Adorers'.
27 McFadden, 'Australia's Eucharistic Adorers'.
28 Interview, Gabrielle Power-West, 23 November 2023.
29 Dunphy, *An Australian Mustard Seed: The Sisters of Perpetual Adoration.*
30 The epidemic lasted well into the 1950s. In the year 2000 Australia was declared free of poliomyelitis.
31 *Catholic Leader,* 19 June 1947, 7.
32 Mother Philomena to Archbishop Duhig, 1 July 1947, BAA. The letter is addressed to the Archbishop at Chicago, Illinois. Despite nervousness about air travel, Archbishop Duhig returned to Australia after his visit to the United States. However, hardly had he done so as T. P. Boland points out in *James Duhig* (St Lucia: University of Queensland Press, 1986), 320, that he set out again for Europe and Ireland on 15 September 1947. Therefore there would have been very little time to resolve the matters brought up by Mother Philomena.
33 'Proposals for Establishment of Xavier Catholic Home for Crippled Children and Management Thereof', Clause 10, BAA.
34 Archbishop Panico to Mother Philomena, 11 September 1946, SPAA.
35 The Congregation for the Propagation of the Faith was involved because, at this point, Australia was still regarded as a 'missionary country'.
36 Archbishop Panico to Mother Philomena, 31 October 1947, SPAA.
37 McFadden, 'Resumé of 100 Years'. Lillian Gertrude Donnelly of Mitchell, Queensland, took the Religious name of Sister Immaculata. She was born in 1912 and died in 1976. Sister Gerard (Margaret Dolan) was born in Mullumbimby, NSW m 1917 and died in 1979; Sister Michael (Mary Brosnan) was born in Toowoomba, Qld, in 1916 and died in 2002. The announcement by the Archbishop of Papal Approbation was recorded in the *Catholic Leader* on 18 January 1948, 1.

Chapter Six

1 *Catholic Leader*, 19 May 1949, 4.
2 Edward Michael Hanlon (1887–1952) was born in Brisbane of Irish migrant parents and served as Premier of Queensland from 1946 until his death. See Douglas Blackmur, 'Edward Michael (Ned) Hanlon (1887–1952)', the *Australian Dictionary of Biography,*<https://adb.anu.edu.au/biography/hanlon-edward-michael-ned-10411> accessed 5 June 2024.
3 *Catholic Leader*, 27 October 1949, 8. Archbishop Paul Marella served as Apostolic Delegate to Australia, New Zealand and Oceania from 1948 to 1953.
4 Sister Augustine (Elizabeth Dobie) was born in Scotland in 1885 and entered the Sisters of Perpetual Adoration in September 1914. She died on 28 April 1974. Sister Cordelia (Elizabeth Constable) was born in 1914 and entered in 1932. She died in 1997. Sister Matthew (Alice Ives) was born in 1921 and entered in 1943. She died in 1992.
5 Dympna McFadden RPA, 'Resumé of 100 years', 1974, Sisters of Perpetual Adoration Archives (SPAA).
6 Minutes of the Meeting of the Executive of the Xavier Home for Crippled Children, 15 November 1949, BAA.
7 McFadden, 'Resumé of 100 years'.
8 The Franciscan Missionaries of Mary were founded in India in 1877 by Hélène de Chappotin (1839–1904). There they provided medical care to women who, because of the practice of *purdah* segregating women from men, were unable to have contact with male doctors. They quickly spread around the world, and today offer a variety of services to women and children.
9 McFadden, 'Resumé of 100 years'.
10 Ipswich, now a city, is situated on the Bremer River about 40 kilometres south-west of Brisbane. It is part of the Archdiocese of Brisbane.
11 Dr John Flynn was born in Ipswich in 1870, and died from influenza in 1919, after serving for 25 years on the hospital's surgical staff (*Queensland Times,* 26 February 1920, 6).
12 TP Boland, *Quiet Women* (Deception Bay Qld: Refulgence Publishers, 1974), 317.
13 Sister Aloysius (Jessie Wallis) was born in 1920 and entered the Sisters of Perpetual Adoration in 1940. She died in 2017.
14 Monsignor Michael Baldwin was born in Waterford, Ireland, in 1872. He was parish priest of Ipswich from 1929 until his death on 27 June 1951.
15 Chris Hanlon's unpublished biography of Father Basil Bergin (1915–1969) records that he was assistant priest in the Ipswich parish from 1942 to 1951 and was appointed first parish priest of Ekibin in October that year, BAA.
16 McFadden, 'Resumé of 100 years'.
17 Bishop Patrick O'Donnell was, at the time, coadjutor to Archbishop Duhig. His consecration had taken place on 17 March 1949.In his article on Patrick O'Donnell in *Good Shepherds 1859–2009: The Catholic Bishops of Brisbane* (Brisbane: Brisbane Archdiocesan Archives, 2009), 73–94, DW Martin records that he was born in County Tipperary, Ireland, in 1897, the youngest of sixteen children. He succeeded as Archbishop of Brisbane when James Duhig died on 10 April 1965. He resigned as Archbishop when he turned seventy-five years of age in 1973 and died in November 1980.
18 McFadden, 'Resumé of 100 years'.
19 Diary of Sr Augustine Dobie RPA (incomplete), SPAA. The diary does not have daily entries and reads rather as a record with dates interspersed.
20 Diary of Sr Augustine Dobie.
21 Sister Gabriel (Aileen Moloney) was born on 18 February 1892 and entered the Sisters of Perpetual Adoration in January 1920. She was Mother General from 1955 until 1967 and died 17 September 1983. Sister Augustine (Elizabeth Dobie—See Endnote 4); Sister Stanislaus (Dorothy Ryan) was born in 1911, entered in 1933 and died in 1999; Sister Kevin (Mary Lewis) was born in 1911, entered in 1932 and died in 1997.

22 Letters to Archbishop Duhig, BAA. For example, in letters written in 1955 and 1956, two Sisters, unaware that others may have brought up the issue, complained about the factional nature of authority structures and the lack of transparency in leadership groups, noting unrest having been 'brewing' for years among ordinary Sisters.
23 Chris Hanlon, 'Robert John Flynn', unpublished biography, BAA: 'Robert John Flynn was born in Ipswich, on 23 February 1902; the son of Dr. & Mrs. John Flynn . . . He died in St Vincent's Hospital, Toowoomba, 22 July 1980.'
24 McFadden, 'Resumé of 100 years'
25 Diary of Sr Augustine Dobie.
26 Chris Hanlon, 'Timothy Molony', unpublished biography, BAA: 'Timothy Molony was born at Feakle, Co. Clare, Ireland, on 14 May 1891 . . . He served as parish priest of Ipswich from 1951 to 1975 . . . He died on 17 June 1976.'
27 Diary of Sr Augustine Dobie.
28 Diary of Sr Augustine Dobie.
29 Chris Hanlon, 'Denis Power', unpublished biography, BAA: 'Denis Power was born in Waterford, Ireland, on 4 March 1924 . . . He served at St Mary's Ipswich from 1951 to 1955 . . . He died on 23 December 2007.
30 McFadden, 'Resumé of 100 years'
31 *Queensland Times,* 30 June 1952, 2.
32 *Queensland Times,* 30 June 1952.
33 Diary of Sr Augustine Dobie.
34 Mother Philomena, 'Quinquennial Report to the Holy See', BAA.
35 Sister Eucharia (Margaret Mary Kingston) was born in 1910 and entered the Sisters of Perpetual Adoration in 1938. She died in the year 2000.
36 McFadden, 'Resumé of 100 years'.
37 Diary of Sr Augustine Dobie.
38 Diary of Sr Augustine Dobie.
39 *Queensland Times,* 26 October 1954, 2.
40 Jan Tranter RSJ, 'Memories of Father Woods—Interviews with Sister Dympna RPA and Other Sisters', 1986. Mary Leavy (Sr Josephine) was born in 1861 and entered the Sisters of Perpetual Adoration on 6 May 1882.
41 Julian Woods, 'Of Obedience' in *Rules and Constitutions of the Congregation of the Blessed Sacrament,* 1873, SPAA.
42 'Mother Maria Joseph', 'Reminiscences of Various Sisters', collected by Dympna McFadden, SPAA.
43 *Catholic Leader,* 1 September 1955, 6. The Holy Name Society is a lay confraternity that traces its beginnings to the early 15th century when members followed a rule laid down by the Spanish Dominican preacher Didacus of Victoria. It had its Australian foundation in Adelaide in 1921.
44 Woods, 'Objects of the Congregation' in *Rules and Constitutions of the Congregation of the Blessed Sacrament.*
45 McFadden, 'Resumé of 100 years'.

Chapter Seven

1 In the early 1900s, Mother Stanislaus had arranged for Sister Mary Magdalen (Mary Rafter, 1880–1958) to receive training in accountancy. She had held the role of Congregational Bursar for over twenty years when Sister Gabriel took her place.
2 The Catholic Women's League (CWL) was founded in England by Margaret Fletcher in 1906. Her aim was to provide a forum where educated Catholic women could bring a Catholic perspective to public affairs. The movement came to Adelaide in 1914 and soon spread to other Australian states. Within two decades, it had spread to most Commonwealth countries.

3 Kathleen Burrow MBE (1899–1987), a leading Catholic laywoman, had founded the Graham-Burrow School of Physical Education with her sister Anne in 1926. It served Catholic schools and institutions all over the country. Kathleen was president of the Catholic Women's League of Australia from 1957 to 1959.

4 The Poor Sisters of Mary were refugees from Hungary and came to Australia after World War II. In 1957, due to failing health in the group and unable to obtain new recruits for the work of managing Legion House, they decided to leave Sydney and join other Sisters of their Order who had established a community in Perth.

5 Cardinal Norman Gilroy (1896–1977) was consecrated bishop of Pt Augusta, South Australia, in 1934. Three years later he was appointed as coadjutor to the archbishop of Sydney, Michael Kelly. He became archbishop of Sydney in 1940. On 18 February 1946 Pope Pius XII named him cardinal, the first Australian-born so elevated. He resigned as archbishop in 1971. See T. P. Boland, 'Sir Norman Thomas Gilroy (1896–1977)' *Australian Dictionary of Biography*, <https://adb.anu.edu.au/biography/gilroy-sir-norman-thomas-10308> accessed 1 August 2024.

6 Sister Mary St Peter (Alice McAllister) was born in 1910 and entered the Sisters of Perpetual Adoration in 1938. She died in 1984. Sister Gerard (Margaret Mary Dolan) was born in 1917 and entered in 1942. She died in 1979. Sister Clement (Verna Thomas) was born in 1925 and entered in 1951. She died in 1995. Sister Gemma (Hazel Lincoln) was born in 1924 and entered in 1954. She died in 2013. Sister Immaculata (Lillian Donnelly) was born in 1912 and entered in 1942. She died 1976. Sister Angela (Elizabeth Turvey) was born in 1924 and entered in 1955. She died in 2016.

7 The Congregation of the Blessed Sacrament was founded by St Peter Julian Eymard in Paris, France, in 1856. The Blessed Sacrament Fathers arrived in Melbourne in 1929. In 1953 Cardinal Gilroy blessed and opened the Church of the Blessed Sacrament at their new monastery in Haymarket, Sydney. In 1964 the church was rebuilt and dedicated to St Peter Julian Eymard. See Damien Cash, *The Road to Emmaus: A History of the Blessed Sacrament Congregation in Australia* (Kew East, Vic.: The Congregation of the Blessed Sacrament in Australia, 2007).

8 Father Carmelo *Micallef* (1930–2015) came from Malta to the Archdiocese of *Brisbane in 1959).* He served as chaplain to Villa Maria from February 1960 to April 1965. Sisters of Perpetual Adoration Archives (SPAA).

9 Interview, Gabrielle Power-West, Brisbane, 23 November 2023.

10 *Catholic Leader*, 'Memorial Supplement', 15 April 1965, 31. See also T. P. Boland, 'Irish and Australia: James Duhig, Archbishop of Brisbane, 1917–65', *Good Shepherds 1859–2009: The Catholic Bishops of Brisbane* (Brisbane: Brisbane Archdiocesan Archives, 2009): 49–71.

11 Phillipa Barker RPA, 'The Story of the Sisters of Perpetual Adoration', Archivists' Conference, Brisbane, 2008, SPAA.

12 *Catholic Leader*, 22 July 1965, 5.

13 Dympna McFadden RPA, 'Resumé of 100 years', 1974, SPAA.

14 Father Jeremiah (Dermot) Hogan was born in Ireland in 1903. He died in Melbourne, Australia, in 1986.

15 Denis W. Martin, 'Monsignor John English' in *Priests of 1928*, (Brisbane: Brisbane Archdiocesan Archives, 2003): 201–205, BAA. John English was born in Ireland in 1897. Ordained in 1922, he migrated to Brisbane in 1925. He was Vicar General of the Archdiocese from 1938 until his death in 1968.

16 Archbishop O'Donnell to Apostolic Delegate, Archbishop Enrico, 26 June 1967, BAA. Domenico Enrico (1909–1997) was appointed by Pope John XXIII as Apostolic Delegate to Australia, New Zealand and Oceania in 1962; he served in that post until 1969.

17 Letter to Apostolic Delegate, 26 June 1967.

18 The Code of Canon Law (Washington, DC, Canon Law Society of America, 1999): 631.1

19 Fr Jeremiah Hogan to Monsignor John English, 8 September 1965, BAA.

20 Hogan, 'Report of Visitation of Sisters of Perpetual Adoration', Brisbane 1965, BAA.

21 *Perfectae Caritatis*, 2, 3.

22 *Catholic Leader*, 14 September 1967, 4.

23 Mother Rosarii (Gabriel Ansaldo) was born in Brisbane in 1922 and entered the Sisters of Perpetual Adoration in 1941. She was Mother General from 1967 to 1979. She died in 1989.
24 Sister Philippa (Patricia Barker) was born in 1928 and entered the Sisters of Perpetual Adoration in 1950. She took the name of Sister Philip but in 1973 changed it to the feminine form of Philippa. She died in 2013.
25 *Perfectae Caritatis*, 2.
26 Barker, 'The Story of the Sisters of Perpetual Adoration', referring to *Perfectae Caritatis* 2.
27 Minutes of General Council, 28 September 1967, SPAA.
28 Sister Eucharia (Margaret Mary Kingston) was born in 1910 and entered the Sisters of Perpetual Adoration in 1938. She died in the year 2000. Sister Philomena (Alice McAuliffe) was born in 1933 and entered in 1958. She died in 2019. Sister Monica (Pansy Brown) was born in 1920 and entered in 1948. Tragically, however, she was not able to carry out the catechetics ministry as she died after a short illness on 20 August 1968. The *Catholic Leader*, 29 August, 20, wrote about her death, pointing out that, 'She was a fully qualified teacher and a triple certificated nurse.'
29 Julian Woods, 'Of Employments' in *Rules and Constitutions for the Congregation of the Blessed Sacrament*, 1873.
30 Hogan, 'Report of Visitation of Sisters of Perpetual Adoration'.
31 *Catholic Leader*, 18 April 1968, 3.
32 Seymour Douglas Tooth (1904–1982) was the Minister for Health 1964–1974. He was knighted in 1975.
33 Chris Hanlon, 'John Bonaventure Kitts', unpublished biography, BAA: John Kitts was born in 1910 and died in 1989.
34 McFadden, 'Resumé of 100 years'.
35 Bishop Thomas McCabe (1902–1983) was Bishop of Wollongong, New South Wales, from 1952 to 1974.
36 McFadden, 'Resumé of 100 years'. Sister Dympna (Vera McFadden) was born in 1920. She entered the Sisters of Perpetual Adoration in 1940 and died in 2011.
37 McFadden, 'Resumé of 100 years'.
38 Interview, Sister Philomena McAuliffe RPA, 2007.
39 *Catholic Weekly*, 15 March 1970, 13.
40 *Catholic Leader*, 8 March 1970, 3.
41 McFadden, 'Resumé of 100 years', including scrap-book cuttings from various un-named and un-dated local newspapers, SPAA.
42 Interview, Sister Aloysius Wallis, 2007.
43 Minutes of General Council meeting, 5 May 1973.
44 *Perfectae Caritatis*, 2 and 3.
45 Minutes of General Council meeting, 4 October 1971.
46 *Perfectae Caritatis*, 5.
47 Yvonne Tobin was born in 1940 and entered the Sisters of Perpetual Adoration in 1965. She served as Superior General from 1989 to 2001 and was on General Council from 2001 to 2009. She died in 2023.
48 Minutes of General Council meeting, 25 August 1968

Chapter Eight

1 John Gerry, 'Compassionate Man of God: Francis Rush, Archbishop of Brisbane, 1973–91', *Good Shepherds 1859–2009: The Catholic Bishops of Brisbane* (Brisbane: Brisbane Archdiocesan Archives 2009), 95–131. Francis Rush (1916–2001) was the first Australian-born Archbishop of Brisbane. He was consecrated Bishop of Rockhampton in 1961 and was appointed Archbishop of Brisbane on 5 March 1973. He was installed on 29 May 1973 and retired from this office on 3 December 1991.
2 Minutes of General Council, 12 December 1973, Sisters of Perpetual Adoration Archives (SPAA).

3 *Illawarra Mercury*, 4 March 1974, scrapbook cutting, SPAA.
4 Dympna McFadden RPA, 'Resumé of 100 years', 1974, SPAA.
5 Interview, Sister Aloysius Wallace, 2007.
6 T. P. Boland, *Quiet Women* (Deception Bay Qld: Refulgence Publishers, 1974), 351. Sister Dympna's account of the complex process that led to the naming of Tenison Woods Mountain is given in detail, pages 349–355. Marjorie Walker (1914–2009) joined the John Oxley Library in 1965 and was appointed as Head Librarian in 1976. She retired in 1979.
7 Boland, *Quiet Women*, 353–354.
8 Boland, *Quiet Women*, 355.
9 *Catholic Leader*, 30 June 1974, 6 and 19.
10 McFadden, 'Resumé of 100 years', quoting *Queensland Times*, 21 October 1974. William George Hayden AC (1933–2023) had spent some of his boyhood years at Spring Hill near Brisbane's Villa Maria. He entered parliament in 1961 and became Minister for Social Welfare in 1972. He resigned from parliament in 1988 and was appointed as Governor-General of Australia from 1989 to 1996. He was baptised a Catholic in Ipswich in 2018.
11 Boland, *Quiet Women*, 327.
12 Boland, *Quiet Women*, 9.
13 Dympna McFadden RPA, 'Congregation of the Sisters of Perpetual Adoration of the Most Blessed Sacrament', SPAA.
14 Ric Elliot (1933–1995) was an English-born artist who migrated to Australia. Many of his paintings depict the older areas of Sydney.
15 Refer to Chapter 7.
16 Helen Alfrey was born in 1943, entered the Sisters of Perpetual Adoration in 1972 and was professed on 8 September 1974.
17 Boland, *Quiet Women*, 91.
18 Dympna McFadden RPA, 'History of the Foundation of the Sisters of Perpetual Adoration 1874', SPAA.
19 Boland, *Quiet Women*, 193.
20 See Chapter 2.
21 Minutes of General Council, 1 July 1975.
22 Shirley Hickson (nee Ryan) was born in 1922. She died in 2008. Narelle Hickson was born in 1945. Barbara Hickson was born in 1947 and died in 2024.
23 *Catholic Leader*, 3 July 1983, 1. The article was subsequently reported in the *Catholic Weekly*, Sydney's Catholic newspaper.
24 Minutes of General Council, 25 May 1977.
25 Minutes of General Council, 13 October 1977.
26 Minutes of Community Meeting, Villa Maria Brisbane, 4 July 1980, SPPA.
27 Minutes of General Council, 9 October 1980.
28 Dame Margaret Guilfoyle AC DBE (1926–2020) served in the Australian parliament from 1971 to 1987 and was the first woman to hold a cabinet-level ministerial portfolio. See Guilfoyle, Dame Margaret Georgina Constance (1926–2020), Senator for Victoria, 1971–1987, *Biographical Dictionary of the Australian Senate*, <https://biography.senate.gov.au/guilfoyle-margaret-georgina-constance/> accessed 25 July 2024.
29 David John MacGibbon, (1934–), Senator for Queensland, 1978–1999 in *Biographical Dictionary of the Australian Senate*, <https://biography.senate.gov.au/macgibbon-david-john/> accessed 25 July 2024.
30 *Catholic Leader*, 10 May 1981, 6.
31 *Catholic Leader*, 10 May 1981, 6.
32 Interview, Sister Helen Alfrey, 21 November 2023.
33 Julian Woods, 'Objects of the Congregation' in *Rules and Constitutions of the Congregation of the Blessed Sacrament*, 1873, SPAA.

34 *Catholic Leader*, 13 June 1982, 9
35 Minutes of General Council, 30 November 1981. Father Bill Morris was born in Brisbane in 1943. He was ordained for the Brisbane Archdiocese in 1969. From 1979 to 1984 he was secretary to Archbishop Rush and Director of Vocations. He served as Bishop of Toowoomba from 1992 to 2011. See also Bill Morris, *Benedict, Me and the Cardinals Three* (Adelaide: ATF Press, 2014).
36 Minutes of General Council, 8 August 1985.
37 *Catholic Leader*, 16 October 1983, 4.
38 *Catholic Leader*, 6 October 1985, 9.
39 Jean Duncan was born in 1924 and entered in 1963. She died in 2016.
40 Sister Emmanuel (Patricia Carroll) was born in 1928 and entered the Sisters of Perpetual Adoration in 1949. She died in 2010.
41 Father John Lennon (1930–2006) was later made a Monsignor and served in the Cairns diocese until his death.
42 Beryl Allport (Sister Margaret Mary) was born in 1928 and entered the Sisters of Perpetual Adoration in 1954. She died in 2008. Jennifer Ordish (Sister Anthony) was born in 1947 and entered in 1968. She left the Congregation in 2003 and died in 2022.
43 Minutes of General Council, 13 January 1987.
44 Refer to Chapter 2.
45 The biographies are Margaret M Press RSJ, *Julian Tenison Woods* (Sydney: Catholic Theological Faculty, 1979) and Isabel Hepburn RSJ, *No Ordinary Man: Life and Letters of Julian E. Tenison Woods* (Whanganui New Zealand: Sisters of St Joseph, 1979).
46 Jan Tranter RSJ, 'Foundations: The Forces at Work in the Foundation of the Sisters of St Joseph of Lochinvar, 1883–1913', MA thesis, University of Newcastle. 1988
47 *Catholic Leader*, 30 October 1988, 7.
48 Minutes of General Council, 1 May 1989.The tapes were based on Gerald Arbuckle's book *Out of Chaos* (Sydney: Paulist Press 1988).
49 Minutes of General Council, 29 May 1989. Corpus Christi College has since been re-named Mary MacKillop College and was originally staffed by the Sisters of St Joseph.
50 *Catholic Leader*, 17 September 1989, 8.
51 *Catholic Leader*, 3 December 1989, 5.
52 Transcribed letters of Father Julian Woods and the first Sisters of Perpetual Adoration 1872–1896, 28 April 1874, SPAA.
53 *Catholic Leader*, 22 October 1989, 17. The 'half a dozen' religious institutes referred to include the Sisters of Perpetual Adoration, the diocesan and pontifical congregations of the Sisters of St Joseph and also some defunct groups such as the Brothers of the Sacred Heart and the Solitude of Mary for reformed penitents, both founded in Adelaide in 1868 and dying out in the years following the enforced exile of Father Woods in 1871.
54 Peter Anderson CFC, 'Julian Tenison Woods: Bush Scientist & Geologist', paper given at Symposium on Julian Tenison Woods, Corpus Christi College, 28 October 1989, SPAA. Peter Anderson was born in 1941 and entered the Christian Brothers in 1959. He died in 2021.

Chapter Nine

1 *Catholic Leader*, 11 March 1990, 9.
2 Teen Challenge is a non-profit organisation founded in New York City in 1958 for the rehabilitation of young addicts. It was brought to Australia in 1971 and is now established in each state.
3 Minutes of General Council, 19 February 1991, Sisters of Perpetual Adoration Archives (SPAA).

4 Archbishop John Bathersby (1936–2020) was installed as the sixth Archbishop of Brisbane on 30 January 1992 and retired in 2011. He had previously served as Bishop of Cairns from 1986 until his appointment to Brisbane on the death of Archbishop Rush.
5 Minutes of General Council, 4 August 1992.
6 Minutes of General Council, 10 March 1993.
7 Interview, Michael Lynch, Brisbane, 23 November 2023. Sister Cordelia (Elizabeth Constable) was born in 1914. She entered the Sisters of Perpetual Adoration in 1932 and died in 1997. Sister Michael (Mary Brosnan) was born in 1916. She entered in 1942 and died in 2002. Sister Teresa (Lucy Donovan) was born in 1912. She entered in 1936 and died in 2003.
8 Minutes of General Council, 9 September 1993. At an 'Anointing Mass', the Sacrament of the Anointing of the Sick is administered, generally after the reading of the Gospel, to those who are sick and aging.
9 Minutes of General Council, 5 October 1994.
10 Minutes of General Council, 16 August 1995.
11 Minutes of General Council, 13 November 1995.
12 Yvonne Tobin RPA, Letter to the Sisters, 25 March 1995.
13 Minutes of General Council, 5 February 1995.
14 Minutes of General Council, 5 August 1997.
15 Ozenham Industries is a work of the St Vincent de Paul Society offers training and employment for people who have a disability to provide a variety of services to manufacturing companies, government departments and community groups. Christian Supplies provide religious resources for individuals, parishes, schools and organisations.
16 Yvonne Tobin RPA, Letter to the Sisters, 22 October 1994, SPPA.
17 Minutes of General Council, 31 August 1994. The Daughters of Our Lady Immaculate were the first apostolic Congregation of women to be founded in the Chaldean Rite of the Eastern Church. They were founded in 1922 by Father Antoun Zabuni and now serve in many countries around the world. Their Motherhouse is in Baghdad, Iraq. Since the 1991 economic embargo imposed on Iraq by the UN after the Gulf War, Church resources there had been drained in assisting many thousands of needy families. The Chaldean Sisters, who had lost their schools and other means of support, had taken on supplying altar breads using very old methods.
18 Minutes of General Council, 3 November 1993.
19 Robyn Gugenberger is the sister of Sister Yvonne Tobin and had been business manager for a successful private firm for many years.
20 Minutes of General Council, 5 May 1997. In the early 1990s, a number of Religious Congregations in New South Wales combined to establish Catholic Health Care Services to transfer their health ministries to lay leadership. In 1994 the re-named Catholic Healthcare Australia was given episcopal approval and has since grown to be one of the largest providers of Catholic aged and community services in Australia.
21 Yvonne Tobin RPA, Letter to the Sisters, 12 May 1997, SPPA.
22 *Statutes of the Congregation of the Sisters of Perpetual Adoration of the Most Blessed Sacrament*, Chapter 10, approved by Archbishop Bathersby 6 October 1992.
23 Minutes of General Council, 1 July 1997.
24 Minutes of General Council, 3 September 1997.
25 Yvonne Tobin RPA, Letter to Archbishop Bathersby, 12 November 1997.
26 Canon 684 A.1 and A.2 says that a member in perpetual vows can only transfer from one religious institute to another with the permission of the Congregational Leader of each institute and with the consent of their respective councils. After completing a probation which is to last at least three years, the member can be admitted to perpetual profession in the new institute.

27 Bishop Michael Putney AM (1946–2014) was consecrated auxiliary bishop of Brisbane Archdiocese in 1995. He became Bishop of Townsville in 2001.
28 *Catholic Leader*, 27 September 1998, 7.
29 Minutes of General Council, 15 December 1997.
30 *Catholic Leader*, 21 March 1999, 5. The Canossian Daughters of Charity were founded in Verona, Italy, by St Magdalene of Canossa in 1808. They are now spread throughout the world.
31 Interview, Helen Alfrey RPA, 23 November 2023.
32 Professor John McAuliffe AM (1940–2020) and lawyer Laurie Rogencamp were engaged as consultants by Sister Yvonne Tobin and remained close friends.
33 Philip Wilson (1950–2021) served as Bishop of Wollongong from 1996 until his transfer to Adelaide in 2001. Canon 1291 of the Code of Canon Law states that permission is required for the alienation of property acquired for Church mission and whose value is considerable: that is, above a certain value usually defined in Australia by the Bishops' Conference.
34 Minutes of General Council, 24 July 2000.
35 The Brisbane Archdiocesan Development Fund is a funding institution of the Catholic Archdiocese of Brisbane created in 1969 by Archbishop O'Donnell to fund capital development and pastoral programmes for Church mission.
36 Minutes of General Council, 6 January 1999.
37 Interview, parishioners from the Lutheran Church of St Andrew the Apostle, Brisbane City, 25 Wickham Terrace, 19 November 2023.
38 *Catholic Leader*, 9 April 2000, 7.
39 Margaret Broadbent is a Sister of Mercy who now lives in country Victoria. Her works in stained glass and iconography have won her national acclaim.
40 Gael O'Leary is an internationally renowned sculptor who taught at the Mercy Art and Creativity Centre. In 2009 she established the Bayside Sculpture Centre in Highett, Melbourne. She retired in 2023.
41 Yvonne Tobin RPA, Letter to Co-Adorers, 23 March 2001, SPPA.
42 Archbishop John Bathersby, 'Homily, Blessing of Villa Maria Chapel', 24 March, 2001, SPAA.
43 Jackson Birrell, edited by Tone Wheeler, 'AAA looks at Villa Maria Perpetual Adoration Chapel', <https://www.architectureanddesign.com.au/news/villa-maria-chapel/> accessed 9 August 2024.
44 Exodus 33:7–11.
45 Jan Tranter RSJ, 'Villa Maria Chapel', Sisters of St Joseph Lochinvar newsletter, 20 April 2001, SPAA.
46 The style of this icon is 'Panagia Platytera', a Greek term meaning 'wider' or 'more spacious'. The Orthodox theology of 'theotokos' (that is, mother of God), is depicted poetically: by her conception of the Creator of the Universe in her womb, Mary has become 'more spacious than the Heavens'. The image is one of the most ancient of Christian icons, being found in first-century catacombs where Christians worshipped in times of persecution.
47 Comments made in Visitors' Book in the Villa Maria Chapel, SPAA.
48 Sisters of Perpetual Adoration: Chapter of Affairs 2001, SPAA.
49 The Federation of diocesan Sisters of St Joseph of Perthville, Goulburn, Tasmania, Lochinvar and Whanganui (New Zealand) was formed in 1967 in response to paragraph 22 of *Perfectae Caritatis*: 'Independent institutes and monasteries should, when opportune and the Holy See permits, form federations if they can be considered as belonging to the same religious family. Others who have practically identical constitutions and rules and a common spirit should unite, particularly when they have too few members. Finally, those who share the same of a very similar active apostolate should become associated, one to the other.' The Federation ended when all but the Lochinvar Congregation had merged with the pontifical Sisters of St Joseph by May 2015.
50 Sister Patricia Scully was the first woman to be Vicar for Religious in the Brisbane Archdiocese.

51 Evangelisation Brisbane is an overall organisation of the Brisbane Archdiocese that supports and resources parishes in reaching out to all within the Catholic community to nurture spiritual growth and faith. The Youth and Young Adults section focuses on this area.
52 Minutes of General Council, 27 February 2002.
53 Mark De Battista, 'Eucharistic Congress in Wollongong: a time of blessing', *AD2000,* vol 13, no. 7 (2000): 9. Fr Mark De Battista is a priest of the Diocese of Wollongong.
54 Bishop Peter Ingham (1941–2024) was installed as the fourth Bishop of Wollongong on 25 July 2001.

Chapter Ten

1 List of awards for Camarda & Cantrill Pty Ltd, <https://hipages.com.au/connect/camcan> accessed 17 August 2024.
2 Michael Rego is a Marist Father and now serves in northern New South Wales.
3 Archbishop John Bathersby to Sister Philippa Barker, 22 April 2003, Sisters of Perpetual Adoration Archives (SPAA).
4 The Province House of the Sisters of St Joseph is in Bage Street in the Brisbane suburb of Nundah, and their Nursing Home for the Aged, 'Penola', was nearby. This Nursing Home has since been closed.
5 Meeting of Senior Management, 17 March 2004, SPAA.
6 See Chapter 9, note 20. The New South Wales Sydney Archdiocese and the Armidale, Bathurst, Broken Bay, Lismore, Maitland-Newcastle, Parramatta, Wagga Wagga, Wilcannia-Forbes and Wollongong dioceses make up the ecclesiastical province of Sydney.
7 Minutes of General Council, 22 March 2006.
8 Minutes of General Council, 27 September 2006.
9 Minutes of General Council, 2 September 2002 and Community Diary 15 September 2002, SPAA.
10 Notes of Community Meeting, 7 May 2002, SPAA.
11 Notes of Community Meeting, 25 November 2003.
12 Notes of Community Meeting, 11 Feb 2004.
13 'Rhyl Hinwood: Curriculum Vitae 2022', <https://www.rhylhinwood.net/bio> accessed 20 August 2024. Dr Rhyl Hinwood was appointed a Member of the Order of Australia (AM) in 2006.
14 Community Diary, 22 February 2004, SPAA. Bishop Brian Finnigan was consecrated Auxiliary Bishop of Brisbane Archdiocese on 8 April 2002. He retired from this role on 30 December 2015, and now, in addition to his many other Church activities, regularly offers Mass at the Villa Maria chapel.
15 The Little Rock Scripture Study booklets provide a course for adult faith formation using Catholic biblical scholarship, reflection and life application: <https: //litpress.org/LRSS/Getting-Started/Index?srsltid=AfmBOootZX5ZYwH4cqgcSxiD6qWZm538dvwh2i9_m19-6v551c6_o-jB> accessed 20 August 2024.
16 Kenneth Howell completed a Licentiate in Sacred Liturgy at the Pontifical Institute of Liturgy at Sant' Anselmo in Rome in 1997. As Secretary to Archbishop Bathersby he also served as Director of Worship at St Stephen's Cathedral Brisbane between 1997 and 2005. He was consecrated as seventh Bishop of the Catholic Diocese of Toowoomba in 2023.
17 Vocations Committee Report, July 2002, SPAA.
18 Notes of Community Meeting, 23 March 2005. Lucy Tierney is a Queensland Sister of St Joseph who co-ordinates Virginia Waters Self-Care, an Inner Wisdom Consultancy that offers resources for personal development and spiritual companionship.
19 Minutes of General Council, 25 February 2005. Carmel Pilcher is a Sister of St Joseph who comes from Adelaide and currently lives in Sydney from where she is engaged as a Liturgy and Culture Consultant for parishes and dioceses across Australia and in the Archdiocese of Suva, Fiji.

20 Minutes of General Council, 10 August 2005. Margaret Schiemer RSJ was born in 1932 and was professed as a Sister of St Joseph, Perthville, in 1951. In her later years her main ministries were in adult faith development and retreat work. She died on 15 August 2007.
21 The Second Vatican Council ended in 1965.
22 See Chapter 7.
23 Philippa Barker RPA, Letter to Sisters, 22 October 2002, SPAA.
24 Minutes of General Council, 7 October 2002.
25 Adoration Committee Report, 13 December 2002, SPAA.
26 Notes of Community Meeting, 14 November 2003, SPAA.
27 Jean Cain RSJ was born in 1937 and was professed as a Sister of St Joseph, Perthville, in 1957. She was Congregational Leader of the Sisters of St Joseph, Perthville 2000–2005. She died on 10 May 2022.
28 Jean Cain RSJ to Philippa Barker RPA, 24 April 2004, SPAA.
29 Notes of Community Meeting, 25 April 2004. By 2015, with the exception of the Sisters of St Joseph of Lochinvar, all groups had opted to merge with the 'central' Sisters of St Joseph, and the links with the Lochinvar groups has remained strong. The Beatification of Mary MacKillop took place on 19 January 1995, and both the President of the Federation of the (diocesan) Sisters of St Joseph and the Congregational Leader of the (pontifical) Sisters of St Joseph had played a prominent role at the event. The adjective 'brown' refers to the fact that when the centrally governed Sisters of St Joseph were given final approbation from Rome in 1888, those Sisters who remained diocesan had to change the colour of their habit from 'brown' to 'black'.
30 See Chapter 9, footnote 49.
31 Minutes of General Council, 6 May 2005.
32 Sister Philippa Barker RPA to Archbishop John Bathersby, 9 September 2005, SPAA.
33 Bishop Brian Finnigan to Sister Philippa Barker RPA, 15 January 2006, SPAA.
34 Minutes of General Council, January–April 2006, and 'The Appointment by Archbishop John Bathersby of a Canonical Superior for the Sisters of Perpetual Adoration', July 2006, Brisbane Archdiocesan Archives (BAA). Note: The full title for all Sisters of St Joseph was 'Sisters of St Joseph of the Sacred Heart'. This did not change when some groups became diocesan, except for the Sisters of St Joseph at Whanganui, New Zealand, who changed their title to 'Sisters of St Joseph of Nazareth'.
35 'The Appointment by Archbishop John Bathersby . . . Sisters of Perpetual Adoration'.
36 Sister Berice Livermore is a Sister of Mercy from Singleton, New South Wales.
37 'Memorandum of Understanding: The Archbishop of Brisbane and the Congregational of the Sisters of Perpetual Adoration of the Most Blessed Sacrament and the Congregation of the Sisters of St Joseph of the Sacred Heart, 7 October 2006', SPAA. Sister Chrstine Rowan RSJ from New South Wales was Provincial of South Australian Sisters of St Joseph from 2001 to 2007.
38 *Catholic Leader*, 22 October 2022, 5. Sisters Yvonne Tobin, Helen Alfrey and Philippa Barker had been elected as councillors at the General Chapter.
39 Peter Meneely is a priest of the Brisbane Archdiocese. In 2012 Pope Benedict XVI conferred on him the title 'Monsignor'.
40 'Sisters of Perpetual Adoration of the Blessed Sacrament: Consideration of the Future of the Villa Maria Centres', BAA.
41 Interview, 2 August 2024. Sister Mary McDonald is a Sister of the Good Samaritan, living in Brisbane.
42 'Sisters of Perpetual Adoration . . . Future of the Villa Maria Centres'.
43 Mary Cresp RSJ, *Villa Maria: The Sisters of Perpetual Adoration and Care of the Aged* (Brisbane: Sisters of Perpetual Adoration, 2007). As is required, copies of the 50-page booklet were deposited in the State Library of Queensland, the National Library of Australia and the Queensland Parliamentary Service.
44 *Catholic Leader*, 24 February 2008, 5.

45 Minutes of General Council, 8 February 2007. Groups who practise the 40 Hours Devotion spend time in continuous prayer before the exposed Blessed Sacrament.
46 *Catholic Leader*, 24 February 2008, 3.
47 Sister Margaret Robertson was Provincial of the Queensland Sisters of St Joseph from 2001 to 2007.
48 Sister Moya Campbell was Provincial of the Queensland Sisters of St Joseph from 2007 to 2013.
49 Minutes of General Council, 7 February 2009.
50 *Sacramentum Caritatis*, 84.
51 Interview, Brisbane, 20 April 2007. Sister Regina (Frances Greenhalgh) was born in 1922 and entered the Sisters of Perpetual Adoration in 1965. She died in 2021.
52 Father Jim Smith (1947–2024) was the founder of the Catholic Psychiatric Pastoral Care ministry in Fortitude Valley.
53 Mary Gavin (1921–2014) was the co-ordinator of 'Always People', a group she and Jose Zepeda founded in 1994 in Brisbane to support education, health care and development in communities in various parts of the world. She was also Director of the Centre for Multicultural Pastoral Care in the Archdiocese of Brisbane.
54 Sister Katrina Brill RSJ was Congregational Leader of the Sisters of St Joseph of the Sacred Heart from 2001 to 2007. Sister Catherine Trinh is a Sister of St Joseph based in Sydney and originally comes from Vietnam. The Sisters of the Miraculous Medal were founded for ethnic minority women by French Bishop Gioan Sion Kham, Bishop of Kon Tum, Vietnam, in 1947. Their main work is the education of indigenous girls.
55 Coreen Small had been employed as receptionist at Villa Maria Brisbane and assisted Sister Narelle Hickson there. In 1997 she worked in finance and assumed secretarial duties with Sister Yvonne Tobin at Villa Maria Convent as well as assisting Sister Helen Alfrey.
56 Margaret McKenna RSJ currently lives at Nundah, Brisbane.
57 Minutes of General Council, 31 July 2008.
58 *Catholic Leader*, 21 June 2009, 7.
59 Minutes of General Council, 13 October 2001.
60 Code of Canon Law, 580.
61 Sister Margaret Modde OSF (1920–2010) assisted a number of Religious Congregations in their processes of merger, aggregation and union in Canada and USA. Sister Sharon Holland IHM worked at the Congregation for Institutes of Consecrated Life and Societies of Apostolic Life at the Vatican from 1991 to 2012 when she returned to her Motherhouse in Monroe, Michigan, USA.
62 Memorandum of Understanding . . . 7 October 2006.
63 Minutes of General Council, 7 February 2008.
64 Sister Anne Derwin (1949–2019) was Congregational Leader of the Sisters of St Joseph from 2007 to 2013. Sister Annette Arnold is a Sister of St Joseph from Queensland and was a councillor on the Congregational Leadership Team from 2007 to 2013.
65 Francis Morrisey OMI (1936–2020), an eminent canon lawyer, taught at the Saint Paul University Ottawa and was a founding member of the Canadian Canon Law Society.
66 Minutes of General Council, 25 February 2009.
67 Minutes of General Council, 7 May 2009.
68 Code of Canon Law 123 deals with making arrangements for the extinction of a public juridical person.
69 Minutes of General Council, 7 May 2009.
70 Anne Derwin RSJ, letter to Sisters of Perpetual Adoration, quoting the letter of Archbishop Bathersby, 9 September 2009, SPAA.
71 *Catholic Leader*, 18 October 2009, 7.
72 Some years after aggregation, this group moved to another centre in suburban Brisbane where they could continue their schedule of adoration.

73 Minutes of General Council, 9 September 2009.
74 Therese Wilson RSJ, 'Villa Maria Ministry—Mid-2011 to March 2015', SPAA.
75 Interview, 31 August 2024.
76 Anne Player RSJ ed., *The Archer Letters* (North Goulburn NSW: Sisters of St. Joseph, 1983), Letter 33.
77 Anne Player RSJ (1934–2016) studied the life and works of Julian Woods extensively and edited many of his letters. The Sisters of Perpetual Adoration published the last of this collection, *'Yrs Most Affly': Letters from Father Julian Tenison Woods to Terry and Sarah Tenison Woods 1878–1887* (Brisbane: Sisters Perpetual Adoration, 2008).
78 John 6:35.
79 Jan's works are hung in many galleries around the world. Her portrait of Rachel Ward won the Archibald Packing Room Prize in 2003.

Epilogue

1 Pope Francis: Eucharistic Adoration is the secret to knowing the love of Jesus Christ, https://aleteia.org/2016/10/20/pope-francis-eucharistic-adoration-is-the-secret-to-knowing-the-love-of-jesus-christ Accessed 10 September 2023.
2 *Sacrosanctum Concilium* (Constitution on the Sacred Liturgy), Austin Flannery (ed.), *Vatican Council II: The Conciliar and Post Conciliar Documents* (Dublin: Dominican Publications, 1977), 21.
3 Flannery, *Sacrosanctum Concilium*, 47.
4 Flannery, *Sacrosanctum Concilium*, 46.
5 The encyclical *Mysterium Fidei* ('On the Holy Eucharist') was issued on 3 September 1965.
6 Pope Pius X, encyclical *Quam Singulari*, 1905, 401.
7 Pope Paul VI, *Mysterium Fidei,* 67.
8 Heather Joseph, Interview, Brisbane, 21 November 2023.
9 Michael Kennedy, Interview, Brisbane, 22 November 2023.
10 *Mysterium Fidei,* 39.
11 Flannery, *Unitatis Redintegratio* (Decree on Ecumenism), 11.
12 Pope John Paul II, 'God is Love', 2 October 1985, <https://truedignityofwomen.wordpress.com/2016/12/09/john-paul-ii-on-god-is-love/> accessed 10 September 2024.
13 Paraphrase of *Catechism of the Catholic Church* (New York: Doubleday, 1995), No. 1: 'God, infinitely perfect and blessed in himself, in a plan of sheer goodness freely created man to make him share in his own blessed life. For this reason, at every time and in every place, God draws close to man. He calls man to seek him, to know him, to love him with all his strength. He calls together all men, scattered and divided by sin, into the unity of his family, the Church. To accomplish this, when the fullness of time had come, God sent his Son as Redeemer and Savior. In his Son and through him, he invites men to become, in the Holy Spirit, his adopted children and thus heirs of his blessed life.'
14 Tradition refers to the handing on of the Apostolic faith as found in Scripture and the creeds and doctrines formulated by the early Christian communities.
15 Nicene Creed.
16 Flannery, *Eucharisticum Mysterium* (Instruction on the Worship of the Eucharistic Mystery), 1967, 3c.
17 Interview, Brisbane, 23 November 2023.
18 Interview, Brisbane, 20 November 2023.
19 Pope Franics, *Laudato 'Si*, 85.
20 Pope Francis, *Amoris Laetitia*, 12.

21 Pope Francis, General Audience 15 December 1921, <https://www.vatican.va/content/francesco/en/audiences/2021/documents/papa-francesco_20211215_udienza-generale.html> accessed 10 September 1923.

22 Elizabeth Harrington, 'Adoration', *Liturgy Lines,* Brisbane Archdiocese Office of Liturgy, 2 October 2005.

23 Pope Benedict XV1, *Sacramentum Caritatis*, Post-Synodal Apostolic Exhortation, 2007, 70.

24 St Augustine of Hippo, Sermon 272, <https://www.earlychurchtexts.com/public/augustine_sermon_272_eucharist.htm> accessed 3 June 2004.

25 Pope Francis, 'Eucharistic Adoration Urges You to Care for the Poor', 23 August 2023, <https://www.vaticannews.va/en/pope/news/2023-08/pope-eucharistic-adoration-urges-you-to-care-for-the-poor.html> accessed 11 September 2024.

26 Pope Benedict XVI, *Sacramentum Caritatis*, 71.

27 Ronald Rolheiser, 'When Time Stands Still', 2 April 2018: https://ronrolheiser.com/when-time-stands-still/ . Accessed 23 August 2023.

Sisters of Perpetual Adoration

in order of Profession
Total: 84 Sisters, 1874–1914

Name	Religious Name	Entered	Death
Catherine Gaffney	Stanislaus	1874	1914
Sarah Breen	Mary Joseph	1874	1945
Alice Downs	Francis	1874	1882
Bridget Lillis	Mary John	1875	1942
Miss Oliver	Clare	1876	1891
Louise Lewis	Aloysius	1878	1930
Bridget Hayes	Clare	1880	1883
Emily Francis	Gabriel	1881	1888
Bridget Donoghue	Michael	1881	1892
Bridget McGrath	Raphael	1881	1937
Mary Leavy	Josephine	1882	1955
Sarah Meagher	Maria Joseph	1885	1955
Annie Shannahan	Mary Baptist	1886	1919
Mary Dinan	Clare	1888	1939
Mary McNulty	Juliana	1893	1939
Catherine Breen	Michael	1893	1907
Mary Daly	Margaret Mary	1896	1953

Bridget Meagher	Berchmans	1898	1963
Bridget Kelvin	Agnes	1901	1956
Annie Rinn	Cecilia	1902	1915
Elizabeth Rafter	Anthony	1902	1926
Mary Rafter	Magdalen	1902	1958
Ann Kelvin	Irene	1905	1956
Ellen Callaghan	Philomena	1906	1955
Mary Rodgers	Paschal	1914	1973
Elizabeth Dobie	Augustine	1914	1974
Mary Baggot	Mary Paul	1915	1938
Margaret Murray	Sebastian	1915	1942
Ellen Cummings	Alphonsus	1917	1967
Aileen Moloney	Gabriel	1920	1983
Jean Inverarity	Teresa	1920	1927
Margaret Quinlan	Bernadette	1923	1987
Jane Newman	Bernard	1923	1932
Alicia McSweeney	Veronica	1923	1969
Mary Doody	Rosario	1924	1935
Honoria McElligott	Dolores	1926	1986
Winifred Shortall	Jude	1927	1991
Dorothy Goggin	Patrick	1929	1980
Margaret Donnelly	Brigid	1929	1942
Bridget Tuohey	Christopher	1931	1997
Elspeth Lewis	Kevin	1931	1997
Cecilia Fitzpatrick	Stephen	1932	1966
Elizabeth Constable	Cordelia	1932	1997
Dorothy Ryan	Stanislaus	1932	1999
Ellen Priaulse	Mary St Anne	1933	1980
Lyla Gillen	Benedicta	1935	1987

Lucy Donovan	Teresa	1936	2003
Annie Wust	Antonia	1937	1959
Martha Ziegenfusz	Christina	1937	2001
Margaret Kingston	Eucharia	1938	2000
Alice McAllister	Mary St Peter	1938	1984
Vera McFadden	Dympna	1940	2011
Jessie Wallis	Aloysius	1940	2017
Kathleen Tyler	Mary Paul	1941	2003
Eileen McMahon	Vianney	1941	2001
Lillian Donnelly	Immaculata	1942	1976
Mary Brosnan	Michael	1942	2002
Margaret Dolan	Gerard	1942	1979
Gabriel Ansaldo	Rosarii	1943	1989
Alice Iver	Matthew	1943	1992
Levina Quinn	Evangelist	1943	2015
Veronica Mason	Mark	1944	1974
Catherine McNamara	Assumpta	1947	2001
May Stewart	Ignatius	1947	1974
Pansy Brown	Monica	1948	1968
Patricia Carroll	Emmanuel	1949	2010
Patricia Barker	Philippa	1950	2013
Verna Thomas	Clement	1951	1995
Hazel Lincoln	Gemma	1954	2013
Beryl Allport	Margaret Mary	1954	2008
Elizabeth Turvey	Angela	1955	2016
Theresa McDonald	Leonard	1955	2013
Alice McAuliffe	Philomena	1958	2020
Frances Woods	Xavier	1962	
Jean Duncan	Jean	1963	2016

Frances Greenhalgh	Regina	1965	2018
Catherine Bradshaw	Joseph	1965	1977
Yvonne Tobin	Yvonne	1967	2022
Carmel Bargenquast	Elizabeth	1971	
Helen Alfrey	Helen	1972	
Shirley Hickson	Shirley	1975	2008
Narelle Hickson	Narelle	1975	
Barbara Hickson	Barbara	1975	2023
Joan Mizzi	Raphael	(Transferred from Srs St Joseph 6 Feb. 2000)	

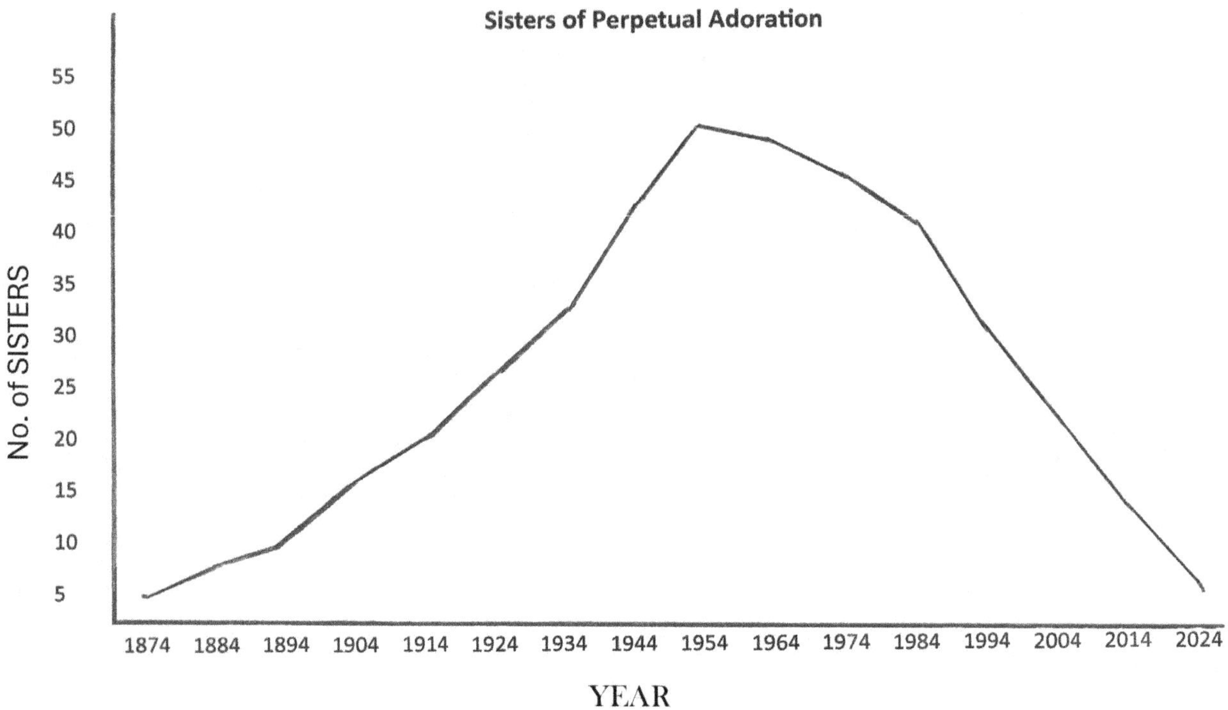

Acknowledgements

It takes a village to raise a child. So, too, to write a book. I am deeply grateful to the following people without whom this book would not have come to be:

- The Sisters of Perpetual Adoration Board of Trustees who asked me to write the history.
- Sister Kristin Johnson rsj (Sisters of Perpetual Adoration Archives), Patrick O'Neill, Adrian Gibb and Brendan Kelly (Brisbane Archdiocesan Archives), Imogen Kennard-King and Liz Sheridan (Congregational Archives of the Sisters of Charity of Australia) and Jo Robertson (Sisters of St Joseph Archives, Mount Street, North Sydney). Your generosity and dedication was over and above the norm.
- David Hilliard OAM whose professional advice and editing was invaluable and gave me assurance. Thank you, David, for the many hours you dedicated to this.
- Gabrielle Waters and Suzanne Ryan who did the final edits—your meticulous attention to detail astounded me. I appreciate the time you gave to this.
- Sister Marie Dowling rsj, Community Leader of the Sisters of Perpetual Adoration. Marie has been my 'right arm'—photographer, courier, consultant, 'researcher *par excellence*'. It was Marie who came up with the title of this book.
- Those who agreed to be interviewed and so graciously shared memories and thoughts: Sisters of Perpetual Adoration Helen Alfrey, Elizabeth Bargenquast, Narelle Hickson, Raphael Mizzi and Xavier Woods; Don Barrett; Sr Margaret Broadbent rsm; Sr Berice Livermore rsm; Robyn Gugenberger; Sr Therese Wilson rsj; Margaret Michael; Gabrielle Power-West; Coreen Small; Co-Adorers, Heather Joseph, Michael Kennedy and Michael Lynch.

- Publisher ATF Press, Hilary Regan, for your encouragement and professional advice.
- My community companion Sr Hun Do rsj whose care and interest sustained me.

All photos, except those otherwise acknowledged, are from the archives of the Sisters of Perpetual Adoration or have been taken by Sisters Marie Dowling or Mary Cresp.

Bibliography

Primary Sources:

(Unless otherwise cited, all sources listed below are held in the Sisters of Perpetual Adoration Archives, Brisbane.)

Bulger, Anne (comp.), 'Memoirs of Reverend J. E. Tenison-Woods'.

Congregation of the Blessed Sacrament, *Rules and Constitutions of the Congregation of the Blessed Sacrament,* 1873.

Congregation of the Perpetual Adoration of the Most Blessed Sacrament, Wexford, *Constitutions of the Congregation of the Perpetual Adoration of the Most Blessed Sacrament*, Wexford, Diocese of Ferns, Ireland.

Eymard, Peter Julian. 'The Real Presence: Eucharistic Meditations', <https://www.ecatholic2000.com/cts/untitled-609.shtml> accessed 1 September 2024.

Hogan, Jeremiah, 'Report of Visitation of Sisters of Perpetual Adoration', 1965, Brisbane Archdiocesan Archives.

Sisters of Perpetual Adoration Community Diary, 2000–2009.

Sisters of Perpetual Adoration, Minutes of General Council of the Sisters of Perpetual Adoration, 1968–2009.

Sisters of Perpetual Adoration, Notes of Community Meetings.

Sisters of Perpetual Adoration of the Most Blessed Sacrament, *Statutes of the Congregation of the Sisters of Perpetual Adoration of the Most Blessed Sacrament.*

'Transcribed letters of Father Julian Woods and the first Sisters of Perpetual Adoration 1872–1896'.

Various interviews, reminiscences, diaries and accounts collected, written and/or edited by Sister Dympna McFadden.

Church Documents:

Catechism of the Catholic Church, New York: Doubleday,1995.

Code of Canon Law, Washington, DC: Canon Law Society of America, 1999.

Council of Trent, Session 13, 'Concerning the Most Holy Sacrament of the Eucharist', <https://www.ewtn.com/catholicism/library/thirteenth-session-of-the-council-of-trent-1479> accessed 3 September 2024.

Flannery, Austin (editor), *Vatican Council II: The Conciliar and Post Conciliar Documents*, Dublin: Dominican Publications, 1977.

Pope Benedict XV1, *Sacramentum Caritatis* (Post-Synodal Apostolic Exhortation), 2007.

Pope Francis, *Amoris Laetitia* (On Love in the Family), 2016.

'Catechesis on St Joseph', General Audience, 15 December 2021, <https//www.vatican.va/content/Francisco/en/audience/2021/documents/papafrancisco_20211 215_udienza-generale.html> accessed 10 September 2023.

'Eucharistic Adoration is the Secret to Knowing the Love of Jesus Christ', < https://aleteia.org/2016/10/20/pope-francis-eucharistic-adoration-is-the-secret-to-knowing-the-love-of-jesus-christ> accessed 10 September 2023.

'Eucharistic Adoration Urges You to Care for the Poor', 23 August 2023, <https://www.vaticannews.va/en/pope/news/2023-08/pope-eucharistic-adoration-urges-you-to-care-for-the-poor.html> accessed 11 September 2024.

Laudato 'Si (On Care for our Common Home), 2015.

Pope John Paul II, 'God is Love', General Audience, 2 October 1985, <https://truedignityofwomen. wordpress.com/2016/12/09/john-paul-ii-on-god-is-love/.> accessed 10 September 2024.

Pope Paul VI: *Mysterium Fidei* ('On the Holy Eucharist'), 1965.

Pope Pius X, *Quam Singulari*, (Concerning the Admittance of Children to the Eucharist), 1905.

Pope Pius XII, *Mystici Corporis Christi*, (The Mystical Body of Christ), 1943.

St Augustine of Hippo, *Sermon 272*, <https://www.earlychurchtexts.com/public/augustine_sermon_272_eucharist.htm> accessed 3 June 2004.

Newspapers:

Age, (Brisbane Catholic newspaper), 1899–1929.

Brisbane Truth, 23 January 1944.

Catholic Leader, 1930–2024.

Catholic Weekly, 15 March 1970.

Horizons (Toowoomba Diocese), 17 February 2017.

Illawarra Mercury, 4 March 1974.

Queensland Times, 26 February 1920, 26 October 1954, 21 October 1974.

Articles:

Birrell, Jackson, Wheeler, Tone (ed.), 'AAA looks at Villa Maria Perpetual Adoration Chapel', <https://www.architectureanddesign.com.au/news/villa-maria-chapel/> accessed 9 August 2024.

Black, Carmel, 'Depression Era', *Queensland Historical Atlas*, <https://www.qhatlas.com.au/content/era> accessed 5 July 2024.

Blackmur, Douglas, 'Edward Michael (Ned) Hanlon (1887–1952)', *Australian Dictionary of Biography*, <https://adb.anu.edu.au/biography/hanlon-edward-michael-ned-10411> accessed 5 June 2024.

Boland, TP, 'Irish and Australian: James Duhig, Archbishop of Brisbane, 1917–65', *Good Shepherds 1859–2009: The Catholic Bishops of Brisbane* (Brisbane: Brisbane Archdiocesan Archives, 2009), 49–71.

'Sir Norman Thomas Gilroy (1896–1977)', *Australian Dictionary of Biography*, <https://adb.anu.edu.au/biography/gilroy-sir-norman-thomas-10308> accessed 1 August 2024.

Byrne, Neil, 'What is Becoming of the People? Robert Dunne, Archbishop of Brisbane, 1882–1917', *Good Shepherds 1859–2009: The Catholic Bishops of Brisbane* (Brisbane: Brisbane Archdiocesan Archives, 2009), 29–49.

De Battista, Mark, 'Eucharistic Congress in Wollongong: a time of blessing', *AD2000*, 13/7 (2000): 9.

Gerry, John, 'Compassionate Man of God: Francis Rush, Archbishop of Brisbane, 1973–91', *Good Shepherds 1859–2009: The Catholic Bishops of Brisbane* (Brisbane: Brisbane Archdiocesan Archives, 2009), 95–131.

Hardon, John A, 'The History of Eucharistic Adoration—Development of Doctrine in the Catholic Church', <https://www.therealpresence.org/eucharist/pea/history.htm> accessed 4 September 2024.

Harrington, Elizabeth, 'Adoration of the Blessed Sacrament', *Liturgy Lines*, Brisbane Archdiocese Office of Liturgy, 2 October 2005.

Hinwood, Rhyl, 'Rhyl Hinwood: Curriculum Vitae 2022', <https://www.rhylhinwood.net/bio> accessed 20 August 2024.

Loch, TS, 'Sir Frederick Aloysius Weld (1823–1891)', *Australian Dictionary of Biography*, <https://adb.anu.edu.au/biography/weld-sir-frederick-aloysius-4829> accessed 25 June 2024.

Martin, Denis W, 'From Altar Boy to Archbishop: Patrick O'Donnell, Archbishop of Brisbane, 1965–73', *Good Shepherds 1859–2009: The Catholic Bishops of Brisbane* (Brisbane: Brisbane Archdiocesan Archives, 2009),73–94.

'Monsignor John English', *Priests of 1928*, (Brisbane: Brisbane Archdiocesan Archives, 2003): 201–205.

McKenna, John H, 'Theology of Adoration', *Vincentiana*, 49/1 (2005): 83–87.

McMullen, Gabrielle and Oakley, Paul, 'Ministerial PJPs Advancing Lay Leadership in the Australian Church', *Australasian Catholic Record*, 97/4 (2020): 450–459.

O'Malley, Timothy P, 'Medieval Assent: Communion of Body and Soul as an Ascending Model for Liturgy', <https://adoremus.org/2021/01/medieval-assent-communion-of-body-and-soul-as-an-ascending-model-for-liturgy/> accessed 1 September 2024.

O'Shea, William, 'Building a Diocese: James Quinn, Bishop of Brisbane, 1859–1881', *Good Shepherds 1859–2009: The Catholic Bishops of Brisbane* (Brisbane: Brisbane Archdiocesan Archives, 2009), 1–28.

Rahner, Karl, 'Meditation: The Eucharist—The Mystery Of Our Christ', <https://thevalueof sparrows.wordpress.com/2014/03/02/meditation-the-eucharist-the-mystery-of-our-christ-by-karl-rahner/> accessed 1 September 2024.

Rolheiser, Ronald, 'When Time Stands Still', 2 April 2018, <https://ronrolheiser.com.when-time-stands-still/> accessed 23 August 2023.

Walker, David, 'The French Influence', *Australasian Catholic Record*, 15/1 (1978): 28–35.

Books:

Arbuckle, Gerald, *Out of Chaos,* Sydney: Paulist Press 1988.

Boland, TP, *James Duhig,* St Lucia: University of Queensland Press, 1986. *Quiet Women*, Deception Bay, Qld: Refulgence Publishers, 1974.

Bradshaw, P, *Early Christian Worship: A Basic Introduction to Ideas and Practice*, London: SPCK, 1996.

Buchanan, Colin, *Justin Martyr on Baptism and Eucharist: Texts in Translation with Introduction and Commentary,* London: SCM Canterbury Press, 2007.

Burley, Stephanie and Teague, Katherine (editors), *Chapel, Cloister and Classroom: Reflections On the Dominican Sisters at North Adelaide,* Adelaide: Lutheran Publishing House, 1993.

Byrne, Neil, *Robert Dunne: Archbishop of Brisbane 1830–1917,* St Lucia: University of Queensland Press, 1991.

Cash, Damien, *The Road to Emmaus: A History of the Blessed Sacrament Congregation in Australia,* Kew East, Vic: The Congregation of the Blessed Sacrament in Australia, 2007.

Cresp, Mary, *Villa Maria: The Sisters of Perpetual Adoration and Care of the Aged,* Brisbane: Sisters of Perpetual Adoration, 2007.

De Lubac, Henri, translated by Semma Simmonds, *Corpus Mysticum: The Eucharist and the Church in the Middle Ages*, London: SCM Press, 2006.

Doherty, Carmel, *Song of Seasons: Father J. E. Tenison Woods*, Wollongong: Sisters of Perpetual Adoration, 1996.

Dunphy, Thomas L, *An Australian Mustard Seed: The Sisters of Perpetual Adoration* (No publication details given. Copy in Brisbane Archdiocesan Archives).

Hardon, John A, *With Us Today: On the Real Presence of Jesus Christ in the Eucharist,* Ave Maria, Florida: Sapientia Press, 2001.

Hepburn, Isabel, *No Ordinary Man: Life and Letters of Julian E. Tenison Woods,* Whanganui New Zealand: Sisters of St Joseph, 1979.

Laracy, Hugh M, *Marists and Melanesians A History of Catholic Missions in the Solomon Islands,* Canberra: Australian National University Press, 1976.

MacKillop, Mary, *Julian Tenison Woods: A Life*, Introduced and annotated by Margaret Press, Melbourne: HarperCollins, 1997.

Morris, Bill, *Benedict, Me and the Cardinals Three,* Adelaide: ATF Press, 2014.

O'Malley, Timothy P, *Real Presence: What Does It Mean and Why Does It Matter?,* South Bend, Indiana: Ave Maria Press, 2020.

O'Neill, George, *Life of the Reverend Julian Edmund Tenison Woods,* Sydney: Pellegrini & Co, 1929.

Pitre, Brant, *Jesus and the Jewish Roots of the Eucharist,* New York: Doubleday, 2011

Player, Anne (editor), *The Archer Letters,* North Goulburn NSW: Sisters of St. Joseph, 1983. *'Yrs Most Affly': Letters from Father Julian Tenison Woods to Terry and Sarah Tenison Woods 1878–1887,* Brisbane: Sisters Perpetual Adoration, 2008.

Press, Margaret M., *Julian Tenison Woods,* Sydney: Catholic Theological Faculty, 1979.

Stone, Darwell, *A History of the Doctrine of the Holy Eucharist*, 2 volumes, London: Longmans, Green & Co, 1909.

Tynan, Patrick, *The Apostle of Brisbane: A Biography of Fr Joseph Augustine Canali,* Toowoomba: Church Archivists Press, 1992.

Woods, Father Julian, *A Guide to Confession and First Communion,* Sydney: Louis Gille & Co, 1875.

Unpublished Works:

Anderson, Peter, 'Julian Tenison Woods: Bush Scientist & Geologist', Sisters of Perpetual Adoration Archives.

Hanlon, Chris, unpublished biographies, 'Denis Power'; 'Father Basil Bergin'; 'John Bonaventure Kitts'; 'Robert John Flynn'; 'Timothy Molony', Brisbane Archdiocesan Archives.

Tranter, Jan, 'Foundations: The Forces at Work in the Foundation of the Sisters of St Joseph of Lochinvar, 1883–1913', MA thesis, University of Newcastle, 1988.

Index

A

B

C

D

E

F

G

H

I

J

K

L

M

O

P

Q

R

S

T

U

V

W

X

www.ingramcontent.com/pod-product-compliance
Lightning Source LLC
Jackson TN
JSHW072259160225
79072JS00012B/90
9781923206823